Citizen Oversight of Law Enforcement

JUSTINA CINTRÓN PERINO, EDITOR

Section of State and
Local Government Law

Cover design by ABA Publishing

10 09 08 07 06 5 4 3 2 1

Cataloging-in-Publication data is on file with the Library of Congress

Library of Congress Cataloging-in-Publication Data

Citizen oversight of law enforcement : legal issues and policy considerations / [edited by] Justina Cintron Perino.
      p. cm.
   Includes bibliographical references and index.
   1. Police administration--United States--Citizen participation. 2. Police--Complaints against--United States. I. Perino, Justina Cintron.
   HV7936.C56C535 2006
   363.2068'4--dc22

                              2006009711

ISBN: 1-59031-623-1

Contents

Foreword   xiii

Acknowledgments   xv

About the Editor   xvii

About the Contributors   xix

Introduction   xxv

Chapter 1
The History of the Citizen Oversight
by Samuel Walker   1

    A. Introduction   1
    B. A Definition of Citizen Oversight   2
    C. Years in the Wilderness: 1920s to 1970   2
    D. Years of Growth: 1970 to 1993   4
    E. Years of Consolidation and Development:
       1993 to the Present   5
    F. Setbacks   6
    G. Sources of Change   7
    H. Conclusion   9

Chapter 2
Alternative Models of Citizen Oversight
by Samuel Walker   11

    A. Introduction: Two Models of Oversight   11
    B. The Citizen Review Board Model   12
    C. The Police Auditor Model   14
    D. A Merger of Roles   16
    E. The Question of Effectiveness   17
    F. Conclusion   20

Chapter 3
Credibility, Impartiality, and Independence in Citizen Oversight
by Richard Jerome 21

A. Introduction 21
B. The Importance of Credibility and Impartiality 23
C. Building Credibility 24
   1. Selection Process for Oversight Agency Members 25
   2. Types of Individuals Selected 29
   3. Maintaining the Support of Stakeholders 32
      a. Police Unions 32
      b. Community Activists and Organizations 33
      c. Police Chief and Police Department Management (Command Staff) 34
      d. Mayor and City Council 34
   4. Expertise and Experience 36
      a. Professional Executive Direct and Professional Staff 36
      b. Expertise on Matters of Police Practices and Procedures 36
      c. Development of Written Procedures and Manuals for Investigations 37
      d. Review and Audit of Internal Processes 38
      e. Reports to the Public 38
      f. Experts and Consultants 38
      g. Policy Recommendations and Identifying Patterns 39
      h. Funding 40
      i. Vacancies 40
      j. Timely Action 41
D. Independence 42
   1. Creation 42
   2. Authority 42
   3. Stability 43
E. Conclusion 45

Chapter 4
Training *by Benjamin Jones* 47

A. Introduction 47
B. The Crossfire of Competing Interests Demands Adequate and Relevant Training 48

C. Adequate and Relevant Training Is Critical to Credible and
    Impartial Citizen Oversight   51
    1. Orientation to the Law Enforcement Agency   52
    2. Citizen Police Academies   53
    3. Ride-Alongs   55
    4. Internal Training Seminars   56
    5. External Training Seminars   56
    6. External Consultants   57
D. Conclusion   58

Chapter 5
Funding and Staffing *by Benjamin Jones* 59

A. Introduction   59
B. Sufficient Staff with Expertise   61
C. Compensation   61
D. Commitment to Reform   62
E. Active and Thorough Agencies   63
F. Independent Agencies   63
G. Agencies Overseeing a Large Law Enforcement Department   64
H. Backlogs   65
I. Operational Expenses   65
J. Training   66
K. Reporting   66
L. Professional Staff   66
M. Conclusion   68

Chapter 6
Access to Information *by Laura J. Cail* 71

Chapter 7
Collective Bargaining and Labor Agreements:
Challenges to Citizen Oversight
by Ronald J. Kramer & Elayne G. Gold 79

A. Introduction   79
B. Collective Bargaining Defined   80
C. Bargaining, Generally   81
D. Discipline and Disciplinary Procedures   82
    1. Bargaining Obligations   82
    2. Contract Issues   85

E. Subpoena Power   88
F. Union Representation   89
G. The New York Experience   90
    1. New York City   90
    2. Syracuse   91
    3. Rochester   93
H. Conclusion   95

Chapter 8
Municipal Subdivision Liability under Section 1983
by J. Rita McNeil   97

A. Municipal Subdivision Liability under Section 1983   97
    1. The Prior Law: Local Governments Could Not
       Be Sued   98
    2. The Current Law: Local Governments May Be Sued   98
    3. General Requirements for Local Government Liability
       under *Monell*   99
       a. Official Policy or Custom Requirement   99
       b. Two Bases of Liability, in Particular, the
          "Policymaker" Basis   99
       c. The Derivative Nature of Local Government
          Liability   100
       d. The Distinction between Official and Personal
          Capacity Suits   101
    4. Local Government Immunity   101
       a. No Qualified Immunity from Compensatory
          Damages: Measure of Compensatory Damages   101
       b. Absolute Immunity from Punitive Damages   103
    5. Supervisory Liability   103
       a. The "Affirmative Link" Requirement for
          Supervisory Liability   103
       b. "State of Mind" Requirements for "Failure to
          Train" Supervisory Liability   104
B. Immunities under Section 1983   105
    1. Absolute Immunity for Municipal Legislators for
       Their Legislative Actions   105
    2. Qualified Immunity   106

        a. Introduction to Qualified Immunity   106
        b. The "Objective" Qualified Immunity Test   106
            i. The Prior Two-Part Test   106
            ii. The Court's Shift to the Objective Test Alone   107
            iii. The Fact-Specific Inquiry Requirement   108
            iv. The Roles of Judge and Jury   109
    3. The Relevance of State Law   110
    4. Interlocutory Appeals from Denials of Defense
       Motions for Summary Judgment on the Basis of
       Qualified Immunity   110
        a. The Leading Case: *Mitchell v. Forsyth*   110
        b. Limited Scope of Interlocutory Appeals   111
        c. Frequency of Interlocutory Appeals   112
    5. Burdens of Pleading and Proof   112
        a. Burden of Pleading   112
        b. Burden of Proof   113

Chapter 9
Los Angeles County Sheriff's Department's Risk Management and
Civil Litigation Management Programs: One Law Enforcement
Agency's Response to High Litigation Costs
by Benjamin Jones & Shaun Mathers   **115**

    A. Introduction   115
    B. Internal Review   116
    C. External Review   117
    D. Toward a Strategic Risk Management Plan   117
      1. Sources of Liability   118
      2. Reexamining Existing Risk Management Philosophies 119
      3. Assessing Existing Systems and Practices   120
    E. Strategic Risk Management   121
      1. Expedited Settlements of Minor Civil Claims   121
      2. Earlier Identification and Intervention of High-Risk
        Incidents and High-Volume and Fee-Driven Litigation 124
      3. Corrective Action to Address Systematic
        Liability Issues   125
    F. Conclusion: The Results   126

Chapter 10
Citizen Complaints and Mediation
by Sue Quinn   127

A. Introduction	127
B. *Mediation* Defined	129
C. Investigations, Audits, and Mediation: Spokes in the Umbrella of Citizen Oversight	129
D. Investigation versus Mediation in Complaints about Individual Officers	130
1. To File or Not to File a Complaint: The Citizen	131
2. To Have a Complaint Filed: The Subject Officer	132
3. The Complaint Lands Here: The Supervisor/Manager	132
E. Mediation: The Un-Investigation	133
F. Shifting from "Exactly What Happened" to Shaping the Future	133
G. To Mediate or Investigate	135
H. Complaints Meriting Mediation	136
1. Examples of Complaints Appropriate for Mediation	138
I. Complaints Meriting Investigation	140
1. Examples of Complaints to Investigate	140
J. To Mediate or Investigate: Values, Risk Management, and Public Policy	140
1. Examples of Complaints to Investigate or Mediate	141
K. Legal Issues in the Mediation of Citizen Complaints	142
L. Resources	143
M. Models	144
N. Outside the Box: Envisioning Other Uses of Mediation in Citizen Oversight	145
1. Examples of Trends	145
O. Conclusion	146

Chapter 11
Community Outreach and Public Education in Citizen Oversight
by Lauri K. Stewart   147

A. Introduction: Why Outreach?	147
B. What Is Outreach?	148
1. Promoting Basic Agency Awareness	149
2. Reporting/Transparency	149

    3. Networking and Relationship Building   149
    4. Soliciting Business   149
    5. Recruiting Volunteers   149
    6. Soliciting Community Input and Involvement   150
    7. Basic Public Relations, Self-Promotion; Build, Maintain, or Restore Public Trust   150
    8. Education   150
    9. Liaising between Citizens, Police; Brokering Improved Relationships   150
   10. Coalition Building and Problem Solving or Prevention   151
C. What Are Your Outreach Goals?   151
D. What Kind of Agency Structure and Resources Do You Have to Work With?   152
E. What Does the Agency Do?   153
F. What Is the Life Stage of the Oversight Agency?   156
    1. The Formative Phase   156
       a. Identifying Stakeholders, Identifying Problems, and Evaluating Needs   157
       b. Researching Models and Best Practices and Educating Stakeholders about Choices   158
       c. Selecting Solutions and Making It Happen   159
    2. Hanging Your Shingle: The Brand New Agency   159
       a. Outreach to the Community   160
       b. Outreach to the Portland Police Bureau   161
    3. The Ongoing Enterprise   161
    4. Crises and Crossroads   163
G. Local Challenges and Outreach Needs   165
H. Conclusion   167

Chapter 12
What to Expect of Outreach: Different Strategies for Different Stakeholders
by Lauri K. Stewart   169

A. Introduction   169
B. Community Outreach and Public Education   170
    1. Complainants   170
    2. Targeted Segments of the Community   171
    3. Neighborhoods and the Community-at-Large   175

C. Elected Officials and Other Agencies   176
    1. Administration/Government Officials   176
    2. City Attorneys   179
    3. Allied Professionals   180
    4. The Police   181
    5. The Unions   183
    6. Command Staff   184
    7. Internal Affairs   185
    8. Rank-and-File Officers   186
    9. Special Units   187

Chapter 13
Nuts and Bolts: Using the Tools of the Outreach Trade
by Lauri K. Stewart   189

A. Introduction   189
B. Outbound Outreach: From the Agency to the Public   190
    1. Written Communication   190
        a. Agency Literature: Brochures and So Forth   191
        b. Web Pages   192
        c. Newsletters   194
        d. Agency Reports   195
C. Regular Reports   195
D. Special Reports   196
E. Nonwritten Forms of Outbound Outreach   197
    1. Informal Discussion and Networking with Individuals 197
    2. Speaker's Bureau: Dog and Pony Show   198
    3. Public Meetings and Case Hearings or Appeals   199
    4. Educational Presentations, Workshops, Seminars,
        Conferences   200
    5. Public Inquiries and Expert Panels: "Meet the Press" 201
F. Outbound Outreach through the Media   202
    1. Wait for the Media to Notice You or Decide to Pay
        Attention to You   202
    2. Press Releases   203
    3. The Active Pursuit of Media Attention   206
        a. Television   207
        b. Radio   208
        c. Videos   209

d. Purchasing Media Attention   209
e. Information Flyers/Bill Stuffers   210
4. Generate or Tap into Current Controversy or
Heightened Emotions   211
G. Inbound Outreach: Listening to and Engaging the Public   212
1. Advisory Committees, Councils, Task Forces, Panels   212
2. Public Forums   213
3. Focused Discussion Formats   215
4. Methods to Get at Very Specific Input   217
5. Hotlines   217
6. Employing Research Methodologies in Outreach   218
a. Surveys/Questionnaires   218
b. Focus Groups   219
c. Telephone Surveys   219
d. Face-to-Face Interviews   219
H. Conclusion: Pulling It All Together   220

Appendix A: Selected Bibliography   223

Appendix B: Listing of Citizen Oversight Agencies in the
United States   235

Table of Cases   259

Index   261

Foreword

Citizen oversight is an integral and important part of the landscape of American law enforcement. The involvement and participation of citizens in the review, investigation, and disposition of complaints of police misconduct has existed in the United States since the late 1920s. Today, more than 100 citizen police oversight agencies have been created across the country in nearly all of the largest cities, and citizen police oversight is spreading in medium- and smaller-sized cities as well as in towns, villages, and counties.

Whether you provide legal counsel to a municipality or department of law enforcement, serve as a member of an oversight agency, or are a municipal official, advocate, or member of the public, this compilation offers you the "nuts and bolts" of citizen oversight of law enforcement—the legal issues and policy considerations.

In this book, you will find important insights into this emerging area of law and public policy as well as practical advice and guidance from national scholars, experts, practitioners, and students of citizen police oversight. A comprehensive appendix of ready resources is sure to complete your oversight library.

Acknowledgments

This book is dedicated to my husband, David, and my son, Gabriel, whose love, support, and patience allowed me to complete this important and timely publication. I love you both very, very much!

I would also like to thank the many people whose input, guidance, and assistance helped to make this book a reality. Thank you to Patricia Salkin, Associate Dean and Director of the Government Law Center of Albany Law School, for hiring me five years ago to work for the only citizen oversight agency in the country to be staffed by a law school, involving me with the ABA Section of State and Local Government Law, conceiving the idea for this book, and encouraging me to go above and beyond. I am truly grateful.

Thank you to the officers, council, and members of the ABA Section of the State and Local Government, who welcomed me with open arms at my very first meeting in Chicago, supported me through the production of this project, especially during times of delay, and are just some of the best lawyers, colleagues, friends, and people that I have had the occasion to know.

Thank you to the staff and law student interns of the Government Law Center for their assistance with this project. In particular, thank you to our former administrative assistant, Ginny Battige, who helped to proofread, edit, and put together the appendices for this book. You are amazing.

Thank you to the ABA Publications staff for their assistance, especially members James Cavicchia and Barbara Leff, in guiding this book through production and marketing. I appreciate your efforts. A special thank you to the State and Local Government Law Section's Publications Liaison, Rick Paszkiet, for his patience and understanding throughout this process.

Thank you to the National Association for Civilian Oversight of Law Enforcement (NACOLE) for providing a national forum for the discussion of critical issues in police oversight and accountability and for serving as a repository for the exchange and sharing of information among the national and international citizen police oversight community. In particular, thank you to the many NACOLE members who offered input, insight, and information in the development of this book.

Last, but certainly not least, I would like to thank each of the contributing authors who gave of their time, energy, experience, and expertise—some of you in the eleventh hour—to complete what we hope will fill an important niche in this evolving area of government law and public policy.

Justina Cintrón Perino

About the Editor

Justina Cintrón Perino is a senior staff attorney at the Government Law Center of Albany Law School. She coordinates the Center's program on citizen oversight of law enforcement and has staffed the Albany Citizens' Police Review Board since November 2000. She also serves on the Adjunct Clinical Faculty at Albany Law School, where she teaches a course on government practice, law, and public policy to students interning in federal, state, and local government agencies and the state legislature. She is the author of several publications in the areas of police oversight, local government, and land use and has lectured on citizen oversight and local government issues. Ms. Perino is an officer of the American Bar Association's Section on State and Local Government Law, serving as the Section's newsletter editor, and holds various positions within the New York State Bar Association, including delegate to the House of Delegates, chair-elect of the Young Lawyers Section, member of the Executive Committee of the Municipal Law Section, and member of the Task Force on Electronic Communications. She is also a member of the Albany County Bar Association and the Capital District Black and Hispanic Bar Association. She received her B.A. degree, magna cum laude, from Boston College in 1997 and her J.D. degree from Albany Law School in 2000.

About the Contributors

Laura J. Cail is currently a third-year law student attending Albany Law School at Union University in Albany, New York, where she is on the dean's list and is a member of Albany Law Review. After working as a professional child caregiver, Miss Cail first entered the legal profession as a member of the support staff for the New York State Unemployment Insurance Appeal Board. Upon the sudden loss of her beloved father, Frederick Cail, Miss Cail chose to pursue her lifelong dream of becoming a lawyer. While working for two insurance defense firms, Miss Cail completed her associate's degree in Advanced Paralegal Studies at Mildred Elley College in Latham, New York, and one year of undergraduate studies at Excelsior College in Albany, New York. Miss Cail then requested, and was granted, early acceptance by Albany Law School, having completed three-fourths of her baccalaureate degree. Miss Cail credits the support of her mother, Gloria Cail, as the reason she has been able to endure the rigors of law school at this stage of her life, and she looks forward to her career in the legal profession.

Elayne G. Gold is a partner at Roemer, Wallens & Mineaux, L.L.P., where her practice is concentrated on representation of public-sector employers, engaging in negotiations, grievance and discipline resolution, day-to-day contract administration, and all labor-relations matters, including the development and delivery of specialized training programs for management and supervisory personnel. Ms. Gold is a trainer for the Capital Region's Zone 5 Police Academy Supervisor School and a frequent presenter to statewide employer organizations on a wide range of labor-related topics. She has been published in the New York State Bar Journal and Capital District Business Review and serves as an occasional lecturer at local colleges, New York State PERB, and Cornell University seminars.

Richard Jerome is the president of Richard Jerome, P.C., a firm providing legal and consulting services specializing in police reform and civil rights. Mr. Jerome is currently the deputy monitor and court-appointed special master for two police reform settlements in Cincinnati, Ohio. Other recent projects included a review of the Portland, Oregon, Police Bureau's officer-involved shootings (with the Police Assessment Research Center); an independent evaluation of the effectiveness of Albuquerque's police oversight system for the Albuquerque City Council; and assistance to the District of Columbia Council on police department responsibilities and standards for handling First Amendment assemblies and demonstrations. From 1997 to January 2001, Mr. Jerome served as deputy associate attorney general. He oversaw the work of the Civil Rights Division and the Community Relations Service, and coordinated the Department of Justice's efforts to promote police integrity.

Benjamin Jones is an attorney in private practice. For the past three years he has served as deputy chief attorney of the Office of Independent Review (OIR) and consults on civilian oversight issues. Created in 2001, OIR is an independent civilian oversight group composed of six attorneys who are retained by the Los Angeles County Board of Supervisors to oversee the Los Angeles County Sheriff's Department. Prior to returning to private practice, Mr. Jones was assistant U.S. attorney in Los Angeles for more than 10 years.

Ronald J. Kramer is a partner representing management in labor and employment law matters in the Chicago office of Seyfarth Shaw. He has been responsible for advising and representing private- and public-sector employers in a wide range of labor and employment issues, including but not limited to employment discrimination charges, investigations, settlements, and lawsuits; employee benefits (ERISA) litigation matters, including benefits claims and multiemployer withdrawal liability assessments; and traditional labor matters such as positive employee relations, union organizing drives, unfair labor practice charges, collective bargaining, strikes, interest arbitration, grievance, and arbitration matters. Mr. Kramer has also served as chief negotiator in collective-bargaining negotiations for numerous clients in their negotiations with unions such as the Laborers, IUOE, Painters, IAM, Teamsters, UFCW, IAFF, FOP, and MAP.

Shaun Mathers is a lieutenant in the Risk Management Bureau of the Los Angeles County Sheriff's Department. A 23-year veteran of the department, Lieutenant Mathers is responsible for the management and oversight of all the department's civil litigation.

J. Rita McNeil is currently the city solicitor for the City of Cincinnati. She graduated cum laude with a bachelors of business administration (B.B.A.) from Howard University in Washington, D.C. She received her J.D. from the Ohio State University College of Law, where she was an OSU Merit Scholar. Ms. McNeil most recently served as director of law for the City of Dayton, Ohio. She has also served in a variety of private- and public-sector capacities, including as the section chief for the Civil Rights Section for the Office of Ohio Attorney General Betty D. Montgomery; a juvenile referee/magistrate in the Franklin County Courts of Common Pleas; an associate with the law firms of Crabbe, Brown, Jones, Potts & Schmidt and Schottenstein, Zox & Dunn; the chief legal counsel for the Ohio Department of Commerce; and assistant deputy legal counsel for Ohio Governor George V. Voinovich. Ms. McNeil is a member of the American, Ohio State, and Cincinnati Bar Associations and serves on Ohio's Minority Development Finance Advisory Board, the Board of International Municipal Lawyers Association, the Governor's Community Service Council, the Board of the Tri-State Adoption Coalition, and is a member of Leadership Cincinnati Class XXVII. She was honored as one of *Business First* magazine's "Forty under 40" and as a distinguished alumni of The Ohio State University College of Law Black Law Students Association.

Sue Quinn has worked for more than 30 years to increase community cohesion and accountability within the justice system. A probation officer and manager from 1974 to 1992, she moved into civilian oversight as this field emerged in the early 1990s in southern California. She staffed San Diego County's Citizens' Law Enforcement Review Board (CLERB) when it opened in May 1992 as its first special investigator and as its acting executive officer from 1995 to 1997. In late 1997 she joined the board of the National Association of Civilian Oversight of Law Enforcement as NACOLE worked to build a networking, educative resource for jurisdictions attempting to develop credible oversight that served communities in the United States. She was NACOLE's first elected president and authored and maintains a number of the tutelary documents on NACOLE's Web site, NACOLE.org. She remains an active NACOLE member and lives in San Diego.

Lauri K. Stewart is the community relations coordinator and mediation program manager for the City of Portland's Independent Police Review. Previously, Ms. Stewart was a victim/witness specialist and Indian Country specialist with the U.S. Attorney's Office, District of Oregon. She has performed research in areas of social science, social services, and public health; taught on the faculty of Lower Columbia College in Washington State; worked as a television and newspaper journalist; and worked as a customer service supervisor. Ms. Stewart has a bachelor's degree in psychology and journalism from the University of Alaska and a master's degree in communications from the Annenberg School at the University of Pennsylvania.

Samuel Walker is the Isaacson Professor of Criminal Justice at the University of Nebraska at Omaha; he is now professor emeritus. His research interests involve police accountability, including citizen oversight of the police, early intervention systems for police officers, and the mediation of citizen complaints against police officers. Professor Walker is the author of 13 books on policing, criminal justice policy, and civil liberties. His most recent book is *The New World of Police Accountability* (2005). He is also the author of *The Police in America: An Introduction* (5th ed., 2005). He is also the author of *Police Accountability: The Role of Citizen Oversight* (2001), *Taming the System: The Control of Discretion in Criminal Justice, 1950–1990* (1993), *Sense and Nonsense about Crime* (5th ed., 2001), *The Color of Justice: Race, Ethnicity, and Crime in America* (with C. Spohn and M. DeLone; 3rd ed., 2003), and *In Defense of American Liberties: A History of the ACLU* (2nd ed., 2000). He is the author of *Early Intervention Systems for Law Enforcement*

Agencies: A Planning and Management Guide (2003), published by the COPS Office of the U.S. Justice Department. He currently serves as coordinator of the Police Professionalism Institute (PPI) at the University of Nebraska at Omaha. The PPI is engaged in a number of projects related to police relations with the Hispanic/Latino community, early intervention systems, national standards for police auditor systems, and a comparative analysis of police accountability in the United States, Latin America, and Europe. PPI reports are available at www.police accountability.org. Professor Walker has served as a consultant to the Civil Rights Division of the U.S. Department of Justice and to local governments and community groups in a number of cities across the country on police accountability issues.

Introduction

An emerging topic in local, state, and federal government law, citizen oversight of law enforcement combines an interesting and exciting blend of legal issues and public policy considerations. From the creation of an oversight agency to the determination of what form it will take, what authority and capacity it should be given, how it should be staffed and funded, how it will operate, what kind of opposition it will receive, how it will be presented to interested stakeholders, and what effect it will have on community–police relations and on the municipality as a whole, the goal of this book is to engage citizen oversight practitioners, especially legal practitioners, in an important and timely dialogue.

In Chapter 1, Samuel Walker, Isaacson Professor of Law at the University of Nebraska at Omaha and the leading national expert in this area, introduces the reader to citizen oversight of law enforcement. Through his historical tour of the oversight movement in the United States, Professor Walker guides the reader through three distinct periods, describing both setbacks and sources of change attributable to the growth and acceptance of the community policing concept.

Following his introduction, Professor Walker presents the reader with two alternative and competing models of citizen oversight: the citizen review board model and the police auditor model. In Chapter 2, Walker addresses the merger of these two models and discusses the current debate around questions of effectiveness.

In Chapter 3, noted police reform and civil rights attorney Richard Jerome sets forth the challenges facing citizen oversight agencies in establishing credibility while maintaining impartiality and independence. He identifies four key factors that are critical to the success of an oversight agency, presents ways in which an agency can build credibility through the selection of agency members, support of the key and interested stakeholders, and the agency's expertise and experience, and discusses the components of an agency's independence.

Citizen oversight consultant and practicing attorney Benjamin Jones discusses the importance of adequate and relevant training in building a credible, impartial, and effective citizen oversight agency in Chapter 4. In this chapter, Jones addresses training through internal agency orientation and citizen police academies, participation in ride-alongs, attendance at internal and external training seminars, and consultation with experts in the field.

Funding and staffing of citizen police oversight agencies is the focus of Chapter 5. In this chapter, Jones contends that an investment of sufficient and appropriate resources not only demonstrates a municipality's commitment to citizen police oversight, it increases the likelihood of an oversight agency's ability to be effective.

In Chapter 6, Albany Law School student Laura Cail presents the challenges faced by citizen oversight agencies in trying to access and obtain information from departments of law enforcement. In this chapter, Cail briefly addresses the tension that exists between the public's right to know public information and the state's interest in protecting information maintained by its law enforcement agencies in an effort to protect the health and welfare of its citizens. Cail also discusses how freedom of information laws can serve as a resource for gathering information.

Chicago labor lawyer Ronald Kramer and New York labor lawyer Elayne Gold describe the impact of collective bargaining and labor law issues on citizen police oversight in Chapter 7. In this chapter, Kramer outlines the general principles of collective bargaining and addresses how public sector labor laws can affect the scope of an oversight agency's power and authority, including its power to investigate and review complaints of misconduct, recommend and impose discipline, and compel testimony and/or the production of records through subpoena. The chapter concludes with Gold's discussion of the experiences of three New York municipalities: New York City, Syracuse, and Rochester.

The correlation between citizen oversight and claims against a municipality for the acts of its law enforcement officers raises several important legal issues. In *City of Canton v. Harris,* the United States Supreme Court held that "the inadequacy of police training may serve as a basis for Section 1983 liability ... where the failure to train amounts to deliberate indifference to the rights of persons with whom the police come into contact."[1] Lower courts have expanded the Supreme Court's deliberate indifference standard "beyond failure-to-train claims to claims based upon a municipality's inadequate system of hiring, supervising, or reviewing [incidents] of police misconduct."[2] A municipality's failure to implement adequate procedures to receive, investigate, and/or resolve citizen complaints against police officers may amount to "deliberate indifference," giving rise to a claim and subsequent liability under Section 1983.[3]

While very little has been written to address these legal issues and the questions they raise, Chapter 8 provides a comprehensive overview of the legal landscape of municipal subdivision liability under Section 1983. Cincinnati City Solicitor Julia "Rita" McNeil begins the chapter with a brief discussion of the state of the law before the seminal case of *Monell v. Department of Social Services* was decided by the United States Supreme Court. McNeil's attention shifts to a detailed treatment of the general requirements of local government liability under *Monell*, and the chapter concludes with a thorough explanation of absolute and qualified immunity defenses to Section 1983 claims.

Chapter 9 offers a case study of one law enforcement agency's approach to dealing with civil claims and lawsuits. In this chapter, Benjamin Jones and Lieutenant Shaun Mathers of the Los Angeles County Sheriff's Department describe the development of two innovative and complementary methods for assessing risk and managing civil litigation.

Advocate, well-known citizen oversight practitioner, and the first elected president of the National Association for Civilian Oversight of Law Enforcement, Sue Quinn explores mediation in citizen police oversight in Chapter 10. In this chapter, Quinn explains mediation as part of the larger citizen oversight umbrella, discusses how mediation rather than investigation can provide a quicker, more respectful, empowering

---

1. City of Canton v. Harris, 489 U.S. 378, 388; 109 S.Ct. 1197, 1204; 103 L. Ed. 2d 412, 426 (1989).
2. Hazel Glenn Beh, Municipal Liability for Failure to Investigate Citizen Complaints against Police, Fordham Urb. L.J. 25, 209, 225 (1998).
3. *Id.* at 210, 225–226.

and cost-effective remedy for certain complaints, outlines guidelines for determining whether to mediate or to investigate a complaint, highlights the legal issues and public policy considerations in citizen police oversight mediation, offers resources for the practitioner, identifies trends, and suggests expanded uses of mediation in police oversight.

In Chapter 11, Lauri Stewart, Community Relations Coordinator and Mediation Program Manager for Independent Police Review in Portland, Oregon, provides a thorough treatment of community outreach and public education in citizen oversight of law enforcement. In this chapter, Stewart defines "outreach," identifies goals and strategies to implement outreach objectives, and addresses challenges based on local needs and circumstances.

Strategies for dealing with different stakeholder groups are the focus of Chapter 12. In this chapter, Stewart presents the issues and challenges faced by a citizen oversight agency as it begins to develop its strategic community outreach and public education plan.

In Chapter 13, a "nuts and bolts" guide to the outreach tools of the citizen oversight trade is provided. With the benefit of hindsight, Stewart offers advice, guidance, and techniques to the citizen oversight practitioner.

The book concludes with a comprehensive appendix of ready resources: a selected bibliography with more than 100 articles, studies, reports, books, treatises, practitioner materials, and Web sites of interest; a detailed listing of U.S. citizen oversight agencies; sample laws, ordinances, bylaws, policies, rules and regulations, complaint forms, and brochures from various citizen police oversight agencies from around the country; and a chart of outreach tools of the trade.

Trends and development within the last 15 years suggest that citizen oversight is a permanent feature of the system of law enforcement in the United States, that there is no "one size fits all" approach to effective citizen oversight—oversight must be designed to address local challenges and meet local needs to achieve its goals, and that within the oversight community there are varying approaches at work to provide ideas, insights, useful information, and practical advice and guidance in this shared experience.

Justina Cintrón Perino

The History of the Citizen Oversight

1

Samuel Walker

A. INTRODUCTION

Citizen oversight is now an established feature of the institutional landscape of U.S. policing. The growth of citizen oversight over the last 35 years represents a dramatic change not only in formal criminal justice institutions but an even more profound change in public expectations about the police and in how police leaders (not the rank and file) respond to citizen input into the complaints process.[1]

By mid-2005 more than 100 oversight agencies covered the police departments in almost every large city in the United States (and consequently a substantial proportion of the population). Additionally, an increasing number of agencies covered county sheriff's departments and police departments in medium-sized cities. The growth of citizen oversight is not confined to the United States. External citizen oversight of the police is virtually univer-

---

1. SAMUEL WALKER, POLICE ACCOUNTABILITY: THE ROLE OF CITIZEN OVERSIGHT (2001). SAMUEL WALKER, THE NEW WORLD OF POLICE ACCOUNTABILITY (2005).

sal in the rest of the English-speaking world and is spreading in Latin America, Asia, and continental Europe.[2]

This chapter provides a brief overview of the history of the movement for citizen oversight in the United States. That history can be divided into three periods: the Years in the Wilderness, from the 1920s through 1970; the Years of Growth, from 1970 to about 1993; and the Years of Consolidation and Development, from 1993 to the present.

B. A DEFINITION OF CITIZEN OVERSIGHT

Citizen oversight of the police is defined here as an agency or procedure that involves participation by persons who are not sworn officers (citizens) in the review of citizen complaints against the police and/or other allegations of misconduct by police officers. It is important to note that in one fundamental respect, all law enforcement agencies in the United States are subject to control and direction by citizens through their elected representatives. This represents the very essence of policing in a democratic society. Mayors, governors, and presidents appoint law enforcement chief executives and have a large say in directing law enforcement agencies under their control through the appointment of agency chief executives and the setting of basic policy. City councils, county boards, state legislatures, and Congress exercise control through the budgetary process. The definition used here is more limited and refers to direct citizen involvement in the citizen complaints process. The nature of that involvement varies considerably among jurisdictions. This does not include involvement in issues of police policy as is the case in many community policing programs.[3]

C. YEARS IN THE WILDERNESS: 1920S TO 1970

From the 1920s through the late 1940s, citizen oversight of the police was a radical idea supported only by a small group of civil liberties activists. The idea first appeared in 1928 when the Los Angeles Bar

---

2. CIVILIAN OVERSIGHT OF POLICING: GOVERNANCE, DEMOCRACY AND HUMAN RIGHTS (Andrew Goldsmith & Colleen Lewis, eds., 2000). *See, e.g.,* the Canadian Association for Citizen Oversight of Law Enforcement (CACOLE) *at* http://www.cacole.ca/.

3. *See, e.g.,* the beat meetings in Chicago. WESLEY G. SKOGAN & SUSAN M. HARTNETT, COMMUNITY POLICING, CHICAGO STYLE (1997).

Association created a Committee on Constitutional Rights to receive complaints about police misconduct. The Committee, however, was an unofficial body with no power. In 1931, the Wickersham Commission report on *Lawlessness in Law Enforcement* recommended creating "some disinterested agency" in each city to help people who had complaints about the police.[4] In New York City, following a racial disturbance in 1935, a mayor's task force recommended "a committee of from five to seven Harlem citizens of both races to whom people may make complaint if mistreated by the police." Mayor Fiorello LaGuardia found this idea too radical, however, and did not accept it.[5]

The first official civilian review board was established in Washington, D.C., in 1948. Although a historically significant innovation, the Complaint Review Board (CRB) was extremely weak and ineffectual. A 1966 report concluded that it had "functioned quietly and infrequently," handling a total of only 54 cases between 1948 and 1964. Far more important was the Police Advisory Board (PAB) established in Philadelphia in 1958. The PAB consisted of a board of citizens who would receive citizen complaints, refer them to the police department for investigation, and then make a recommendation to the police commissioner for action after reviewing the police investigative file. The PAB also handled very few cases (particularly as measured by today's volume of complaints) and had minimal impact on police-community relations.[6]

The movement for citizen oversight exploded into a national issue in the 1960s as the civil rights movement challenged police misconduct in virtually every city. Along with the hiring of more African American officers, the creation of a civilian review board was one of the principal civil rights demands. Demands for civilian review appeared in many cities. The most important response occurred in New York City where Mayor John Lindsay in 1966 expanded the existing Civilian Complaint Review Board (CCRB; created in 1953 as a purely internal procedure) to include four nonpolice members, giving it a 4–3 civilian majority. The

---

4. NAT'L COMM'N ON LAW OBSERVANCE AND ENFORCEMENT, LAWLESSNESS IN LAW ENFORCEMENT 192 (Government Printing Office 1931).

5. The Mayor's Commission on Conditions in Harlem is discussed in THE POLITICS OF RIOT COMMISSIONS 159–95 (Anthony M. Platt ed., 1971).

6. Richard J. Terrill, *Police Accountability in Philadelphia: Retrospects and Prospects,* 7 AM. J. POLICE 79–97 (1988).

police rank and file reacted immediately and sponsored a referendum in November 1966 in which the voters abolished the expanded CCRB.[7]

In Philadelphia, meanwhile, the mayor allowed the PAB to lapse in 1969. By the end of the decade, with the two major civilian review boards abolished, citizen oversight of the police appeared to have no political support and no future.

D. YEARS OF GROWTH: 1970 TO 1993

Citizen oversight quietly revived in the 1970s. Kansas City, Missouri, created the Office of Citizen Complaints (OCC; authorized in 1969; operational in 1970), the first citizen oversight agency to survive to the present day. Like the old Philadelphia PAB, the OCC reviewed police investigations but had no independent power to investigate complaints. Even more important, in 1973, a referendum in Berkeley, California, established the Police Review Commission (PRC), the first oversight agency with independent authority to investigate complaints.[8] That same year Detroit voters created the Board of Police Commissioners (BPC) to govern the police department, and the board established its own complaint review process staffed by nonsworn investigators.[9]

The growth of oversight agencies steadily gained momentum. By 1980 there were about 13 agencies, and by 2000 more than 100.[10] Although the absolute number appears small, these agencies exist in all but a few of the major cities and counties and thereby cover a substantial portion of the population. The maturation of the oversight movement was marked by the creation of professional associations, the International Association of Citizen Oversight of Law Enforcement (IACOLE) in 1985 and later the National Association for Citizen Oversight of Law Enforcement (NACOLE).[11]

The creation of an oversight agency, however, was often just the first stage in a long struggle for legitimacy. The San Francisco OCC was cre-

---

7. ALGERNON BLACK, THE PEOPLE AND THE POLICE (1968).
8. See http://www.ci.berkeley.ca.us/prc.
9. See http://www.ci.detroit.mi.us/police_commissioners.
10. WALKER, POLICE ACCOUNTABILITY, *supra* note 1, at 6.
11. IACOLE has been only minimally functional in recent years. It has been largely supplanted by the National Association for Citizen Oversight of Law Enforcement (NACOLE), *see* http://www.nacole.org/.

ated in 1982, but it faced a combination of bitter opposition from the police union and indifferent support from the mayor's office for many years. It finally established an effective program of activities in the mid-1990s. The Citizens Police Review Board in neighboring Oakland, California, meanwhile, was severely hampered for many years because of noncooperation by police officers and other problems.[12]

E. YEARS OF CONSOLIDATION AND DEVELOPMENT: 1993 TO THE PRESENT

It is not possible to set a precise date for when citizen oversight finally became an established part of U.S. policing and entered into a period of maturation and development, but the year 1993 witnessed a number of important developments.

Most notably, several jurisdictions created police auditors, which emerged as an alternative model of oversight of the police. San Jose, California, established the Independent Police Auditor (IPA) that year, and Seattle created a Police Auditor. New York City, meanwhile, revised the CCRB once again, this time creating an agency fully independent of the police department. Perhaps even more important, Los Angeles County created the office of Special Counsel to the Los Angeles Sheriff's Department (LASD). Merrick Bobb, the Special Counsel, had a broad license to investigate any and all aspects of LASD operations and, over the next decade, established the most impressive record of achievement of any oversight agency.[13] In an even more notable development, Sheriff Lee Baca created the Office of Independent Review (OIR) for the LASD in 2002, making it the only law enforcement agency in the United States with two oversight agencies.[14]

One of the most important indicators of the maturity of the citizen oversight movement was the gradual development of professional standards for agencies along with activities that involved more than just investigating complaints. Although there are still no accepted national standards, a number of local agencies developed their own policies and

---

12. ACLU of Northern California, Failing the Test: Oakland's Police Complaint Process in Crisis (1996).

13. The reports of the Special Counsel are *available at* http://www.parc.info.

14. Los Angeles Sheriff's Department, Office of Independent Review, First Ann. Rep. 2002 at 32 (2002), *available at* http://laoir.com/report1.pdf.

procedures for the review of complaints. The San Jose IPA, for example, developed a set of formal criteria for evaluating whether a complaint investigation was thorough and fair.[15] The Boise, Idaho, Community Ombudsman produced a detailed policy and procedure manual that includes a lengthy policy on the classification of complaints, a clear policy regarding officer cooperation with investigations, the criteria for evaluating evidence and disposing of a complaint, and many other issues.[16] A 1997 referendum in San Francisco established a minimum of one OCC investigator for every 150 sworn officers in the police department.[17] This remains the only formal standard for the staffing of a complaint investigation procedure, either for an oversight agency or a police internal affairs unit. Several oversight agencies—in Minneapolis, New York City, Washington, D.C., among others—created mediation programs as an alternative method of resolving citizen complaints.[18] Finally, the (now-abolished) Minneapolis Civilian Review Authority (CRA) instituted a regular client survey procedure whereby both complainants and police officers subject to investigations could submit anonymous evaluations of how they felt they were treated.[19]

F. SETBACKS

Despite the steady growth of citizen oversight agencies, the movement has suffered a number of significant setbacks, in the form of agencies either failing to function effectively or being abolished altogether. The most important setback was the abolition of the Minneapolis CRA by a new mayor in 2002, despite the fact that the CRA had established a solid record of achievement and was rated highly by both complainants and officers. As a result, citizen complaints were not investigated for about two years until a new complaint procedure was established. The Santa Cruz, California, Citizen's Police Review Board was also abol-

---

15. *See* http://www.ci.san-jose.ca.us/ipa.

16. Boise Office of the Community Ombudsman, *Policies and Procedures* (2001), *available at* http://www.boiseombudsman.org/PoliciesProcedures2001. pdf.

17. *See* http://www.ci.sf.ca.us/occ.

18. Samuel Walker et al., *Mediating Citizen Complaints against Police Officers: A Guide for Police and Community Leaders* (2002), *available at* http://www. cops.usdoj.gov/pdf/e04021486web.pdf.

19. Minneapolis Civilian Rev. Authority, 2000 Ann. Rep. (2000).

ished in 2003 for budgetary reasons. Meanwhile, in Cambridge, Massachusetts, the Police Review and Advisory Board (PRAB) fell into disarray for more than a year as city officials did not appoint members to the board and attempted to merge it with another city agency. The Washington, D.C., CCRB was abolished in 1995, but it had been extremely dysfunctional. It was replaced by a new and more effective review board in 1999.[20]

A number of oversight agencies did not operate effectively. An evaluation of oversight in Albuquerque, New Mexico, found that the Independent Counsel, an auditor-style agency, and the Public Safety Advisory Board (PSAB), an advisory committee, had both failed to use their authorized powers adequately and had achieved little.[21] The Seattle Police Auditor also proved to be a low-visibility and ineffectual agency. The Pittsburgh Office of Municipal Investigations (OMI) was found to be deficient by the court-appointed monitor overseeing the settlement of a federal lawsuit.[22] Over the years, the New York City CCRB has been the subject of critical reports by the New York Civil Liberties Union (NYCLU), the leading advocate of citizen oversight in the city.[23]

G. SOURCES OF CHANGE

Several factors explain the growth of oversight from the 1970s to the present. Clearly, there was a significant change in public attitudes, which was reflected in the political process. In the 1960s, few elected city or county officials supported citizen oversight, and in New York City and Philadelphia, the police unions were able to use their political clout to abolish the agencies that liberal mayors had created. By the 1970s and 1980s, however, several oversight agencies were created directly by the votes in referenda or by city councils in response to a changed political

---

20. *See* http://www.occr.dc.gov/.

21. Samuel Walker & Eileen Luna, An Evaluation of the Oversight Mechanisms of the Albuquerque Police Department (Albuquerque City Council, February 1997). Report available at http://www.cabq.gov/council/abqrpt0.html.

22. The court's judgment was based on the report of the court-appointed auditor. Pittsburgh Police Bureau, Auditor's Eighteenth Q. Rep.: Quarter Ending February 16, 2002 (2002).

23. New York Civil Liberties Union, Five Years of Civilian Review: A Mandate Unfulfilled (1998). New York Civil Liberties Union, A Seventh Anniversary Overview of the Civilian Complaint Review Board (2000).

environment. Whereas in the 1960s, police unions were able to success-fully play the "crime card," arguing that oversight would cripple crime-fighting efforts,[24] by the 1980s such appeals were increasingly trumped by concerns about police accountability.

What brought about this profound change in public attitudes? There have been no academic studies of this question, but the evidence sug-gests a broad change in public attitudes toward official misconduct. On the one hand, incidents of serious police misconduct and the resulting community crises continued to occur in virtually every U.S. city. We can assume that an increasing number of Americans accepted the civil rights activists' argument that a serious problem of police misconduct existed and that the traditional police internal affairs units were not adequate.[25] In the 1960s and early 1970s, such respected authorities as the Presi-dent's Crime Commission[26] and the American Bar Association[27] expressed opposition to citizen oversight. By the 1980s, opposition from such elite sources had vanished.

It is also reasonable to speculate that the shift in public attitudes was influenced by the Watergate scandal and other revelations about official misconduct. A series of federal laws since the Watergate era indicate the growing public concern about the need for oversight of government agen-cies. These include the 1978 Inspector General Act related to a number of federal agencies,[28] a federal law also requiring ombudsmen for nursing homes to ensure quality care for patients,[29] and the 1974 Privacy Act con-trolling how government agencies use information about citizens.

---

24. RACE AND POLITICS IN NEW YORK CITY (Jewell Bush ed., 1971).

25. It is noteworthy that public opinion polls on the issue of racial profiling in recent years have found a significant number of white Americans agreeing that profiling exists.

26. PRESIDENT'S COMMISSION ON LAW ENFORCEMENT AND ADMINISTRATION OF JUSTICE, TASK FORCE REP.: THE POLICE (Government Printing Office 1967).

27. AMERICAN BAR ASSOCIATION, STANDARDS RELATING TO THE URBAN POLICE FUNCTION 1.148–1.150 (Little, Brown, 2d ed. 1980).

28. PAUL C. LIGHT, MONITORING GOVERNMENT: INSPECTORS GENERAL AND THE SEARCH FOR ACCOUNTABILITY (Brookings Institution 1993).

29. JO HARRIS-WEHLING et al., REAL PEOPLE, REAL PROBLEMS: AN EVALUA-TION OF THE LONG-TERM CARE OMBUDSMAN PROGRAMS OF THE OLDER AMERI-CANS ACT (1995).

There was also an important change in attitudes among the police. Through the 1960s, police chiefs adamantly opposed citizen oversight, and the International Association of Chiefs of Police (IACP) issued formal resolutions to that effect.[30] By the late 1980s, however, most police chiefs did not publicly oppose the creation of oversight agencies (although many were probably not enthusiastic about the concept). The community policing idea, which swept the country, held that police departments needed to establish partnerships with local communities and solicit public input regarding neighborhood problems. In this context, it became difficult if not impossible for a chief to then argue against citizen input with regard to complaints.

Local police unions remained fierce opponents of citizen oversight. The New York City Patrolmen's Benevolent Association (PBA) sponsored the 1966 referendum that abolished the citizen-dominated CCRB. Unions continued to fight the creation of oversight agencies but, as the growth of oversight indicates, were increasingly unsuccessful. Opposition also took the form of lawsuits challenging subpoena power or other features of oversight agencies, but these were also mostly unsuccessful. The most significant form of hostility was simple noncooperation, in some cases in violation of ordinances requiring cooperation.

Finally, the fact that a movement for citizen oversight of the police arose in other English-speaking countries in the 1970s and has since spread to other parts of the world suggests that the demand for oversight is not a unique U.S. phenomenon, but rather a reflection of common concern about controlling police misconduct in all urban industrial societies.[31]

H. CONCLUSION

The movement for citizen oversight fought a decades-long and bitter battle to gain legitimacy both as an idea and as a practical reality. That battle is now largely won, and the movement now faces new challenges, including the development of accepted professional standards for oversight agencies and performance measures that can indicate whether or

---

30. International Association of Chiefs of Police, *Police Review Boards,* THE POLICE CHIEF 12 (February 1964).

31. Goldsmith & Lewis eds., *supra* note 2.

not an agency is operating effectively. Citizen oversight is a major innovation in U.S. law enforcement. The growth of oversight agencies has transformed the institutional landscape of policing, requiring historically closed police departments to deal with external, citizen-run agencies on a routine basis.

Alternative Models of Citizen Oversight | 2

Samuel Walker

A. INTRODUCTION: TWO MODELS OF OVERSIGHT

The growth and development of citizen oversight has resulted in two general models of oversight agencies.[1] The traditional model can be labeled the *citizen review board*. This involves an agency that is independent of the police department and has the authority to receive and investigate citizen complaints against police officers. The alternative model can be labeled the *police auditor*. Police auditors are charged with the responsibility of auditing or monitoring the policies and procedures of the police department. Although they audit the citizen complaint process, they are not primarily responsible for investigating complaints.[2]

---

1. The different models are explained in detail in SAMUEL WALKER, POLICE ACCOUNTABILITY: THE ROLE OF CITIZEN OVERSIGHT (2001); and SAMUEL WALKER, THE NEW WORLD OF POLICE ACCOUNTABILITY (2005). A roster of current oversight agencies, with contact information, is available on the Web site of the National Association for Civilian Oversight of Law Enforcement (NACOLE), *at* http://www.nacole.org.

2. Agencies are described in detail in WALKER, POLICE ACCOUNTABILITY, *supra* note 1.

Enormous variations within each model exist with regard to source of legal authority, structure, designated powers, and activities. The picture is further complicated by the fact that in practice the two models are not entirely mutually exclusive. Some citizen review boards engage in activities that are the primary responsibility of police auditors, whereas some police auditors undertake investigations of individual cases.

B. THE CITIZEN REVIEW BOARD MODEL

The citizen review board, which has been the traditional demand of civil rights activists, involves an agency independent of the police department with responsibility for receiving and investigating citizen complaints. Review boards then send recommendations regarding the disposition of the complaint (e.g., sustained, not sustained, unfounded, or exonerated) to the police department for action. Review boards do not have the authority to impose discipline themselves. Review boards are independent municipal or county agencies, whose members are appointed, typically by the mayor and/or city council or county board of supervisors. Most review boards have some full-time professional staff, although some have or have had no staff.

Review boards are based on the assumption that police internal affairs units do not conduct thorough and fair investigations of citizen complaints and, consequently, do not succeed in disciplining guilty officers or deterring future misconduct. Innumerable investigations by government agencies and public interest groups—from the 1968 Kerner Commission[3] to the 1991 Christopher Commission[4] and various ACLU reports[5]—have documented the shortcomings of internal police complaint procedures. The principal failings include: (1) not publicizing the complaint process, (2) turning away many citizens who express a desire to file a complaint, (3) failing to locate and identify potential witnesses

---

3. Nat'l Advisory Comm'n on Civil Disorders, Report (1968).

4. Christopher Commission, *Report of the Independent Commission on the Los Angeles Police Department* (1991), *at* http://www.parc.info/reports/pdf/chistophercommision.pdf.

5. *See, e.g.,* ACLU of Northern California, A Campaign of Deception: San Jose's Case Against Civilian Review (1992).

to an incident, (4) asking leading questions to officers and hostile questions to complainants, (5) giving an automatic preference to officers' statements, and (6) reaching dispositions that are not supported by the facts of the case.

Advocates of citizen review boards argue that complaint investigations conducted by an independent agency and by investigators who are not sworn officers will necessarily be more independent, thorough, and fair than investigations by police internal affairs units.[6] In terms of their basic orientation, citizen review boards embody a *criminal trial model* of citizen oversight. They investigate citizen complaints for the purpose of determining guilt or innocence and then recommend punishment of guilty officers. The investigative process is bound by elaborate rules of procedure designed to protect the rights of accused officers.[7] It is assumed that punishment of guilty officers will both render justice in the immediate case and also deter future misconduct.

Examples of citizen review boards with full authority to receive and investigate complaints include: the New York City Civilian Complaint Review Board (CCRB);[8] the Washington, D.C., Office of Police Complaint (OPC), formerly the Office of Citizen Complaint Review (OCCR);[9] and the San Francisco Office of Citizen Complaints (OCC).[10] A number of other review boards do not independently investigate complaints but instead review the investigative files completed by the police internal affairs unit. These agencies include the Kansas City Office of Community Complaints (OCC).[11]

---

6. The issue of what constitutes "independence" has not been adequately discussed in the literature on citizen oversight. *But see* Richard J. Terrill, *Alternative Perceptions of Independence in Civilian Oversight,* 17 J. POLICE SCI. & ADMIN. 77–83 (1990); and WALKER, POLICE ACCOUNTABILITY, *supra* note 1, at 61–67.

7. The criminal trial model is explained in greater detail in WALKER, POLICE ACCOUNTABILITY, *supra* note 1.

8. *See New York City Civilian Review Complaint Board, at* http://www.nyc.gov/html/ccrb/home.html.

9. *See District of Columbia Office of Police Complaints, at* http://www.occr.dc.gov.

10. *See San Francisco Office of Citizen Complaints, at* http://www.ci.sf.ca.us/occ.

11. *See Office of Community Complaints, at* http://www.kcpd.org/kcpd2004/OCC.htm. In an earlier classification scheme, review boards without independent power to investigate complaints are defined as Class II systems. *See* WALKER, POLICE ACCOUNTABILITY, *supra* note 1.

C. THE POLICE AUDITOR MODEL

The alternative model of oversight is the *police auditor model*.[12] In this model, the police department retains responsibility for receiving and investigating citizen complaints, whereas the auditor has the responsibility for examining or monitoring the department's complaint process for purposes of quality control. Some auditors are able to request additional investigation in cases in which they find the police investigation inadequate and to recommend changes in police department policies and procedures. Auditors publish periodic reports that reflect their activities and provide an important element of openness or transparency for the police department in question.

As of 2005, 13 police auditors in the United States covered 12 law enforcement agencies (the Los Angeles County Sheriff's Department has two separate auditors). This represents about 10 percent of all citizen oversight agencies. Examples include the San Jose Independent Police Auditor (IPA),[13] the Special Counsel to the Los Angeles County Sheriff's Department,[14] and the Boise Community Ombudsman. The newest is the Denver police auditor, which began operating in mid-2005.[15]

It is important to distinguish police auditors from other agencies that investigate police departments. The traditional blue-ribbon commission (e.g., the Kerner Commission, the Christopher Commission) is a temporary agency that disbands after issuing its final report. The historic limitation of blue-ribbon commissions is that they have no power to even monitor implementation of their recommendations, much less enforce them. Police auditors have the capacity to conduct follow-up investigations, and although they cannot compel implementation of their recommendations they do have the power to publicly expose implementation failures.[16]

---

12. The role of police auditors in relationship to other police accountability mechanisms is described in detail in WALKER, NEW WORLD, *supra* note 1, at ch. 6.

13. *See* Office of the Independent Police Auditor, *at* http://www.ci.san-jose.ca.us/ipa.

14. The reports of the Special Counsel are available *at* Police Assessment Resource Center, *at* http://www.parc.info.

15. *See Boise Community Ombudsman, at* http://www.boiseombudsman.org.

16. Samuel Walker, *Setting the Standards: The Efforts and Impact of Blue Ribbon Commissions on the Police, in* POLICE LEADERSHIP IN AMERICA: CRISIS AND OPPORTUNITY 354–70 (William A. Geller ed., 1985).

A police monitor, on the other hand, is a court-appointed official responsible for ensuring implementation of a court-ordered consent decree or memorandum of agreement. Monitors have been appointed following settlements of federal *pattern or practice* suits under Section 14141 of the Violent Crime Control Act.[17] The responsibility of a monitor is limited to the specific terms of the court-ordered settlement and to the lifetime of the settlement.

Finally, some police departments in the United States (Detroit, Los Angeles, San Francisco, Kansas City, and St. Louis) are governed by police commissions. Although they technically represent a form of citizen oversight, these commissions have generally not taken a direct role in handling citizen complaints. Indeed, one of the major criticisms of the Los Angeles Police Commission has been its deference to the police department.[18]

Unlike citizen review boards that focus on individual complaints, the principal role of police auditors is on organizational change. In a process known as *policy review,* auditors investigate problems in the complaint process or some other aspect of police procedures and recommend corrective action to the chief executive.[19] The San Jose IPA, for example, made a total of 48 recommendations between 1993 and 2000, almost all of which were adopted by the San Jose Police Department.[20] Over the course of 11 years, Merrick Bobb, the special counsel to the Los Angeles County Sheriff's Department (LASD), has investigated more than 25 separate issues in the LASD. These include a use of deadly and physical force, foot pursuits, sexual harassment, racial and

---

17. *See* Violent Crime Control and Law Enforcement Act, 42 U.S.C.A. § 14141 (2005). The activities of the Special Litigation Section of the Civil Rights Division of the U.S. Justice Department under this provision are *available at* http://www.usdoj.gov/crt/split.

18. The Los Angeles Board of Police Commissioners has been criticized for years for being too deferential to the Los Angeles Police Department. Joe Domanick, LAPD: To Protect and to Serve 151–53 (1995).

19. Policy review is discussed in detail in Walker, Police Accountability, *supra* note 1; and Walker, New World, *supra* note 1.

20. San Jose Independent Police Auditor, 2001 Year End Report 66–71 (2002), *available at* http://www.sanjoseca.gov/ipa/2001%20YER.html.

gender issues related to promotions, the operations of the department's early intervention system, conditions in the jails, and so on.[21]

Mike Gennaco, head of the Office of Independent Review (OIR) in the LASD, explained the strategy guiding his office:

> To change behavior effectively, an oversight body *must look beyond the particular cases of misconduct to systemic issues implicating policy and training* [emphasis added].... Accordingly, OIR endeavors to use individual cases to identify ambiguities in policy, laxity in enforcement, and deficiencies in training. Whenever policies and practices can be reformed to eliminate potential civil rights violations and future liability, it will directly benefit the people of Los Angeles County.[22]

An important feature of police auditors is the capacity for sustained follow-up on issues to determine whether or not policy recommendations have been adopted. This capacity addresses not only the historic limitation of blue-ribbon commissions but also the more general problem of sustaining reforms that have been implemented—a problem that has plagued police reform for generations.[23]

D. A MERGER OF ROLES

As already mentioned, the roles of citizen review board and police auditors are not entirely mutually exclusive, and there is some overlap in terms of activities. The San Francisco OCC, a review board, also engages in auditor-style policy review and has made a number of policy recommendations over the years, including a total of 12 in 1999.[24] Similarly, the New York City CCRB and the Washington, D.C., OPC have made

---

21. The reports are *available at* www.parc.info. The achievements of the Special Counsel are discussed in WALKER, NEW WORLD, *supra* note 1.

22. LOS ANGELES SHERIFF'S DEPARTMENT, OFFICE OF INDEPENDENT REVIEW, FIRST ANNUAL REPORT 2002 32 (2002), *available at* http://laoir.com/report1.pdf.

23. This issue is discussed at length in WALKER, NEW WORLD, *supra* note 1.

24. *See San Francisco Office of Citizen Complaints, at* http://www.ci.sf.ca.us/occ.

policy recommendations on important issues. The Boise Ombudsman conducts investigations of critical incidents and has issued follow-up reports on several controversial cases. Additionally, a staff member is notified and does an immediate *rollout* to shootings and other critical incidents.[25] The Office of Internal Review in the LASD also conducts immediate rollouts and follows up on particular incidents that appear problematic.[26]

The Seattle Office of Professional Accountability (OPA) has a particularly ambiguous role. The OPA director is in charge of the police department's internal affairs unit but, by ordinance, must be a non-sworn employee. In short, the OPA is both an "outsider" and an "insider" with respect to the Seattle Police Department. In addition to responsibility for supervising internal complaint investigations, the OPA director has also issued a number of policy reports on issues of use of force and racial profiling that are similar to reports issued by other police auditors.[27]

E. THE QUESTION OF EFFECTIVENESS

The development of alternative models of citizen oversight has prompted a debate over their respective effectiveness. It should be noted, however, that this debate has been conducted in the absence of systematic empirical data. There are no studies evaluating the effectiveness of any citizen oversight agency, much less any comparative studies of different agencies. Consequently, the debate has been conducted largely on the basis of assumptions about effectiveness of different approaches, supported by fragmentary and often impressionistic evidence.

Discussions of effectiveness have generally failed to take into account the different goals of oversight. There are seven major goals:[28] (1) to ensure independent and fair investigations of citizen complaints, (2) to sustain a properly high rate of complaints in favor of complain-

---

25. *See Boise Community Ombudsman, at* http://www.boiseombudsman.org.

26. *See County of Los Angeles Office of Independent Review, at* http://laoir.com.

27. *See Seattle Police Department Office of Professional Accountability, at* http://www.ci.seattle.wa.us/police/opa.

28. *See* WALKER, POLICE ACCOUNTABLITY, *supra* note 1. The earlier book identified six goals.

ants, (3) to produce proper discipline of officers guilty of misconduct, (4) to deter future misconduct, (5) to provide a satisfactory experience for both complainants and officers, (6) to promote a climate of openness or transparency for the police department, and (7) to enhance the overall professionalism of the police. Most of these issues have not been investigated, and no comprehensive evaluation of an oversight agency takes all or even most of them into account.

The old debate over citizen oversight centered on the question of the legitimacy of oversight. The traditional opponents of citizen oversight, mainly the police, argue that citizen involvement is dysfunctional because it undermines effective police management.[29] This argument has been undermined by the community policing movement, which places great emphasis on citizen input into police strategies and tactics.[30] The police have also argued that citizens lack sufficient expertise in policing to be able to judge complaints. This argument, however, ignores the historic role of juries in which lay people are asked to make judgments about disputed incidents after hearing both sides of the matter. Finally, the police have argued that being "second-guessed" by citizens will deter them from effective police work. There is no evidence to support this argument, however.

Most of the political (as opposed to the academic) debate over oversight has focused on the *sustain rate,* the percentage of complaints sustained in favor of the complainant. Although advocates of oversight point out that internal complaint procedures sustain only about 10 to 13 percent of complaints, the evidence indicates that oversight agencies have roughly similar sustain rates. A number of experts, including this author, argue that citizen complaints are inherently difficult to sustain.[31] There are generally neither independent witnesses nor objective forensic evidence (e.g., medical records) that would facilitate a clear resolution. Consequently, most complaints are the proverbial "swearing contests," with each side making allegations that are not supported by independent evidence. These problems affect both internal police affairs units and citizen review boards alike. The advocates of police auditors argue

---

29. Americans for Effective Law Enforcement, Police Civilian Review Boards (1982).

30. David Bayley, Police for the Future (1994).

31. See the argument in Walker, Police Accountability, *supra* note 1.

that because complaints are inherently difficult to sustain, it is not advisable to use the sustain rate as a performance measure for oversight agencies and that other measures should be developed.

The present debate about the effectiveness of oversight centers on the question of the relative merits of the review board and police auditor models. Critics of the auditor model argue that auditors are essentially powerless because they have no power to conduct independent investigations.[32] For some review board advocates, police auditors are suspect by virtue of the fact that the model first appeared as a political compromise. In San Jose and Seattle, police auditors were adopted as an alternative to review boards that civil rights activists demanded.[33] Additionally, auditors cannot compel police departments to adopt their policy recommendations. Auditor model advocates reply by pointing out that review boards also have only the power to make recommendations regarding the disposition of complaints and have no power to impose discipline on officers.[34]

The advocates of the police auditor model argue that focusing on organizational change is far more likely to improve policing in the long run than is handling individual complaints. Focusing on individual officers, as review boards do, makes the lowest-ranking members of a police department scapegoats for larger organizational problems. Law professor Barbara Armacost argues that "it is unfair to lay the moral responsibility for police misconduct solely at the feet of individual officers."[35]

Police auditor advocates argue that changes in police department policies and procedures, such as the use of force policies, the handling of the canine unit, or how critical incidents are investigated (issues that have been investigated by existing auditors), are likely to result in long-term improvements in policing and prevent misconduct from occurring

---

32. ACLU OF NORTHERN CALIFORNIA, *supra* note 5.

33. WALKER, POLICE ACCOUNTABILITY, *supra* note 1, at ch. 2.

34. In most jurisdictions, granting an oversight agency the power to impose discipline would require changes in city or county charters and possibly state law. Additionally, many police accountability experts, including this author, argue that taking the power to discipline officers away from police chiefs would be inadvisable and likely to undermine accountability in the long run.

35. Barbara Armacost, *Organizational Culture and Police Misconduct,* 72 GEO. WASH. L. REV. 493 (2004).

in the future. Additionally, they argue that the policy review process and the publication of their reports open up historically closed police organizations and create a critically needed element of transparency with regard to the police department.

In *The New World of Police Accountability,* Walker argues that the role of the police auditor is not only consistent with other reforms designed to enhance police accountability (e.g., use of force reporting, improved citizen complaint procedures, early intervention systems) but also plays an important role in reinforcing them. Police auditors in Los Angeles County and Philadelphia, for example, have investigated and reported on the extent to which use of force reporting procedures and early intervention systems are functioning as intended.[36]

The arguments in favor of police auditors, it must be said, have not been validated by independent research. The special counsel to the Los Angeles County Sheriff's Department is the only oversight agency that has offered data indicating its effectiveness. It has documented, for example, a decline in civil litigation and payments arising from police misconduct claims and also a substantial decline in the use of the LASD canine unit and a reduction in the number of citizens bitten by the unit's dogs.[37]

F. CONCLUSION

There are presently two basic models of citizen oversight of the police. The emergence of competing models and the resulting debate over their relative effectiveness are indicators of the maturity of the oversight movement. At present, there are no systematic evaluations that permit a definitive judgment about the effectiveness of either model or even about particular programs or activities within each model. Developing appropriate performance measures and sponsoring independent research are the most important issues facing the citizen oversight movement.

---

36. WALKER, NEW WORLD, *supra* note 1.

37. LOS ANGELES SHERIFF'S DEPARTMENT, SPECIAL COUNSEL MERRICK J. BOBB ET AL., ELEVENTH SEMIANNUAL REPORT 77–83 (October 1999), *available at* http://lacounty.info/11threport.htm; and LOS ANGELES SHERIFF'S DEPARTMENT, SPE-CIAL COUNSEL MERRICK J. BOBB ET AL., FIFTEENTH SEMIANNUAL REPORT 97–108 (July 2002), *available at* http://www.parc.info/projects/pdf/July02reporttext.pdf.

Credibility, Impartiality, and Independence in Citizen Oversight

3

Richard Jerome

A. INTRODUCTION

The challenges facing citizen oversight entities are great. Can they be effective in reviewing and prompting change in a law enforcement agency when those agencies are traditionally insular and suspicious of outsiders, jealous of their own authority to manage and discipline their members, and those members have legitimate, but oftentimes overwhelming, procedural rights and protections for their actions? Can they maintain credibility with groups in the community that have widely different, and sometimes polar opposite, views of the police and still retain the support of the oversight agency's appointing authority? Can they make appropriate and difficult determinations relating to individual citizen complaints for which the facts are in dispute and for which there is often little independent evidence? And, how can they do it on a shoestring budget (sometimes no budget at all) with limited staff (if they are lucky enough to have staff)?

Over the last decade, citizen oversight of the police has gained in numbers and public acceptance. Yet it remains controversial with police rank and file, and its effectiveness is often a matter of dispute. Although the expectations for citizen oversight bodies are high, those expectations are too often not fulfilled. Certainly there have been failures and problems with citizen oversight of police departments, but there have been successes, too.

As noted in an earlier chapter, there are a wide variety of types of citizen oversight. This makes broad pronouncements about what works more difficult. There are also difficulties in measuring success, as there are multiple goals of citizen oversight, some of which may be in conflict.[1] A number of commentators have endorsed particular types of citizen review, such as monitors and auditors. These may indeed be more effective in critically evaluating police practices and enhancing accountability in police investigations of misconduct. The auditor/monitor model may do less well, however, in providing a public forum for community concerns about police practices and giving citizens with complaints an opportunity to be heard.[2] Moreover, even police auditors and monitors face difficulties in getting their recommendations adopted and obtaining adequate funding. Whichever type of oversight entity is chosen, it is important to ask if there are factors that predict success, or at least contribute to its possibility.

---

1. *See, e.g.*, Cheryl Beattie & Ronald Weitzer, *Race, Democracy and Law: Citizen Review of Police in D.C., in* CITIZEN OVERSIGHT OF POLICING: GOVERNANCE, DEMOCRACY AND HUMAN RIGHTS 41 (Andrew Goldsmith & Colleen Lewis eds., 2001), on the conflict between goal of impartial review of complaints and goal of representing community interests.

2. *See* Merrick Bobb, *Citizen Oversight of the Police in the United States*, 22 ST. LOUIS U. PUB. L. REV. 151 (2003); Samuel Walker, *New Directions in Citizen Oversight: The Auditor Approach to Handling Citizen Complaints, in* PROBLEM-ORIENTED POLICING (Tara Shelley & Anne Grant eds., Police Executive Research Forum 1998); PolicyLink, *Community Centered Policing: A Force for Change* 78 (2001), *available at* http://www.policylink.org/pdfs/ForceForChange.pdf; City of Sacramento Blue Ribbon Citizens Committee, *Report of the Blue Ribbon Committee on Selected Police Practices* (1998).

There are a number of key factors that are critical to the success of a citizen oversight agency. These include: (1) ensuring sufficient authority for the agency and the organizational capacity to carry out that authority, (2) establishing the agency's credibility and impartiality, (3) managing the stakeholders' expectations of the agency, and (4) effectively conducting outreach to the public. Earlier chapters have addressed the goals of citizen oversight, the forms that such oversight can take, and the appropriate powers that a citizen oversight entity might possess. This chapter will focus on how citizen oversight entities can establish credibility with the police, the public, and its appointing authority, and how they can maintain their independence and impartiality.

B. THE IMPORTANCE OF CREDIBILITY AND IMPARTIALITY

With a few exceptions, citizen oversight entities lack the power to discipline police officers directly. When addressing individual complaints of police misconduct, the outcomes of the deliberations of most citizen oversight agencies are recommendations back to the chief of police or city manager on the disposition of complaints and the imposition of discipline.[3] This is true whether or not agencies are citizen review boards

---

3. There are some police commissions, such as the Los Angeles Police Commission and the Detroit Police Board, for which the citizen authority is the deciding entity for officer discipline. These are rare, however. Although community activists often lament the fact that citizen oversight bodies do not have the authority to discipline officers directly, most academics and practitioners acknowledge that the best avenue for police integrity is a police executive who sets an ethical tone for the department and holds his or her officers to account. The ability of the chief to impose discipline is necessary for that to occur. *See, e.g.,* HERMAN GOLDSTEIN, POLICING A FREE SOCIETY 174 (1977) ("Given the decentralized and dispersed nature of police organizations, it is utterly hopeless to attempt to control police conduct other than by making the administrative system work. No court or specially constituted citizen body, based outside the police agency, can possibly provide the kind of day-to-day direction that is essential if the behavior of police officers at the operating level is to be effectively controlled.").

that only hear appeals from police department internal affairs divisions, oversight entities that conduct their own investigations, or auditor/monitor models that oversee and in some cases directly participate in internal affairs investigations. Similarly, oversight entities generally do not have the power to change police department policies. Instead, they report and recommend. To accomplish their objectives, citizen oversight bodies must rely on the strength of their reputation and on their powers of persuasion.

Citizen oversight agencies are created: (1) to provide an objective review of citizen complaints, either through an initial investigation or an appeal from an investigation of the police department; (2) to make recommendations for improving police policy and practice, especially with respect to police integrity; (3) to serve as a public forum for community concerns regarding the police department; and (4) to increase public trust in the police and improve police-community relations. None of these functions can be accomplished effectively if the entity is viewed as:

- biased (either toward police or against police),
- untrained or ill-informed,
- lacking status within the government, or
- ineffectual and powerless.

As will be discussed below, the credibility necessary to effectively serve as a check on police misconduct depends on both the actual powers and performance of the agency and the perceptions of the community.

C. BUILDING CREDIBILITY

There is no playbook for establishing credibility. Rather, it stems from a combination of factors: who the members of the oversight entity are, how they were selected, what powers they have, their relations with other political officials such as the mayor and council, and, most importantly, what they do.

1. Selection Process for Oversight Agency Members

It seems obvious, but who is selected to be on the oversight board or to be the auditor/monitor makes a tremendous difference. The process by which they are selected may also have an impact on the type of persons selected and on whether they are perceived to be independent by members of the public.

For citizen review boards, most jurisdictions have the mayor appoint board members because the oversight entity is normally viewed as an executive agency or advisory body within the government. It is important that the mayor's selections be viewed as balanced. If the mayor is not perceived as interested in police reform, it will be difficult for the appointments to be viewed that way.

In many cases, the city council will have the power to confirm the mayor's selections. A number of cities provide that city council members make the initial nominations to the oversight body, with the appointments made by the mayor. A few cities have a mixed selection whereby some members are selected by the council and others by the mayor. The table below illustrates a sample of agencies with a variety of selection methods.[4]

---

4. A good source of information on oversight agencies is the roster of agencies listed on the Web site of the National Association of Citizen Oversight of Law Enforcement (NACOLE), *at* http://www.nacole.org.

City	Agency	Number of Members	Appointment Process
Albuquerque, N.M.	Police Oversight Commission	7 members	Appointed by mayor, from nominations by City Council[5]
Baltimore, Md.	Citizen Review Board	9 voting members, 3 nonvoting members	Appointed by mayor, confirmed by City Council
Cincinnati, Ohio	Citizen Complaint Authority	7 members	Mayoral appointment, City Council confirmation
New York City	Citizen Complaint Review Board	13 members	Hybrid system[6]
San Francisco	Police Commission	9 members	Hybrid system with appointments by Board of Supervisors and mayor
Seattle, Wash.	OPA Review Board	3 members	Mayor appoints
Washington, D.C.	Citizen Complaint Review Board	5 members	Mayor appoints, with council approval

---

5. The POC's seven members are appointed by the mayor, with the advice and consent of the City Council. Each Council member nominates one individual, and the mayor appoints five POC members from among the nine nominations, plus two additional members. Nominees may not have been employed in law enforcement for two years prior to their appointment.

6. New York City's Citizen Complaint Review Board has one of the more complicated appointment structures. It is a 13-member board. Of these, five are appointed directly by the mayor; five are appointed by the mayor, but nominated by New York's City Council, one to represent each of New York's five boroughs; and three Board members are nominated by the police commissioner. The three Board members nominated by the police commissioner are

There have been no empirical studies assessing whether or not the method of appointment has an impact on the agency's actions. However, involving the city council in the appointment is viewed by some as adding to the independence of the entity.[7]

In 2003, San Francisco passed a charter amendment, Proposition H, that amended the way that the Police Commission in San Francisco is selected.[8] The San Francisco Police Commission oversees the Police Department (SFPD) and the Office of Citizen Complaints, the agency that investigates complaints against members of the SFPD.[9] Before Proposition H, the Police Commission consisted of five members who were appointed by the mayor.

Some commentators criticized earlier appointments because the mayor was not viewed as sufficiently "reform minded." The Police Commission and the Office of Citizen Complaints were also criticized for their lack of authority and independence.[10] To address these concerns,

---

permitted to have prior law enforcement experience. The other members may not have been law enforcement professionals or be former employees of the NYPD, although they can be former prosecutors.

7. *See* Sam Walker, *Oversight and Accountability: A Statement of Principles, at* http://www.policeaccountability.org/statementopa.htm ("Members should be appointed by both the mayor and the city council. This guarantees that all parts of the community will be represented and that no one person or faction will control the board."); PolicyLink, *supra* note 2, at 79. Recent efforts to create citizen oversight entities have reflected this debate over the method of selection. In St. Louis, Missouri, the creation of a citizen review board in May 2004 was controversial with some activists because the mayor has the power to appoint all of its members, whereas earlier proposals would have created a hybrid board with both appointed members and elected members. Doug Moore & Bill Bryan, *Police Board Sets Up Review Panel,* St. Louis Dispatch, May 20, 2004, at C1.

8. *See Proposition H, Police Commission/Office of Citizen Complaints, City of San Francisco, at* http://www.smartvoter.org/2003/11/04/ca/sf/meas/H.

9. The Police Commission also hears appeals from suspensions of police officers of less than 10 days and tries and hears cases of police termination and suspensions of more than 10 days.

10. Mark Schlossberg, Roadmap to Reform—Strengthening the Accountability Mechanisms of the San Francisco Police Department (2003).

the American Civil Liberties Union (ACLU) of northern California and other community groups mounted a political campaign to change the way the Police Commission was appointed.[11]

Proposition H expanded the Police Commission from five members to seven, with four members nominated by the mayor and confirmed by the Board of Supervisors and three members nominated by the Rules Committee of the Board of Supervisors and confirmed by the full Board of Supervisors. There was a well-funded campaign on both sides, with the local police union vigorously opposing the change.[12] Proposition H was seen as making a difference in whether the Commission would be "more independent," in the ACLU's view, or "more political," in the view of the police union and the city's main newspaper.[13] Passed in November 2003, it may still be too early to tell whether or not this change will have the impact its supporters intended. Recent statements of the appointed Police Commission members suggest, however, that they view Proposition H as sending a distinct message: "When voters passed Proposition H, they wanted to see some fairly substantial changes in the Police Department."[14]

Miami-Dade County, Florida, has gone a step further in adjusting its appointment process to obtain community representation on its citizen oversight body. The Independent Review Panel (IRP) of Miami-Dade County consists of nine members, five of whom are chosen from lists provided by organizations in the community. The Community Relations Board, the Community Action Agency, the Miami-Dade League of Women Voters, the Miami-Dade County Bar Association, and the

---

11. Proposition H also made changes to the powers of the OCC and the procedures for handling citizen complaints.

12. Jaxon Van Derbeken, *Police Department Reform on San Francisco Ballot,* S.F. CHRON., Oct. 21, 2003, at A15.

13. An editorial in the San Francisco Chronicle opposed the effort to "give the supervisors power over the commission and the police chief. Such a move would further dilute the lines of responsibility for departmental actions and misconduct and subject the commission to the politics that the best police departments seek to avoid." S.F. CHRON., Oct. 27, 2003, at A24.

14. Rachel Gordon, *New-Look Police Commission Carries Big Broom: Broad Changes Seen in Cops' Accountability*, S.F. CHRON., May 19, 2004, at B9. *See also,* Rachel Gordon, *Watchdog Gets More Autonomy*, S.F. CHRON., May 27, 2004, at B4.

Miami-Dade Police Chief's Association each submit three names to the Board of County Commissioners. The Board must select one IRP member from each of the five lists. The five panel members selected in this manner then themselves select the remaining four members of the IRP.[15]

2. Types of Individuals Selected

City ordinances or other governing statutes generally do not specify the qualifications or professions of the persons appointed to the oversight body. There are notable exceptions to this rule, however. The Citizens Complaint Authority in Cincinnati, Ohio, and the Citizens Police Review Board in Oakland, California, are both required to have at least one member under the age of 25; this person is usually a student. In San Francisco, at least one of the mayor's appointees must be a retired judge or attorney with trial experience.

The backgrounds of the members of citizen oversight bodies are probably as broad as there are careers and professions. They include lawyers, doctors, mental health workers, businesspersons, members of community organizations, clergy, and advocates for the homeless.

One significant question is whether or not persons with law enforcement experience should be included as members or be explicitly excluded. Most agencies exclude persons who have worked as law enforcement professionals or who have been employed by the agency being reviewed. Some include police officers from the agency it will be reviewing, whereas others exclude personnel from the agency being reviewed but do not limit other law enforcement personnel, either from another jurisdiction or federal law enforcement or retired officers.

In Pittsburgh and New York City, at least three members of the oversight entity must have prior law enforcement experience, but they may not be currently employed with the police department. The Police

---

15. MIAMI-DADE, FLA., COUNTY CODE art. IC, § 2–11.42, PolicyLink, *supra* note 2, at 87–88. The Key West, Florida, Citizen Review Board has a similar appointment process, with community organizations recommending names for four of the Board's members to the City Commission. The Commission appoints the four members and selects the remaining three positions. Alyson Motley, *18 Nominated for Cop Board*, KEYNOTER, Feb. 26, 2003.

Complaints Board, formerly the Citizen Police Review Board, in Washington, D.C., is an example of a board that includes an active officer from the Metropolitan Police Department, chosen by the chief of police. The Citizen Review Board in Baltimore, Maryland, includes three non-voting members, consisting of one representative each from the Fraternal Order of Police, the Vanguard Justice Society, and the Baltimore City Police Commissioner.[16] A 1995 study estimated that 26 percent of citizen review boards then in existence had sworn police department members.[17]

Including appointees who have a connection to the police department raises concerns about the independence of the oversight entity and the ability of that member to overly influence or obstruct the decisions of the board. On the other hand, having members with law enforcement experience brings a level of knowledge of police procedure to an entity that often is criticized as being uninformed about the realities of policing. Advocacy organizations such as the ACLU take the position that oversight boards should not have a police member.[18] Although having a police department member or former member on an oversight body may diminish the perception of independence, there has been little research on whether it has led to gridlock or obstruction.

What should the jurisdiction be looking for in an appointee to an oversight body? Miami-Dade's ordinance lists the qualifications for its Independent Review Panel members as follows: "a qualified elector of Miami-Dade possesses a reputation for civic pride, integrity, responsibility and has demonstrated an active interest in public affairs and service."[19] Valuable qualities include: standing in the community; a reputa-

---

16. *See* Baltimore Civilian Review Board, *at* http://www.ci.baltimore.md. us/government/crb/. The Citizen Police Complaint Office in Indianapolis similarly has three nonvoting police officer members, *see* http://www.indygov.org/ eGov/City/DPS/CPCO/home.htm.

17. Samuel Walker & Betsy Wright, *Citizen Review of the Police, 1995: An Analysis of Roles, Structures, and Procedures* (presentation at the Annual Meeting of the Academy of Criminal Justice Sciences, Boston, MA) (1995), *in* SAMUEL WALKER, CITIZEN REVIEW: RESOURCE MANUAL, POLICE EXECUTIVE RESEARCH FORUM (1995).

18. Professor Sam Walker takes a similar position, *see* Walker, *supra* note 7.

19. MIAMI-DADE, FLA., COUNTY CODE art. IC, § 2–11.43(A).

tion for fairness and integrity; experience on other boards; and balance among the board's members in terms of their perspectives, experiences, and backgrounds. Diversity is extremely important, especially because issues of race and policing invariably will come before the board. The CCRB in New York City and the Police Internal Investigations Auditing Committee (PAIC) in Portland, Oregon, among others, explicitly include diversity in their ordinances as a goal for appointments.[20]

Although the members of the board should be viewed as representing community standards and bringing a "citizen's" perspective on police practices, there is a danger that nominating persons who have been "activists" on police matters will color the perception of the board as "antipolice" or having a specific agenda. Conversely, the nominees should avoid being viewed as too "propolice" and tied in with the establishment. Many will not have had significant experience in dealing with law enforcement issues, but as members of a government body, some previous experience in government or management will be helpful.

The considerations for selecting a monitor or auditor are similar. In this case, however, the jurisdiction is making a professional appointment rather than a volunteer one. Prior experience is, therefore, even more important. The Los Angeles Sheriff's Office Special Counsel (monitor) was previously the executive director of the commission that examined police misconduct in the county.[21] The director of the Office of Independent Review for the Sheriff's Department, the entity that audits and reviews internal affairs investigations at the LASD, is a former assistant United States attorney who had prosecuted police misconduct cases. In Sacramento, the director of Office of Police Accountability previously was a police officer and an investigator for Berkeley's oversight board. In Seattle, the civilian auditor for the Office of Professional Accountability is the former United States attorney. In San Jose, the newly appointed independent police auditor is a licensed private

---

20. Lack of diversity can be a flash point for a citizen review board. Although the Police Commission in San Francisco came into office with new vigor, *supra* note 8, there was controversy that none of the Police Commission members were Hispanic. Tyche Hendricks, *Latinos Demand Voice on Policing,* S.F. CHRON., Apr. 27, 2004, at B4.

21. Merrick Bobb was also Deputy General Counsel to the Christopher Commission, examining the practices of the Los Angeles Police Department.

investigator and has had a career in citizen oversight for the last 22 years, whereas the former auditor had been a criminal trial attorney and a special agent with the United States Drug Enforcement Agency before being appointed to that office. Denver's new police monitor is a former prosecutor who worked on police misconduct cases.

3. Maintaining the Support of Stakeholders

Police oversight entities are often created in the wake of high-profile incidents of police use of force or other revelations of police misconduct. Seldom will they be established without political struggle and significant debate within the community. Conflicts between community advocates and police management and the police union usually lead to compromises over the agency's authority. (The almost-universal debate over whether oversight entities should or should not have subpoena authority testifies to these struggles.) It is, therefore, not surprising that oversight agencies often launch with fanfare but hit stormy seas quite quickly. Criticism from both sides is common,[22] and lawsuits challenging the agency's actions and authority are not infrequent.[23] Oversight entities and board members should be prepared for these challenges.

a. *Police Unions*

Relations with unions representing rank-and-file officers are often the most problematic. Oversight agencies need to be clear that their deliberations will be fair and objective and will protect officers' due process rights. A major concern for police unions is that citizen oversight agencies become a venue for "police bashing," especially if agency meetings include an open public comment period with no constraints. They also have objected to public discussions of individual personnel matters,

---

22. In their review of the Albuquerque Police Oversight Commission, Richard Jerome and the PARC found that "the POC is viewed, incorrectly in our view, as 'anti-police' by many members of the police force. In sharp contrast, the POC is considered ineffective by civil rights advocates and community activists." *Police Oversight Project, City of Albuquerque* 3 (May 2002), *available at* http://www.parc.info/projects/pdf/abqreport.pdf.

23. *Id.* at 14–15.

such as complaints. In the case of complaints that are determined to be unfounded, officers feel that negative and false information about them has been given to the public. A balance must be struck between the personal privacy rights of the officer and the complainant and the public interest in transparency and disclosure of police department practices.[24]

Oversight agencies also need to affirmatively reach out to the union and the rank and file. Although agency officials may not be able to disabuse officers of the notion that only someone who has "walked a beat" can fairly judge police behavior, at least the agency can convey an understanding of the difficulties and dangers of police work. Winning over the union may be impossible, but neutrality and acceptance (even if grudging) is the goal. The director of the Office of Police Accountability in Sacramento states: "In order to maintain good relations between the OPA and police officers, the OPA Director has continued to make roll-call appearances, tour police facilities, participate in ride-alongs, make repeated presentations at the Police Academy and meet with individual officers when they have requested it."[25]

b. *Community Activists and Organizations*

Relations with community activists can be just as rocky. They may view oversight board members as their "representatives" and may expect them to "take on" the police. Having pushed for police oversight, they may be disillusioned by the agency's lack of power and effectiveness. (It is not unusual for citizens to believe that the police oversight agency should be able to fire police officers who they believe have engaged in misconduct.) In reviewing complaints, however, objective and impartial handling of individual cases is more important than being seen as an

---

24. In Albuquerque, the airing of individual appeal hearings on public access television was one reason cited for officers not participating in Police Oversight Commission hearings. *Id.* at 60–61.

25. CITY OF SACRAMENTO, OFFICE OF POLICE ACCOUNTABILITY, 2003 ANNUAL REPORT, *available at* http://www.cityofsacramento.org/cityman/pdfs/2003_OPA_Annual_Report.pdf.

advocate for the community.[26] Given the limitations of an agency's authority, there is a need to be clear about what it can and cannot do and to set realistic expectations. Again, outreach is crucial, as civil rights organizations, community organizations, and activists are an oversight agency's natural allies and will be needed to buttress support with the agency's appointing and funding authority.

c. *Police Chief and Police Department Management (Command Staff)*

The third important stakeholder in police oversight is the chief of police, along with his or her command staff. Maintaining a professional relationship with the chief and other police executives will set the tone for the agency's relations with the department. Police chiefs can send a message to their commands and to the troops that they expect cooperation with and respect for the oversight agency. Or, the chiefs can send the opposite message (explicitly or not). The oversight agency also will be working directly with the internal affairs division or bureau. To accomplish oversight effectively, the agency will need access to the police department's files and records and to its officers. It is best if this access is spelled out in the governing ordinance or charter of the agency. If it is not, however, the agency should try to hammer out written procedures for access and cooperation with the police department, perhaps through a memorandum of understanding.

d. *Mayor and City Council*

Finally, the support of the mayor and city council is essential. It is these officials who will have the ultimate say over whether or not the recom-

---

26. Beattie & Weitzer, *supra* note 1, at 41, 52; *see also* EMMA PHILLIPS & JENNIFER TRONE, BUILDING PUBLIC CONFIDENCE IN POLICE THROUGH CITIZEN OVERSIGHT, 7–8 (Vera Institute of Justice, September 2002), *available at* http://www.vera.org/publication_pdf/177_336.pdf ("In order for those judgments [on officers and citizens involved in misconduct complaints] to be accepted as legitimate by both the police and the public, the oversight agency must be widely regarded as impartial and objective. And to achieve such a status, the agency has to function in a deliberate and pragmatic fashion, resisting impulses to advocate wider social change or to amplify public outrage that led to its creation.").

mendations and findings of the agency are accepted and implemented. In the aftermath of a high-profile police incident, such as a fatal officer-involved shooting, or string of incidents, there is tremendous pressure to respond to community demands for police oversight. Too often, political authorities in a jurisdiction agree to citizen review because of demands to "do something" about the police, but they do not give it sufficient authority or support. Commentators have noted numerous ways in which governments give "lip service" to police oversight but fail to deliver on its promise. They can accede to police demands to limit the agency's structure, powers, and capacity to deliver accountability; starve the agency for resources; fail to make timely appointments; and ignore reports.[27] Conversely, they can provide the political support for police oversight that will enable the agency to work effectively.

In a number of notable examples (San Francisco, Seattle, New York City, and Albuquerque), dissatisfaction in the community over the existing police oversight has led to successive increases in the powers of the citizen oversight agency. These efforts have not always succeeded. The structure and powers of an agency, by themselves, are not sufficient. Factors external to the agency include the extent of polarization in the community over police functions, the strength of police unions, and the "political will" of the governing officials of the city to hold the police department accountable for misconduct. Without this political will, police oversight will likely fall short no matter how the agency is structured.[28] A National Institute of Justice study of citizen review puts it this way: "The talent, dedication, and flexibility of the key participants—in particular, the oversight system's director, chief elected official, police chief or sheriff, and union president—are more important to the procedure's success than is the system's structure."[29]

---

27. *See* Colleen Lewis, *The Politics of Citizen Oversight: Serious Commitment or Lip Service,* in CITIZEN OVERSIGHT OF POLICING, *supra* note 1, and the examples she cites from Australia, Canada, and the United Kingdom.

28. *Id.;* SAMUEL WALKER, POLICE ACCOUNTABILITY: THE ROLE OF CITIZEN OVERSIGHT (2001).

29. PETER FINN, CITIZEN REVIEW OF POLICE: APPROACHES AND IMPLEMENTATION, xi (U.S. Department of Justice, Office of Justice Programs, Nat'l Institute of Justice March 2001), *available at* http://www.ncjrs.org/pdffiles1/nij/184430. pdf.

It is a political tightrope that must be walked with care. Agency officials must be prepared to lobby for support, develop allies, master arguments, and persevere through tough times. As noted in the next section, the best remedy is a job well done.

4. Expertise and Experience

a. *Professional Executive Direct and Professional Staff*

Whether or not the police oversight entity conducts initial investigations of citizen complaints, there is no question that having a professional executive director or staff enhances the agency's ability to function effectively. If the agency does conduct investigations, professional staff is a necessity. It is untenable for volunteer members with other full-time jobs, meeting at most on a weekly basis, to conduct thorough, complete, and impartial investigations of often complicated police incidents on their own.[30]

b. *Expertise on Matters of Police Practices and Procedures*

Oversight agency members must themselves be well informed on matters of police practices and procedures. How else can the agency counter the critique that oversight board members or staff lack experience in police work? The opponents' mantra of "you can't understand the cop's job unless you've been a cop" must be answered. Although part of the rationale of citizen review is that it is citizens, as citizens, reviewing police action, nothing is served if board members are start-

---

30. The largest oversight agency in the country is the CCRB in New York City. Lead supervisors for NYC CCRB investigative teams generally have at least 15 years of law enforcement or other investigative experience and come from a range of agencies, including the IRS, the DEA, the INS, and the Federal Defenders Service. *See* NEW YORK CITY CIVILIAN COMPLAINT REVIEW BOARD, STATUS REPORT JANUARY–DECEMBER 2003, 5 (June 2004), *available at* http:// www.nyc.gov/html/ccrb/pdf/ccrbann2003.pdf. The Office of Citizen Complaints in San Francisco has a statutorily mandated ratio of one line investigator for every 150 sworn police officers. SAN FRANCISCO, CALIF., CITY CHARTER § 4.127. In Cincinnati, the ordinance creating the Citizens' Complaint Authority mandates a minimum of five professional investigators.

ing from scratch in learning about and evaluating police practices. Board members should obtain as much training as possible, and they should start with the jurisdiction's police procedures and observe training in the police academy. They should seek out additional training from prosecutors and city or county attorneys, police unions, civil liberties experts, and plaintiffs' attorneys. Training on use of force issues and on investigative standards is particularly important. The National Association for Citizen Oversight of Law Enforcement (NACOLE) is another excellent source of training and training materials for citizen oversight bodies.

c. *Development of Written Procedures and Manuals for Investigations*

Oversight agencies that conduct their own investigations should develop written procedures and manuals for their investigations. These should include templates and checklists to document investigative activities, ensure the thoroughness of the investigation, and provide for a level of uniformity in the analysis and write-up of the investigations. There are several sources for best practices on citizen complaint investigations.[31] For agencies that hear appeals from internal affairs investigations and findings, procedures for the appeals need to be developed. Hearings before a citizen oversight entity are most effective when their purpose is a review of the initial investigation, an opportunity for the complainant to provide input to the entity and answer questions, and an opportunity to bring a citizen perspective to the process. Although other models envision an adversarial "minitrial" with witnesses, these proceedings are time-consuming (and backlog producing) and are likely to heighten the tensions that already exist between the police and the oversight entity.

---

31. *See* National Association for Civilian Oversight of Law Enforcement, *Investigation, Monitoring and Review of Complaints: A Practitioner's Case Study Guidelines* (Annual Conference, October 5–9, 1999), *available at* http://www.nacole.org/investigative%20guidelines2.html; Lou Reiter, Law Enforcement Administrative Investigations (2d ed., 1998); Department of Justice, *Principles for Promoting Police Integrity* (2001), *at* http://www.ncjrs.org/pdf-files1/ojp/186189.pdf, among others.

d. *Review and Audit of Internal Processes*

Perhaps the most effective role played by citizen review is the improvement it can bring to the police department's own internal processes through public review, audit, and outside perspective.[32] A critical function of any citizen oversight entity is to review the police department's complaint process to ensure that it comports with national best practices in terms of openness and access, tracking and documentation, investigation, adjudication, and disposition.

e. *Reports to the Public*

Public reports, at a minimum annually, are a significant tool in building an oversight agency's credibility. These reports should describe not only the activities of the oversight entity, they should also provide the public with a source of information on complaints trends or patterns, police use of force, and other police practices. Annual reports should be disseminated widely, certainly to the media outlets in the jurisdiction, and should be posted on the Web sites of both the oversight agency and the police department.

f. *Experts and Consultants*

Some areas of police practice, such as investigations of officer-involved shootings, require specialized expertise. Volunteer boards cannot conduct shooting investigations well, and they should not try, but they can review the results of the police department's shooting investigations. Even more effective is having professional staff members review the police investigations and report to the board. In Portland, Oregon, in response to concerns about officer-involved shootings, the City Council authorized the city auditor to hire an expert consultant to review five years of police shooting investigations. The auditor's Independent Police Review (IPR) Division issued a request for proposals and selected the Police Assessment Resource Center (PARC) to conduct the review. The

---

32. *See* Merrick Bobb, *Citizen Oversight of the Police, supra* note 2; Jerome & PARC, *Albuquerque Police Oversight Project, supra* note 22; Phillips & Trone, *supra* note 26.

depth and thoroughness of the review led to its acceptance by both the community and the police department.[33]

g. *Policy Recommendations and Identifying Patterns*

Making recommendations on policy issues and identifying patterns of complaints or uses of force is another central role of citizen review.[34] The city's and the police department's responses to those recommendations then have to be tracked and reported. The San Jose police auditor and the Los Angeles County Sheriff's Department (LASD) monitor are often cited as examples to emulate.[35] Areas that have been addressed by the LASD special counsel include use of force training, early warning/identification systems, the canine unit, risk management, officer-involved shootings, foot pursuits, and jail conditions.[36] Other agencies to issue specific reports on police practices include Philadelphia's Integrity and Accountability Officer (police discipline system, officer-involved shootings); New York City's CCRB (failure of officers to identify themselves when requested, execution of no-knock warrants, and strip searches);[37]

---

33. Police Assessment Resource Center, *The Portland Police Bureau: Officer-Involved Shootings and In-Custody Deaths* (August 2003), *at* http://www.parc.info/pubs/pdf/ppbreport.pdf; Maxine Berstein, *Kroeker Promises Changes,* THE OREGONIAN, Aug. 27, 2003, *available at* http://www.oregonlive.com/special/kendrajames/index.ssf?/special/oregonian/kendrajames/082703.html.

34. *See* PolicyLink, *supra* note 2, at 80–81.

35. The LASD special counsel uses various consulting experts for his reports, including a psychologist and sociologist and active and retired police executives, among others, for his reviews.

36. LOS ANGELES SHERIFF'S DEPARTMENT, SPECIAL COUNSEL MERRICK J. BOBB ET AL., ELEVENTH SEMIANNUAL REPORT (October 1999) (use of force training; canines), *available at* http://lacounty.info/11threport.htm; THIRTEENTH SEMIANNUAL REPORT (December 2000) (medical care to inmates in the Los Angeles County Jails), *available at* http://www.parc.info/pubs/pdf/sheriffreport13.pdf; FOURTEENTH SEMIANNUAL REPORT (October 2001) (officer-involved shootings), *available at* http://www.parc.info/projects/pdf/mbobb14.pdf; and FIFTEENTH SEMIANNUAL REPORT (July 2002) (early identification system; canines), *available at* http://www.parc.info/projects/pdf/July02reporttext.pdf.

37. *See Refusal to Provide Name and/or Shield Number: An Analysis of an Allegation, at* http://www.nyc.gov/html/ccrb/pdf/nmshldanalysis.pdf; *Policy Recommendation Memorandum—CCRB Case 200104846, at* http://www.nyc.gov/html/ccrb/pdf/200104812pg.pdf; and *CCRB Strip Search Procedures, at* http://www.nyc.gov/html/ccrb/pdf/stripsearchletter.pdf.

the Office of Police Complaints in Washington, D.C. (report on disor-
derly conduct arrests);[38] and Seattle's Office of Professional Accountability (racially biased policing).[39]

h. *Funding*

Oversight agencies must have at least a minimum level of funding. It
serves little purpose for a city to create a volunteer oversight board,
provide it with no staff and no budget, and expect it to have any impact.
"Poorly resourced accountability institutions can only create illusions
of action."[40]

i. *Vacancies*

Vacancies also can diminish an agency's ability to function as well as the
public's perception of the importance attributed to the agency by the
mayor and the city. In Cambridge, Massachusetts, four of the five positions on the Police Review and Advisory Board were vacant for more
than two years. Several residents brought suit against the city to fill the
vacancies, and in 2004 the mayor finally made the appointments.[41] In
Oakland, vacancies at the Citizen Police Review Board in 2002 led the
chair of the board to publicly appeal to the mayor for replacements.[42]

---

38. *See* www.occr.dc.gov/occr/frames.asp?doc=/occr/lib/occr/pdf/disorderly_
conduct_policy_recommendation.pdf.

39. *See Report on Seattle's Response to Concerns about Racially Biased
Policing* (June 2003), *at* http://www.cityofseattle.net/police/OPA/Docs/Biased-
Policing.pdf.

40. Lewis, *supra* note 27, at 33. *See also,* PolicyLink, *supra* note 2 ("Community oversight entities must be provided with the human and financial
resources necessary to carry out their charge effectively. The alternative—insufficient staff and an inadequate budget—will doom the oversight process.").

41. Deborah Eisner, *Activists Sue over Cop Board,* CAMBRIDGE CHRON., May
6, 2004. Deborah Eisner, *Two Years Later, Healy Names Police Board,* CAM-
BRIDGE CHRON., June 3, 2004.

42. CITY OF OAKLAND, CITIZENS' POLICE REVIEW BOARD, 2002 ANNUAL
REPORT, 23, *available at* http://www.oaklandnet.com/government/citizens/
2002AnnualReport.pdf ("In 2002, Board vacancies and absences prevented
any cases from being heard by nine members."). In 2002, one of the board's
hearings was canceled for lack of quorum. In his November 15, 2002, letter to
Mayor Jerry Brown, the Chair of CPRB, William Hubbard, urged the Mayor

Staff vacancies can also handicap the agency. In Oakland, "staff turn-over resulted in the Board having to rely on only two to three investigators (as opposed to the budgeted four) for most of the year."[43] In Cincinnati, a vacancy in the Citizen Complaint Authority's executive director position for eight months severely hampered its ability to function.[44]

j. *Timely Action*

To maintain public confidence in the oversight process, timely action on complaints and reports are necessary. A large backlog and overly long lead times before decisions are issued squander an agency's credibility with both the police department and the public. The former Citizen Complaint Review Board in Washington, D.C., is an example. The D.C. board was created as an investigative agency, with subpoena powers and full evidentiary hearings, and operated from 1982 to 1995. The problem was that it was required to hold a hearing for every case. Although hundreds of complaints were filed every year, the board could only conduct approximately 30 hearings each year. By 1987, it had a backlog of more than 1,000 cases.[45] Despite legislation in 1992 to address the backlog, which expanded the Board's membership to 21 members and gave it powers to decide cases summarily without a hearing and to conciliate less serious cases, the backlog persisted. When the city encountered a fiscal crisis in 1995, it abolished the agency. At the time of its closure, the CCRB had 770 pending cases, most of them more than two years old.

---

to fill positions as quickly as possible. "Given that any action by the Board requires five (5) affirmative votes, those vacancies have a substantial adverse impact on the Board's ability to perform its duties in an effective and efficient manner." *Id.* at Appendix B.

43. *Id.* at Executive Summary.

44. CITY OF CINCINNATI, INDEPENDENT MONITOR, FIFTH QUARTERLY REPORT, 78–79 (April 2004), *available at* http://www.gabsnet.com/cincinnatimonitor/ City_of_Cincinnati_Independent_Monitor's_Fifth_Quarterly_Report_April_ 1_2004.pdf.

45. *See, generally,* Beattie & Weitzer, *supra* note 1.

D. INDEPENDENCE

One of the central purposes of citizen oversight is to increase the public's confidence that police activities (and specifically police misconduct) will be reviewed impartially and by someone outside the police department. The independence of the agency is, thus, an inherent value of citizen oversight.

1. Creation

There are a number of components to an agency's independence. First, is the agency established by charter or ordinance, or is it a creation of the mayor or the police chief? To the extent possible, the independence of the office should be clearly covered in the legislation creating the oversight office. The director or the board of the oversight office should not report to or be supervised by the police chief. The agency should also be free to talk without constraint to the media, civil rights organizations, community leaders, elected officials, and others.

2. Authority

Second, how much authority does it have? The agency should be able to make recommendations on policy, and it should be able to accept complaints directly from the public. It should also have access to and be able to review information and files contained at the police department. There is also the question of what actions the agency can take when it disagrees with decisions of internal affairs and the chief of police. In Cincinnati and in Albuquerque, when the oversight agency reaches a different result from the police chief, the disparate recommendations go to the city manager for a decision. Also, the agency's recommendations should reflect solely the view of the agency's director or board and should not be subject to editing by the police department or political officials prior to their publication.[46]

---

46. In a somewhat related vein, the Albuquerque police chief's controversial decision to reverse the outcome of complaints that had already been decided by the prior chief and the city's oversight entity led the City Council to change its oversight ordinance.

3. Stability

A third component of independence is the stability of the agency. As noted in the previous section, frequent turnover and vacancies undercut an agency's effectiveness. A fixed term for agency board members or the auditor or monitor can contribute to this stability. Staggering the terms of board members will also prevent the wholesale replacement of the board or multiple vacancies at the same time. Fixed terms should also be at least two years, given the time needed to learn the agency's procedures. In Albuquerque, the independent review officer was appointed under a one-year contract, which was unduly disruptive. A study of the oversight system recommended that the term be specifically defined in the Police Oversight Ordinance and that it be at least two years. The San Jose independent police auditor has a four-year term.[47] The San Jose auditor also cannot be removed by the mayor but can only be removed by a vote of more than 10 members of the Board of Supervisors for cause.[48] Similarly, San Francisco's Proposition H limited the mayor's powers to remove Police Commission members without the approval of the Board of Supervisors.

One of the more interesting experiments in independent citizen review is occurring in Cincinnati, Ohio, a city in which police-community tensions have been manifest for many years. In 2001, Cincinnati experienced three days of unrest and civil disturbances after the fatal shooting of a black teenager by a white officer. One year later, in April 2002, the city, a class of African American plaintiffs, and the local police union (FOP) signed an agreement to implement police reforms called the Collaborative Agreement (CA). The city also entered into a Memorandum of Agreement (MOA) with the U.S. Department of Justice at the same time, resolving allegations of a pattern or practice of excessive force.

A principle reform of both the CA and the MOA was the creation of a new entity to investigate police conduct, the Citizens Complaint Authority (CCA). The mission of the CCA "is to investigate serious interventions by police officers, including shots fired, deaths in custody,

---

47. SAN JOSE CALIF., CITY CHARTER § 809.
48. *Id.*

major uses of force, and to review and resolve all citizen complaints in a fair and efficient manner. It is essential that the CCA uniformly be perceived as fair and impartial, and not a vehicle for any individuals or groups to promote their own agendas."[49] The requirements of these agreements were then codified in the city ordinance creating the CCA.

The CCA is an independent city agency directed by a board of citizens and staffed by a professional executive director and a minimum of five professional investigators. CCA investigations are conducted independent of the police department, and police department officers are required to answer CCA questions. The ordinance and the agreements also require CCA access to police department files and records. The results of CCA's investigations and recommendations are forwarded to the city manager at the same time as those of the chief of police, and the city manager is required to take appropriate action within 30 days of receiving CCA recommendations.

In a development that is unique to Cincinnati, representatives of the plaintiff class and of the FOP participated in the selection of the CCA's executive director and investigators. The parties to the agreement jointly reviewed the qualifications developed for the positions, helped publicize the positions, reviewed resumes, and participated in interviews of candidates for both the executive director and investigator positions. Selection of the executive director was a consensus choice.

The establishment and implementation of the CCA has not been without bumps in the road. There have been disputes over access to police department files and databases, the role of CCA in criminal investigations, the promptness with which complaints were sent to the CCA when they were received by the police department, and the resignation of its first executive director, with an interim director for eight months.[50] However, with a new executive director now in place, it is hoped that the CCA can make a difference in the community's confidence in police oversight.

---

49. Collaborative Agreement, In Re Cincinnati Police Department, ¶ 55, No. C-1-99-317 (S.D. Ohio 2001), *available at* http://www.usdoj.gov/crt/split/cincinoafinal.htm.

50. *See* QUARTERLY REPORTS OF THE CITY OF CINCINNATI INDEPENDENT MONITOR, *available at* http://www.cincinnatimontitor.org.

E. CONCLUSION

Maintaining the credibility and independence of a citizen oversight agency depends on its ability to address and accomplish the goals of citizen oversight. Jurisdictions should assess whether the police oversight system has: (1) helped to strengthen the relationship between the community and the police, (2) increased public confidence in the police and police oversight, and (3) enhanced the satisfaction of complainants and officers in the police complaint process.[51] Unfortunately, there is no easily transferable formula for success. Rather, the components of success are largely dependant on local circumstances. In the end, citizen oversight of police may not be perfect, but—as they say of getting older—it is better than the alternative.

---

51. Jurisdictions around the country are increasingly conducting surveys or focus groups of the public, complainants, and officers to assess police department performance and to solicit input. Surveys of complainants should examine whether they feel their complaints were fairly investigated and addressed and whether they believe they contributed to holding the police department accountable for officers' behavior.

Training

Benjamin Jones

4

A. INTRODUCTION

The circumstances that result in the creation of a citizen oversight group and the cross fire of interests that represent the support for "transparency" in a law enforcement agency, and the opposition to such transparency, dictate that a credible and an impartial citizen oversight group receive adequate and relevant training to be effective. Throughout the citizen oversight movement, *transparency*, the shine of a public flashlight into law enforcement agencies' internal processes by persons who are not sworn officers, and the permission of citizen input into decisions regarding the findings of officer misconduct have been consistent goals of the public's desire for citizen oversight of law enforcement agencies.[1] Recently, the public's demand for transparency has become more sophisticated.

In addition to demanding insight into when law enforcement agencies investigate and discipline their own,

---

1. *See, e.g.,* SAMUEL WALKER, POLICE ACCOUNTABILITY: THE ROLE OF CITIZEN OVERSIGHT (2001), 5, 21; NATIONAL COMMISSION ON LAW OBSERVANCE AND ENFORCEMENT, LAWLESSNESS IN LAW ENFORCEMENT (1931); *Reviews Get Bad Review: Audit Criticizes Internal Reviews by Eugene Police,* THE REGISTERED-GUARD, May 22, 2004, at A16.

the public has begun demanding insight and input into when and how those law enforcement agencies conduct internal investigations of alleged officer misconduct and what role an agency's management practices contribute to officer misconduct.[2] The quality of the internal investigations and the issue of whether internal affairs investigators investigating police misconduct allegations are independent have also become key components to the public's desire for citizen oversight of its law enforcement agencies.[3]

B. THE CROSSFIRE OF COMPETING INTERESTS DEMANDS ADEQUATE AND RELEVANT TRAINING

Citizen oversight groups must receive adequate and relevant training, or preparation, to succeed during the inevitable storms that will threaten their mission and existence and the public safety. The vast majority of citizen oversight groups are born of tumultuous times, and such groups oversee law enforcement agencies during public crises.[4] Typically, high-profile or media-captured police conduct or misconduct, a string of high-profile police scandals, or a pattern of perceived police misconduct that results in either a large civil payout or criminal charges fuels the public's cry for transparency and accountability of its law enforcement agencies. These recent incidents and their aftermath illustrate the point:

- In 2003, police officers fatally shot a 15-year-old developmentally disabled child who would not drop a knife inside his home. The shooting gripped the city and sent signals of unrest through its black community. Potential settlement talks of a multimillion-

2. *See, e.g.*, WALKER, *supra* note 1, at 39–40.

3. *See, e.g.,* Carol Draeger, *Review Boards—A Mixed Bag: Local NAACP Chapter Leads Push for Citizen-Run Investigations,* TRIBUNE (South Bend, Indiana), Sept. 27, 2004; *Reviews Get Bad Review: Audit Criticizes Internal Reviews by Eugene Police,* THE REGISTERED-GUARD, May 22, 2004, at A16; Lloyd Williams, *Investigating the Police,* JAMAICA GLEANER, May 4, 2004.

4. *See, e.g.*, WALKER, supra note 1, at 19–44.

dollar lawsuit included subjecting police officers to increased citizen oversight.[5]

- In 2003, two police officers were arrested on charges of rape and kidnapping. One of the officers was convicted in February 2004 of coercion, harassment, and official misconduct involving 10 women and one man. The second officer is scheduled to go to trial on charges of rape, sexual abuse, kidnapping, and coercion involving 14 women.[6]

- In 2004, after 20 years of studies, investigations, and analyses of racial profiling, a longtime public frustration in the city over incidents of racial profiling resulted in demands for police to end the practice and for the establishment of a citizen review board to monitor police conduct. A recent two-year study of traffic stop data collected by the city police officers evidenced that police stop black motorists more frequently than white motorists based on their percentage of the population and that officers search Latino motorists significantly more often than white motorists, even though officers are no more likely to find contraband on minority motorists.[7]

- In 2003, a former police chief killed his wife and himself. Subsequent revelations suggested that the former police chief's career should have ended after a credible rape allegation against him in 1998. The former police chief kept his job because the law enforcement agency's internal affairs investigation concluded that the rape allegation was "not sustained."[8] This incident has spawned a wrongful death lawsuit and a well-publicized legal battle to keep

---

5. April M. Washington & Javier Erik Olvera, *Cochran, Mayor Meet, Attorney Urges City to Fire Cop Who Shot, Killed Paul Childs,* ROCKY MOUNTAIN NEWS, Feb. 18, 2004.

6. *Reviews Get Bad Review: Audit Criticizes Internal Reviews by Eugene Police,* THE REGISTERED-GUARD, May 22, 2004, at A16.

7. Rebecca Nolan, *Vigil Demands That Police End Racial Profiling,* THE REGISTER-GUARD, Sept. 23, 2004, at A1.

8. *Tacoma Needs Civilian Review of Police,* THE NEWS TRIBUNE, Sept. 29, 2004, at B6.

secret records of an administrative investigation into alleged misconduct by 32 city and police department employees.[9]

When such events occur in an environment in which the public believes that its law enforcement agency has failed to curb the misconduct among its ranks, the public loses confidence in its local law enforcement agency and demands greater transparency and accountability.[10] To meet the public's demands for transparency and assist in the restoration of the public's confidence in its law enforcement agency, citizen oversight groups must pursue their missions with a high degree of credibility and impartiality.

Generally, law enforcement agencies and law enforcement officers' unions are opposed to citizen oversight or review of agency policies, practices, and decisions.[11] The common refrain is that citizens—nonsworn persons—are unfamiliar with the intricacies of law enforcement and would be unable to determine appropriate or inappropriate police conduct or understand and appreciate the challenges confronted by law enforcement officers.[12] A related common contention is that to make unbiased determinations and to ensure that a law enforcement agency conduct its internal investigations fairly and thoroughly, a citizen oversight group needs to study a broad range of subjects—from constitutional law cases involving police conduct to the history of law enforcement.[13] Concerns that a citizen oversight group could potentially be overwhelmed with complaints of officer misconduct or focus solely on officers, and not on senior law enforcement personnel, have also been

---

9. Sean Robinson, *Judge Calls Fight over Brame Records "Embarrassing,"* The News Tribune, Sept. 17, 2004, at B1.

10. *See, e.g.,* Lloyd Williams, *Investigating the Police,* Jamaica Gleaner, May 4, 2004.

11. *See, e.g.,* Michelle Charles, *Citizen Review of Police Called a Bad Idea,* St. Croix Source, May 19, 2004.

12. *See, e.g.,* Justin Mason, *Martin Weighs in on Cost, Need for Cops Review Board,* Reformer (Brattleboro, Vermont), Oct. 1, 2004. In addition, contrary to this contention, citizens compose, in whole or in part, civil service commissions and police rights boards, which often deal with the intricacies of law enforcement operations and whether a law enforcement agency's disciplinary actions were consistent with its internal policies and relevant law.

13. *See, e.g.,* Mason, *supra* note 12.

cited as grounds for opposing citizen oversight of law enforcement agencies.[14]

Because citizen oversight groups are usually in the middle of the cross fire of competing interests between what the public demands and what most law enforcement agencies and unions desire, citizen oversight groups' effectiveness, or value, is dependent largely on monitoring and reporting with a high degree of credibility and impartiality. Especially, when a crisis occurs, the public demands transparency, or public disclosure and accountability of a law enforcement agency's internal processes relative to allegations or complaints of officer misconduct. In contrast, most law enforcement agencies and unions seek to avoid such transparency. In light of these competing interests, both the public and the law enforcement agencies and unions will closely scrutinize the work of citizen oversight groups. To ensure unbiased and quality oversight, provide valuable assistance to the law enforcement agencies, and assist in the restoration of the public's confidence in its law enforcement agencies, citizen oversight groups must receive adequate and relevant training. Such training will assist a citizen oversight group in maintaining its credibility and impartiality in the performance of its oversight functions. A citizen oversight group's credibility and impartiality will determine its success—the value to the public and the law enforcement agency—during those public crises.

C. ADEQUATE AND RELEVANT TRAINING IS CRITICAL TO CREDIBLE AND IMPARTIAL CITIZEN OVERSIGHT

Adequate and relevant training is a critical component to enhancing the effectiveness of citizen oversight and transparency. Such training can assist a citizen oversight group to cultivate a foundation built on knowledge and openness, which results in a better understanding of a law enforcement agency and its operations and culture and a more effective and active monitoring of internal investigations of officer misconduct allegations. To understand the law enforcement agency and its culture, it is necessary for citizen oversight members to become oriented, in detail, about the agency. Moreover, to monitor internal investigations

---

14. *See, e.g.,* Charles, *supra* note 11.

of complaints or allegations of officer misconduct, citizen oversight members should be well versed in how to conduct a thorough and fair investigation and be familiar with national trends regarding the oversight of such internal investigations. The more citizen oversight members learn about a law enforcement agency and the more such members understand the developments and best practices in citizen oversight, credible citizen oversight and a higher level of transparency should result.

1. Orientation to the Law Enforcement Agency

To provide credible and impartial oversight of a law enforcement agency, citizen oversight members should learn all aspects of the agency's operations and decision-making processes. The law enforcement agency's operations include its policies and procedures for contacting members of the public, using lethal and/or nonlethal force, arresting persons, transporting persons and recording those contacts, and its training and monitoring of officers in the performance of their official duties and in the officers' level of knowledge of relevant agency policies. Citizen oversight members should engage the law enforcement agency's management and officers in discussions on a wide range of topics related to how the law enforcement agency personnel functions internally and in the community.

In addition, citizen oversight members should learn the processes employed by the law enforcement agency in conducting its internal investigations and making relevant determinations. If a citizen oversight group is to do more than catalog complaints or allegations of officer misconduct and actively oversee an internal investigation for quality and consistency issues, then the oversight group must have a detailed understanding of the processes the law enforcement agency employs to decide, among other things, (1) which complaints or allegations to investigate, (2) which agency unit investigates which complaints or allegations, (3) which policy violations to charge or investigate, (4) the sufficiency of evidence necessary to sustain a policy violation, (5) which charges are sustained or not sustained, (6) the appropriate level of discipline for the sustained policy violations, (7) any reduction in discipline during a grievance phase, and (8) the existence and effectiveness of any checks and balances to ensure the agency's thoroughness, fairness, and consistency in the investigation and imposition of discipline. Ideally, in order to learn all aspects and without compromising law enforcement personnel's privacy protections, citizen oversight members should have access to all training provided to the law enforcement agency's management and officers and to meetings and documents in which the law enforcement agency's management discusses any and all aspects of complaints, allegations, and investigations of officer misconduct.

This orientation of the law enforcement agency should occur at the inception of the citizen oversight group's monitoring process and should continue throughout the citizen oversight group's existence. As the law enforcement agency changes, the citizen oversight group may have to refine its process and focus. Citizen oversight groups must maintain sufficient independence and knowledge of the law enforcement agency to adapt to a changing organization.

2. Citizen Police Academies

Within the last 10 years, citizen police academies have become a popularly employed tool by local police departments to foster cooperation with their respective communities.[15] Although citizen police academies offer a window into a police department's operations and fieldwork, such academies alone have limited usefulness to citizen oversight members as a relevant preparatory training tool.

Typically, in an effort to build a partnership with the community a police department will provide citizen police academy participants with a glimpse into the department's operations. A citizen police academy usually offers classes for two or three hours once a week for 8 to 12 weeks.[16] The police department selects which officers or citizen person-

---

15. *See, e.g.,* Allentown Police Department, *Allentown Police Department Civilians Police Academy, at* http://www.allentownpa.org/text/police_civ_acad. htm; Sergeant James M. Goss, Atlantic City Police, *Creating a Citizen Police Academy, at* http://www.communitypolicing.org/publications/artbytop/w5/ w5goss.htm; Colonie Police Department, *Civilian Police Academy, at http:// www.colonie.com/police/cpacademy.html;* Edison Police Department, *Edison Civilian Police Academy, at* http://www.edisonnj.org/police/cpa.asp; Kissimmee Police Department, *Civilian Police Academy, at http://www.kissimmee.org/ departments/pd/academy.asp.*

16. *Id.*

nel conduct the classes, and the selected officers or personnel provide a cursory overview of police operations.[17] The overview typically covers the following topics: (1) patrol duties, (2) criminal investigations, (3) constitutional law, (4) hiring practices, (5) traffic duties, (6) uses of force, (7) forensic investigations, and (8) possibly internal affairs.[18] Time constraints preclude a detailed analysis of these and other topics. The laudable and often-cited goal of the citizen police academies relates to building a partnership between the police departments and their respective communities and encompasses (1) fostering cooperation between the police and academy participants, (2) dispelling misconceptions of how police departments operate by explaining why police officers act as they do, and (3) creating "neighborhood ambassadors" who spread positive information about the police departments to their neighbors.[19]

The advantages of members of citizen oversight groups participating in citizen police academies are clear. First, citizen oversight members learn about the law enforcement agency operations from agency members. Second, as participants in a citizen police academy, citizen oversight members become better acquainted with law enforcement officers' perspectives of police fieldwork and decisions.

The limitations of citizen police academies as a training tool for citizen oversight members, however, are equally clear. Citizen oversight members, who are responsible for ensuring transparency to the public regarding the methods by which a law enforcement agency internally investigates allegations and public complaints of police misconduct, typically require a deeper knowledge of police conduct or misconduct and internal investigating processes and procedures than the cursory discussions the citizen police academies impart. Moreover, unless citizen oversight members have independent and previous investigatory experience, citizen police academies may provide only one perspective of law enforcement investigations.

Because of time constraints, citizen police academies devote much of their focus on the methods law enforcement agencies employ to investigate members of the public and not their own officers. At citizen police

---

17. *Id.*
18. *Id.*
19. *Id.*

academies, these time constraints and law enforcement agencies' desire to foster a positive image of themselves within the community do not generally encourage a critical and detailed examination of the individual or patterns of officer misconduct or allegations of such officer misconduct and the methods by which a law enforcement agency internally investigates officer misconduct complaints or allegations.

For example, citizen police academies may review different categories of force and when they may use force; however, citizen oversight members may find it necessary to probe further into why the force was used, what events or officer decisions preceded the use of force, and whether or not the specific force used was appropriate or excessive. Such further probing may also require a critical examination of how the law enforcement agency internally investigates those issues. Citizen police academies typically do not critically examine their agency policies, training, and best practices. However, when appropriate, an independent and effective citizen oversight group may seek to make recommendations to change—or at least publicly report on—the existing policies, training, and best practices and not necessarily buy into them. Whatever the limitations citizen police academies may present as a sole training tool for citizen oversight members, such limitations do not support disregarding them as a component of a citizen oversight group's training program.

3. Ride-Alongs

Although not a new or an advanced training technique, a ride-along can be an opportunity for citizens to gain a real-time perspective of how law enforcement officers conduct themselves within the communities their agency serves. During a ride-along, a citizen rides along with a law enforcement officer during his or her patrol shift. The ride-along should provide a citizen insight into how officers interact with members of the public and how officers often make split-second decisions, which may have significant consequences. It may also provide a citizen with insight into particular officers who work within a law enforcement agency. To increase the chances of receiving the best benefits, a citizen oversight member should participate in several planned and unplanned ride-alongs. By participating in several ride-alongs, the citizen oversight member has a wide variety of officers within a law enforcement agency from which to learn, and by participating in unplanned ride-alongs, the citizen oversight member increases his or her likelihood of learning from unrehearsed interactions with a member of the law enforcement agency. The result should enhance the citizen oversight members' understanding of how the law enforcement agency's personnel conduct their business and provide citizen oversight members with another method to assess the performance standards or expectations cultivated by the law enforcement agency and its management.

4. Internal Training Seminars

Learning about a law enforcement agency should include attending the agency's internal training programs. A law enforcement agency's internal training seminars on ethics, uses of force, and investigative methods offer a citizen oversight member insight into how and what the law enforcement agency teaches its officers and management as well as the agency's culture. In addition, the internal training seminars provide a citizen oversight member with an understanding of the agency's expectations for its officers' performance standards or conduct. Furthermore, by attending internal training seminars, citizen oversight members can also begin to identify the agency's experts in specific areas, develop a rapport with those experts and other members of the law enforcement agency, and build their credibility within the law enforcement agency.

5. External Training Seminars

In an effort to increase its familiarity with the current dialogue on a variety of civil rights and law enforcement oversight issues and demonstrate its commitment to independent and credible oversight, a citizen oversight group should participate in a myriad of seminars and/or conferences related to these issues. Participation in these seminars and/or conferences will assist the citizen oversight group to further develop effective processes and procedures and to accomplish its mission of overseeing the law enforcement agency. Often members of other citizen oversight groups have encountered issues that may initially appear new or challenging to less experienced citizen oversight members. The attendance at national conferences can assist representatives of a newly created citizen oversight group discussing and determining such issues as

(1) the role of citizen oversight groups and its influence on increased police accountability, (2) the development of an effective working relationship with law enforcement unions, (3) the review of biased law enforcement and its related claims, and (4) various perspectives on methods for monitoring and reviewing a law enforcement agency's internal investigations of allegations of officer misconduct, and ethics in the decision-making process and discipline process.

6. External Consultants

Recently, citizen oversight groups have begun to use external consultants, or citizen oversight experts, to prepare for reviewing and monitoring law enforcement agencies as another component of the oversight groups' training program.[20] As the public demand for transparency has become more sophisticated, citizen oversight groups have taken extra measures to increase their investigative skills. External consultants may discuss such topics as different procedures for the intake of citizen complaints, reviewing and conducting internal investigations, assessing the credibility of witnesses, and analyzing the law enforcement agency's internal regulations and policies.[21] Some external consultants may also lead less experienced citizen oversight members through a hands-on review and investigation of a test officer misconduct case.[22] In addition, external consultants may discuss issues dealing with when to review and investigate an allegation of officer misconduct, how to communicate with members of the law enforcement agency, relevant time limitations during which an internal investigation must be completed, and citizen oversight groups' community outreach.[23] These issues may be of unique concern to citizen oversight groups who are tasked with providing transparency of law enforcement agencies and who may need to report publicly their findings and recommendations.

With quality oversight, the citizen oversight group will demonstrate, through its analyses and recommendations, a high level of credibility

---

20. *See, e.g.,* J.J. Hysell, *National Group Coaches Police Oversight Board* (Feb. 21, 2004), *at* keysnews.com.
21. *Id.*
22. *Id.*
23. *Id.*

and impartiality. Whether a citizen oversight group conducts its own investigations or reviews a law enforcement agency's internal investigative file regarding an allegation or a complaint of officer misconduct before or after an agency's decision is made about whether the officer's misconduct constituted a policy violation and about whether a level of discipline is necessary and appropriate, the citizen oversight members' ability to analyze internal investigative files and deliberate and discuss the relevant aspects of an adequate or inadequate investigation is critical to reporting confidently and competently to the public about whether the law enforcement agency followed its protocols during internal investigations, whether a particular internal investigation was fair and thorough, and whether an officer was held accountable for any misconduct.

D. CONCLUSION

Although the creation of a citizen oversight group to assist in the restoration of the public's confidence in a local law enforcement agency is not new, the evolution of training programs to prepare a citizen oversight group has resulted in opportunities for better trained citizen oversight members. Internal orientation, including citizen police academies and ride-alongs, remains a strong component of an orientation process for citizen oversight groups; however, as the public has demanded transparency of law enforcement agencies' internal processes related to methods and timeliness of internal administrative investigations and ranges of discipline, the use of external consultants to provide relevant training to citizen oversight groups and the participation of citizen oversight members in external seminars and conferences have recently begun to complement the traditional forms of citizen training. Adequate and relevant training of citizen oversight members may not alone guarantee credible and impartial oversight; however, such training establishes a solid foundation from which credible and impartial becomes an integral aspect of a citizen oversight group's function and mission.

Funding and Staffing   5

Benjamin Jones

A. INTRODUCTION

An adequate and independent budget and staff are essential to the effective and efficient operation of a citizen oversight entity and to the restoration or enhancement of the public's confidence in law enforcement. Often created in response to a controversy—whether a high-profile incident or a pattern of conduct—in which the public perceives and questions the appropriateness of law enforcement action and response to the controversy, citizen oversight agencies result from the public's demand for increased "transparency" and accountability of law enforcement agencies and their officers. Because of either the perceived law enforcement misconduct or the perceived law enforcement agency's failure to curb the controversial misconduct, the public confidence in the law enforcement agency deteriorates.[1] In these controversial situations, the public demands effective, credible, efficient, and independent citizen oversight of its law enforcement agency.

---

1. *See, e.g., Charter Change Crucial for Denver Cop Reform: Vote Yes on Referred Question,* ROCKY MOUNTAIN NEWS, Oct. 11, 2004, at 1A.

To meet the public's demand for effective, efficient, and independent citizen oversight and to begin the process of restoring or enhancing the public's confidence in its law enforcement agency, government must send a clear mandate of its commitment to substantial and meaningful citizen oversight reform. The government's reform efforts must take into consideration the existence of competing interests: the public's demand for greater transparency and accountability of its law enforcement agency versus the law enforcement agency and its unions' resistance to the same.[2] Adequate funding and staffing of its citizen oversight entity are key elements, evidencing the government's commitment to effective and efficient citizen oversight of the law enforcement agency. By adequately funding and staffing its citizen oversight entity, the government sends a clear message to all interested parties that it is committed to citizen oversight and enhances potential of the citizen oversight entity to be independent and effective—that is, diligent, credible, and impartial. A citizen oversight entity's independence, effectiveness, and credibility should be reflected in the reality and public perception of its relationship with the law enforcement agency and the agency's operations. Adequate investment in the citizen oversight entity can assist in the restoration or enhancement of the public's confidence in its law enforcement agency. Conversely, the inadequate funding and staffing of a citizen oversight entity can significantly undermine the perception of the commitment to and the credibility and effectiveness of citizen oversight.

Ideally, the adequacy of the budget and staffing of a citizen oversight entity should send a critical message: Citizen oversight of the law enforcement agency is not simply window dressing. First, the adequate funding of citizen oversight should place the public on notice of the priority of a strong commitment to transparency and accountability of the law enforcement agency. A substantial investment in citizen oversight demonstrates to the public that the reform is a legitimate and well-conceived, long-term concept and not a superficial attempt to placate a concerned public in the short term.

---

2. *See, e.g.,* Michelle Charles, *Citizen Review of Police Called a Bad Idea,* St. Croix Source, May 19, 2004; Justin Mason, *Martin Weighs in on Cost, Need for Cops Review Board,* Reformer (Brattleboro, Vermont), Oct. 1, 2004.

B. SUFFICIENT STAFF WITH EXPERTISE

For example, if citizen oversight of a law enforcement agency includes taking complaints or receiving allegations of officer misconduct, a citizen oversight entity should have sufficient funding to arrange the taking of complainant's statements in person. The in-person interviews are generally more thorough than telephone interviews and imply a more credible investigation of a complaint or allegation of officer misconduct. In-person interviews also send a message to all parties—the complainant, the law enforcement agency, and the public—that the citizen oversight entity will pursue such complaints of officer misconduct with a high degree of professionalism, and as a result, the parties to this type of investigation will have confidence in the outcome. Therefore, the adequacy of a citizen oversight budget should include adequate funding to ensure a sufficient staff in number and expertise to conduct such in-person interviews and professional and credible officer misconduct investigations.

C. COMPENSATION

Second, a citizen oversight budget should consider competitive compensation of citizen oversight members and professional staff to acquire the requisite members' focus and expertise necessary for timely and thorough citizen oversight. Effective and credible citizen oversight members have an obligation to be vigilant and thorough, and this is especially true where the citizen oversight entity's review relies mainly on the law enforcement agency's internal investigators or where there may be discrepancies between what was written in a report and what actually occurred.[3] Thorough citizen oversight requires a substantial commitment of time to review, monitor, and deliberate the law enforcement agency's internal operations, investigations, policies, procedures, and practices. Providing this type of citizen oversight can require time, in addition to the actual oversight function, or additional efforts or incentives to acquire citizen oversight members with the requisite level of expertise.

---

3. *See, e.g.,* David Porter, *Review Panel Revved Up? Make Elusive Promise of Justice a Reality,* ORLANDO SENTINEL, Sept. 25, 2004, at A23.

Although citizen oversight agencies can function well with volunteer members, the concept of compensating citizen oversight members should not be ignored. Compensating citizen oversight members can expand the pool of potential citizen oversight candidates—persons willing to dedicate their time and expertise to citizen oversight. Volunteer citizen oversight members are usually retired persons or community members with firm ideas on law enforcement conduct or professionals, who may not be able to devote as much time as necessary to provide detailed citizen oversight.

The more often citizen oversight members meet to review and deliberate complaints, allegations, or internal investigations regarding law enforcement personnel misconduct, the more likely a compensation package may be necessary to attract persons who will devote the requisite expertise, time, or energy for effective, credible, and impartial citizen oversight. If a citizen oversight entity will conduct spot audits or review completed internal investigative files and meet and deliberate once a month, compensation becomes less of an issue. If, however, a citizen oversight entity will review internal investigations on a continuous basis and meet and deliberate daily, compensation becomes more of an issue. In addition, compensating citizen oversight members may assist the less experienced citizen oversight members to meet the time demands for training or may give the more experienced citizen oversight members an incentive to participate in the oversight functions.

D. COMMITMENT TO REFORM

Third, the adequate funding of citizen oversight can place the law enforcement agency and its unions on notice of the substantial commitment to reform, which may lead to a higher degree of cooperation between them. Law enforcement agencies and their unions tend to take seriously recommendations or suggested reforms from citizen oversight agencies that are well funded. A well-funded citizen oversight generally can devote more time and effort to their oversight functions and may even function on a full-time basis, and, consequently, the review of and deliberation about a law enforcement agency's internal operations, investigations, policies, procedures, and practices are thorough and complete. The adequate investment in citizen oversight generally yields more effective citizen oversight and better recommendations to the law enforcement executive management and the public.

E. ACTIVE AND THOROUGH AGENCIES

Although there is no magic formula for determining adequate funding and staffing requirements, there are certain truths. First, a more active and thorough citizen oversight entity will require a greater investment of funds. If the public desires a citizen oversight entity to catalog and report claims or allegations of law enforcement personnel's misconduct, few citizen oversight members or staff will be required. However, if the public expects the citizen oversight entity to actively monitor and thoroughly review a law enforcement agency's internal investigatory processes, more citizen oversight members and staff will be necessary. Greater funding will be required if citizen oversight members meet daily versus monthly to review and deliberate on a complaint, an allegation of officer misconduct, or a law enforcement agency's internal investigation of the complaint or conduct. For example, if citizen oversight members will monitor a law enforcement agency's internal investigations from inception to conclusion, or "cradle to grave," and if they may be required to respond to an officer-involved shooting incident at a moment's notice, the citizen oversight's budget should include funding for cellular telephones and/or business cars so that the responding citizen oversight member can receive telephone notification of a shooting and travel to the shooting scene.

F. INDEPENDENT AGENCIES

Second, the more independent the citizen oversight entity is from the law enforcement agency, the more it will require a greater investment of funds. If the citizen oversight entity conducts its own investigations, it will need independent and/or experienced investigators to conduct the witness interviews and to collect any evidence relevant to the allegations or claims of personnel misconduct. If the citizen oversight entity reviews or spot audits the law enforcement agency's internal investigations, it will not need investigators. However, the citizen oversight entity will then depend entirely on the law enforcement agency's pace and quality of investigation.

In addition, whether the citizen oversight entity will receive complaints or allegations of personnel misconduct directly from the public or rely on the law enforcement agency to receive the complaints or allegations directly from the public may impact the level of funding. If the citizen oversight entity receives misconduct complaints or allegations directly from the public, the number of clerical staff to process these complaints or allegations increases. To create independence in reality and in perception—unless there are other indicators of independence, such as citizen oversight funding outside the law enforcement agency, professional citizen oversight members, or reporting to an entity other than the law enforcement agency—the citizen oversight members and staff should have office space and telephone capacity separate from the law enforcement agency. If complainants from the public or the law enforcement agency have to go to or call the same law enforcement agency whose officer engaged in the alleged misconduct, those complainants may be reluctant, for a number of reasons, to report the alleged officer's misconduct.

G. AGENCIES OVERSEEING A LARGE LAW ENFORCEMENT DEPARTMENT

Third, citizen oversight entities covering larger law enforcement agencies will require a greater investment of funds. A larger law enforcement agency may require the citizen oversight entity to review and monitor a larger number of complaints, allegations, or internal investigations of personnel misconduct or law enforcement personnel. Averaging the number of internal investigations or complaints or allegations of personnel misconduct over a specified number of years may provide an effective indication of annual caseloads in the future. The calculation of future annual caseloads could impact the number of citizen oversight members who make up the oversight entity and review or monitor the internal investigators.

If the oversight entity conducts its own investigations, the calculation of future annual caseloads would affect the number of investigators hired to conduct those investigations. If the citizen oversight entity accepts complaints or allegations directly from the public, the calculated figure would affect the number of clerical staff to accept and record the initial complaints or allegations of misconduct. Related determinations may be whether the citizen oversight entity analyzes and monitors internal investigations of all personnel, sworn and nonsworn, within the law enforcement agency and whether a ratio of one citizen oversight member per specified number of agency personnel can provide an effective indication of annual caseloads in the future. All of these factors impact the funding of a citizen oversight entity.

H. BACKLOGS

Fourth, a large backlog of officer misconduct complaints, allegations, and investigations will require a greater investment of funds. If a backlog of internal investigations or complaints or allegations exists, the backlog may require additional citizen oversight members or professional staff to review and analyze the backlog cases or allegations. A common complaint from complaining citizens and subject officers is that they have to wait too long before learning whether or not there was violation of the law enforcement agency's policy; a related complaint is that there are substantial delays in conducting the internal investigations.[4] A citizen oversight entity's inability to substantially reduce or clear a backlog of internal investigations, complaints, or allegations may quickly create the perception of ineffectiveness. This perception may exist even though the citizen oversight entity's inability to reduce the backlog may be directly related to inadequate funding and staffing issues.

I. OPERATIONAL EXPENSES

For a citizen oversight entity to operate credibly and impartially, an adequate budget should including funding for operational expenses in addition to acquiring and maintaining the appropriate type and number of staff members. A separate and secure office space and the necessary utilities will require funding. Office equipment, such as computers, photocopiers, telephones, facsimiles, cars, cellular telephones, paper, pens, pencils, and audio and video recording equipment will require funding.

---

4. *See, e.g., Police Turning More Attention to Complaints,* THE TENNESSEAN, Feb. 14, 2004.

J. TRAINING

Keeping citizen oversight members abreast of developing legal and citizen oversight trends requires funding for the cost of computer research facilities and continuing education training, including seminars and conferences, and should result in more effective and credible citizen oversight.

Moreover, funding for relevant expert witnesses and citizen oversight experts should enhance the quality of the review and oversight of internal investigations and increase the level of the public and law enforcement agency's confidence in the recommendations from the citizen oversight entity. If a citizen oversight entity conducts its own officer misconduct investigations or relies on the law enforcement agency's investigators, there may be occasions when the citizen oversight entity requires further specialized knowledge regarding an issue, such as blood alcohol, drug, or forensic science information. If appropriate and necessary, the citizen oversight entity may need funds to retain an expert from the relevant area of inquiry to complete its review or investigation of the alleged officer misconduct. In its office operations and public reporting requirements, the citizen oversight entity may require funding for expert fees.

To help citizen oversight members in reviewing and monitoring or independently investigating complaints or allegations of officer misconduct, funding for training of citizen oversight members by citizen oversight consultants may be required. Such training helps to build confidence in the investigative process and provides a heightened level of public transparency.

K. REPORTING

To provide public transparency of the law enforcement agency, a citizen oversight entity should be prepared to make its recommendations public. Whether the dissemination of a citizen oversight entity's findings and recommendations are in hard copy or electronic form, funding will be necessary to cover expenses for either traditional publication of the findings or recommendations or a Web site.

L. PROFESSIONAL STAFF

To function credibly and competently, citizen oversight agencies require sufficient and stable professional staff. A citizen oversight entity's expertise, size, role, and caseload will impact size and expertise of its staff. Whether lawyers or nonlawyers, members of citizen oversight entities should have experience or training in conducting or supervising investigations or have detailed knowledge of the law enforcement agency. If citizen oversight members do not have such training or knowledge, their agency should consider professional staff members with investigatory training or knowledge of the specific law enforcement agency. If there is a need for investigators with law enforcement experience, the selected investigators should be independent of the law enforcement agency; otherwise, the lack of such independence will cloud any perception of impartiality and independence of the citizen oversight entity and its functions.

A citizen oversight entity's size and caseload will affect the size and type of its staff members. If necessary, a citizen oversight entity should include the following:

- A sufficient number of experienced or trained citizen oversight members who will be responsible for providing the actual citizen oversight function for the public;
- A sufficient number of experienced or trained independent investigators, or funding to hire or contract such investigators on an as-needed basis, if a citizen oversight entity's responsibilities include conducting its own investigations of a law enforcement agency's personnel;
- An executive assistant to the citizen oversight members, who will coordinate efforts and preparations for any public hearings on complaints or allegations of law enforcement personnel's misconduct, if a citizen oversight entity's responsibilities include conducting public hearings on officer-misconduct complaints or allegations;
- A sufficient number of policy analysts, who will accumulate relevant statistics for internal and external use and coordinate the preparation and release of a citizen oversight entity's reports to the public regarding a law enforcement agency's internal operations and investigations of personnel misconduct complaints or allegations;
- A sufficient number of research analysts, who will conduct legal and news research to keep citizen oversight members informed of developments on relevant legal and citizen oversight issues;

- A sufficient number of clerical staff, who will receive and organize initial complaints or allegations of law enforcement personnel misconduct and who will answer telephones and ensure the efficient office operations; and
- A sufficient number of informational technology personnel, who will establish and update a citizen oversight entity's Web site and address any computer-related issues, or adequate funding to contract such expertise on an as-needed basis.

If the citizen oversight entity is large or has a heavy caseload, then a larger professional staff may be necessary. To avoid a backlog or deficient review of internal investigations or complaints or allegations of misconduct, the citizen oversight entity may have a large number of members. Each member may require a certain level of staff support. To ensure effective, credible, and efficient citizen oversight, a sufficient number of staff members are needed to support adequately the entire citizen oversight entity.

M. CONCLUSION

The role of the citizen oversight entity will impact the size and type of its staff members. If the citizen oversight entity is to receive directly complaints or allegations of misconduct from the public or law enforcement personnel, it will require a large enough number of clerical personnel to receive the complaints and refer the complaints to a citizen oversight member. In this context, the citizen oversight entity may also require additional investigators to conduct in-person interviews of the complainants. If the citizen oversight members will conduct complete reviews of internal investigations (i.e., "cradle to grave"), they will need an adequate staff or assistants to receive the law enforcement agency's initial requests for investigation, to catalog and track the receipt and progress of those internal investigations, and to prepare the citizen oversight members' comments regarding the status and findings of those findings for public dissemination.

Moreover, if the citizen oversight entity has a reporting requirement, it may require professional staff with different types of expertise. A policy analyst or staff member with some experience in statistics could assist in accumulation and analysis of relevant statistics for internal use and/or public dissemination. A staff member with information technology experience may be necessary for servicing and updating the citizen oversight entity's computers and/or update the information on the citizen oversight entity's Web site.

Unless there are other protections of independence, citizen oversight agencies require an adequate and independent budget and staff to function effectively, efficiently, and credibly. Created to restore or enhance the public's confidence in its law enforcement agencies, citizen oversight agencies must be prepared to deliver and support their findings and recommendations under close scrutiny. An inadequate allocation of resources undermines a citizen oversight entity's ability to deliver credible information relative to transparency and accountability of the law enforcement agency's response to allegations or complaints of personnel misconduct and internal investigations of the same.

Access to Information

6

Laura J. Cail

Citizen oversight agencies generally operate in a manner analogous to a trial court, an appellate court (albeit a non-judicial version of either), or a governmental policy-making body. At a trial court level, the fact finder (generally a jury) requires sufficient information to form an opinion. Although a court may deem circumstantial evidence to be sufficient,[1] the point is that the fact finder cannot pull a decision from thin air or render a *chance verdict.* Similarly, an appellate court cannot reach a decision without a sufficiently complete record.[2] And who among us would want a governmental body to decide policy issues without being adequately informed? How can a citizen oversight agency be expected to reach an informed decision without the ability to gather ample information regarding the complaint before it? Despite the clear and obvious need to acquire information, problems arise because obtaining information from a police department can be a difficult task.

---

1. *See generally,* Desert Palace, Inc. v. Costa, 539 U.S. 90, 123 S.Ct. 2148 (2003).

2. *See, e.g.,* Commonwealth v. Basemore, 560 Pa. 258, 278–79, 744 A.2d 717, 729 (2000).

A citizen oversight agency is established by one or more enabling laws.[3] These laws may be general or quite detailed. In the 1970s, Berkeley, California, established a police review commission (in other words, a citizen oversight agency) when the voters approved an ordinance through the process of initiative.[4] Berkeley attempted to accomplish a task that was virtually unheard of in the 1970s and is just as unusual today. Within the ordinance was specific language enumerating the citizen oversight agency's power to obtain information and/or documentation to aid in its decision-making process.[5] In 1976, however, a taxpayer suit was brought against Berkeley, in which the Division 2, First District Court of the Court of Appeal for California struck down, inter alia, the information-gathering provision in the ordinance because it was in direct conflict with the city charter, which required "that everything pertaining to administrative services go solely through the city manager."[6]

Berkeley's attempt to provide its citizen oversight agency with broad (excepting any right-to-privacy conflicts) information-gathering powers had failed.[7] That failure was unrelated to the power to gather information; rather it was the result of the conflict between Berkeley's city charter and the ordinance.[8] Almost 30 years have passed, and municipalities have chosen to refrain from attempting to emulate Berkeley's early effort. Year after year, citizen oversight entities are formed, but their enabling legislation is silent with regard to their ability to gather infor-

---

3. *See, e.g.,* Albany, N.Y., Code §§ 42–332—§§ 42–352 (2002) (enabling Albany, New York's Citizens' Police Review Board (CPRB) to operate by stating the intent of Albany's Common Council to create the CPRB, as well as its reasons for doing so, and by outlining various details of the CPRB's operation, such as the appointment and training of members, the quorum requirement, the members' responsibilities, and the process for filing and reviewing a complaint).

4. Brown v. City of Berkeley, 57 Cal. App.3d 223, 227, 129 Ca. Rptr. 1, 2 (Court of Appeal, First Dist., Div. 2 1976).

5. *Id.* at 223, 234–35, 129 Ca. Rptr. 1, 6–7 (referring to Section 10(c), in which "the ordinance provides the Commission with the power 'to request and receive promptly [that which] it may deem necessary in carrying out any of its responsibilities under the ordinance from any office or officer or department of the city government.'").

6. *Id.* at 223, 234, 129 Ca. Rptr. 1, 6–7.

7. *Id.* at 223, 129 Ca. Rptr. 1.

8. *Id.* at 223, 234, 129 Ca. Rptr. 1, 6–7.

mation. A citizen oversight agency may include information-gathering procedures for its day-to-day operations, but when its enabling statutes have been silent regarding this process, those procedures have no legal relevance. This creates a statutory void, which can only be filled by one vehicle: the applicable freedom of information law.

For the remainder of this chapter, it will be assumed that a citizen oversight agency does not operate under a distinct or independent information-gathering power. That being so, a citizen oversight agency is viewed, in the eyes of the law, and treated as any private citizen would be. In short, a citizen oversight agency enjoys and is limited to the same access to governmental information as any private citizen (or private group representing the public) within the same jurisdiction.

Obtaining information from police agencies can be very difficult or, at times, impossible. Over the years, attorneys general, as counsel for the states, have had to address questions regarding the abilities of police departments to withhold information when those departments deem it necessary to do so, notwithstanding the obligations of those departments to make information available to the public in general[9] and, at times, to citizen oversight entities, specifically.[10] An opinion from the attorney general's office of North Dakota explains the difficulty in dealing with the issue:

---

9. 1976 Wash. AG LEXIS 26 (failing to actually answer the question regarding public access to certain records under the state law and, instead, stating "that each demand for access to public records (including police records) ... [should] be placed before the courts ... for resolution on the basis of all of the pertinent facts of the particular case."); 1980 Ky. AG LEXIS 585 (answering, in the affirmative, whether the police department had the right to refuse to release "[a]ll records and documents relating to complaints filed against Louisville police officer, Robert Whitaker ..." to The Courier Journal & Louisville Times Company); 2003 Tex. AG LEXIS 8665 (advising the City of Austin that the requested information was confidential and must be withheld from the public, since "the requested information pertain[ed] to an internal affairs division investigation that ha[d] not resulted in disciplinary action against any officer.").

10. 2001 N.C. AG LEXIS 20 (concluding that, while the pertinent section of Charlotte's City Code did not *require* disclosure to the Citizens Review Board, it did *permit* disclosure of various types of information regarding police records, including the dispositions (and the facts relied upon) of current and previous misconduct charges against police officers).

[W]e are dealing with ... a matter of balancing public policy regarding the public's undeniable general right to know public information with a public policy that the state's efficient operation of law enforcement agencies is necessary and vital for the protection of the health and welfare of its citizens.[11]

The Federal Freedom of Information Act (FOIA) was originally enacted in 1966 to cure the ills of the public disclosure section of the Administrative Procedure Act,[12] which was seen as a "withholding statute rather than a disclosure statute."[13] However, Congress recognized the danger associated with complete disclosure and drafted "specific exemptions from disclosure under ... FOIA."[14] It is emphasized that the United States Supreme Court has held "that Congress did not design the FOIA exemptions to be *mandatory* bars to disclosure."[15] Stated differently, although federal agencies *may* withhold records in accordance with the exemptions, they are not required to do so. That is also generally true under state freedom of information laws.

Metaphorically speaking, governmental records are stored behind a locked door rather than an impenetrable wall. The question is does a citizen oversight agency compel or perhaps encourage a police department to open the door (when they have not attempted, as in Berkeley, to obtain a key)? The FOIA may provide some magic words, but those words must be expressed in the correct language.

Because police departments fall within the domain of the state and local governments, not the federal government, the FOIA does not apply to requests for information from a police department.[16] Each

---

11. 1979 N.D. AG LEXIS 103 (explaining that not *all* police records are subject to North Dakota's open record law).

12. 5 U.S.C. § 1002 (1964).

13. Patricia L. Andel, *Inapplicability of the Self-Critical Analysis Privilege to the Drug and Medical Device Industry,* 34 SAN DIEGO L. REV. 93, n. 162 (1997).

14. *Id.* at n. 169 (referencing the FOIA exemptions, which are enumerated in 5 U.S.C. § 552(b)).

15. Chrysler Corp v. Brown, 441 U.S. 281, 293 (1979) (emphasis added).

16. Lynne Wilson, *The Public's Right of Access to Police Misconduct Files,* *at* http://www.nlg.org/npap/research_papers/LWpublicaccess.wpd (last visited Jan. 17, 2005).

state, however, has enacted its own freedom of information law.[17] Because most of the states' freedom of information laws[18] have been modeled after the FOIA, the state courts are often guided (or in some instances, misled) by the federal case law in this area.[19]

Exemptions abound in state freedom of information laws and differ from state to state.[20] The majority include exemptions regarding law enforcement and investigatory information.[21] Some require a showing that releasing the information is likely to cause harm, whereas others have no such requirement and provide broad exemptions.[22] These exemptions are frequently litigated,[23] especially when newspapers are seeking information from law enforcement agencies.[24] Two common exemptions are often used to protect the information contained in police files: those pertaining to the protection of privacy and those pertaining to interference with the investigative process.[25] That being said, it is noteworthy that many of the states include, as part of their freedom of information law's legislative intent, a mandate for liberal construction of the law, in

---

17. *See generally,* Burt A. Braverman & Wesley R. Heppler, *A Practical Review of State Open Records Laws,* 49 GEO. WASH. L. REV. 720 (1980–81) (providing a detailed, but slightly antiquated, overview of this subject).

18. A comprehensive list of State Freedom of Information statutes is available at Fed. Proc. § 38:23; however, this source is lacking Mississippi's Freedom of Information statute, Miss. Code Ann. § 25-61-1 (1999), perhaps because Mississippi was the last state to adopt a State Freedom of Information law.

19. Lynne Wilson, *The Public's Right of Access to Police Misconduct Files,* at http://www.nlg.org/npap/research_papers/LWpublicaccess.wpd (last visited Jan. 17, 2005); *see also* Braverman & Heppler, *supra* note 17, at 720, 727.

20. Braverman & Heppler, *supra* note 17, at 720, 740–41.

21. *Id.* at 720, 740.

22. *Id.* at 720, 741.

23. *Id.*

24. *See generally,* Sheridan Newspapers, Inc. v. City of Sheridan, 660 P.2d 785 (1983); Allsop v. Cheyenne Newspapers, Inc., 39 P.3d 1092 (2002); Newspapers, Inc. v. Breier, 89 Wis.2d 417, 279 N.W.2d 179 (1979); Worcester Telegram & Gazette Corp. v. Chief of Police of Worcester, 58 Mass. App. Ct. 1, 787 N.E.2d 602 (2003); Shuttleworth v. City of Camden, 258 N.J. Super. 573, 610 A.2d 903 (1992).

25. Lynne Wilson, *The Public's Right of Access to Police Misconduct Files,* at http://www.nlg.org/npap/research_papers/LWpublicaccess.wpd (last visited Jan. 17, 2005).

favor of disclosure, as well as language indicating the importance of a well-informed public regarding governmental affairs.[26]

It is rare for a citizen oversight agency to challenge, in a court of law, denial of requested information. Because a citizen oversight agency typically has the same rights of access as any private citizen (or private group representing the public) requesting information under freedom of information, an extensive body of case law can be applied.

Therefore, in a state whose freedom of information law is modeled after the FOIA, decisions may be based on the state law, but, in addition, a court may be persuaded by federal case law or even that of other states that have modeled their freedom of information laws on the FOIA. In consideration of the breadth of possibilities, this chapter has been presented through generalities but will now briefly focus on two states, Florida and New York, because an analysis of all 50 states could not be served by one chapter.

Florida is a strongly pro-access state. This is evidenced by the fact that Florida enacted public-records legislation more than a half-century before freedom of information became a national trend. Moreover, that state has chosen to make the public's right of access to governmental information a fundamental state constitutional right.[27] The Brechner Center, a nationally and internationally recognized resource regarding freedom of information issues, notes that "Florida's open government laws are some of the strongest in the nation."[28] Florida specifically designates the custodian of public records as the person responsible for supervising the release of information.[29] Florida also imposes penalties for violating the state's freedom of information laws.[30] It does not, however, include specific time frames in which the information must be provided or clearly denied.

---

26. *Id.*
27. Sandra F. Chance, *Florida Government in the Sunshine: A Citizen's Guide, at* http://brechner.org/citizen's%20gui.pdf (last updated Sept. 16, 2004) (referring to Section 24, which was added to Article I's Declaration of Rights in Florida's State Constitution).
28. *Id.*
29. F.S.A. §119.07(1)(a) (2004) (the Custodian of Public Records is defined in F.S.A. §119.011(5) (1996)).
30. F.S.A. §119.10 (2004).

New York is neither strongly pro-access nor strongly anti-access. New York provides access for its citizens by way of statutes;[31] there is no constitutional provision regarding public access to government information within New York's state constitution. New York's law provides that "each agency shall ... [make records] available,"[32] within certain enumerated exceptions, and provides direction concerning the time and manner in which government agencies must grant or deny access.[33]

This brief comparison illustrates how freedom of information laws can differ from state to state and, therefore, how a citizen oversight agency's ability to access police records can differ depending upon the applicable freedom of information laws. Unless a governmental entity provides Berkeley-like information-gathering powers in its citizen oversight agency's enabling laws, its citizen oversight agency may have no choice but to be limited by a freedom of information law.

This is not intended to suggest that a citizen oversight agency is completely powerless. The majority of state freedom of information laws operate under a presumption of access. Perhaps just as important, most of those laws are permissive in that they permit, but do not require, agencies to withhold information falling within an exemption. That factor can be critical, particularly when the court of public opinion clamors for answers and action.

This brings us back to the locked door metaphor. Sometimes the best way to unlock a door is by being friends with the person on the other side. When a citizen oversight agency does not maintain a good relationship with its police department, success in obtaining records is less likely. As is so well stated in the old axiom "you can attract more flies with honey than with vinegar," it may be said that diplomacy is a citizen oversight agency's most useful method of obtaining the information needed to function well and serve the public.

---

31. New York's Freedom of Information Law (and its various subparts) is contained within Article 6 of the Public Officers Law (Chapter 47).
32. N.Y. Pub. Off. Law § 87(2) (2003).
33. N.Y. Pub. Off. Law § 89(3) (2004) (legislating a response time of five business days from the receipt of a written request).

Collective Bargaining and Labor Agreements: Challenges to Citizen Oversight

7

Ronald Kramer
Elayne G. Gold

A. INTRODUCTION

Collective bargaining and labor agreements can present challenges to a citizen oversight agency's credibility, impartiality, authority, and effectiveness.[1] In those cases where law enforcement agencies and/or police officer unions oppose citizen oversight, they sometimes rely upon collective bargaining and labor agreements to (1) prevent the creation of an oversight agency, (2) limit the scope of the agency's power and authority, (3) discourage police officer cooperation in the oversight process, (4) deny access to officer personnel records, (5) prohibit the disclosure of the identity of officers who are the subject of citizen com-

---

1. *See* Justina R. Cintrón Perino, *Developments in Citizen Oversight of Law Enforcement,* 36 URB. LAW. 387, 390 (2004).

plaints, (6) and prevent the imposition of discipline based upon the recommendation of an oversight agency.[2]

The credibility, impartiality, authority, and effectiveness of a citizen oversight agency will depend, in part, on the municipality's awareness and understanding of the legal and policy issues presented when its police officers are represented by a union for purposes of collective bargaining, especially in those states with statutes governing public-sector labor relations.

B. COLLECTIVE BARGAINING DEFINED

Collective bargaining in the public sector is generally defined the same way as it is in the private sector:

> the performance of the mutual obligation of the employer and the representative of the employees to meet at reasonable times and confer in good faith with respect to wages, hours, and other terms and conditions of employment, or the negotiation of an agreement, or any question arising thereunder, and the execution of a written contract incorporating any agreement reached if requested by either party, but such obligation does not compel either party to agree to a proposal or require the making of a concession.[3]

In the context of citizen oversight of law enforcement, collective bargaining may include: (1) the obligation to bargain with the police union over the actual decision to create a citizen oversight agency—*decisional bargaining,* and/or (2) the obligation to bargain with the union over what effect or impact the creation of a citizen oversight agency will have on the officers it represents—*effects/impacts bargaining.*[4] Additionally, the parties to a labor agreement, reached through

---

2. *Id.*

3. 29 U.S.C.A § 158(d) (West, 2005).

4. *E.g., County of Cook (Cook County Hosp.),* 2 P.E.R.I. § 3001 (1985) (noting Illinois public labor relations act requires employers to bargain over decisions and their impact on when those decisions involve mandatory subjects of bargaining); *City of Detroit,* 7 MPER § 25, 074 (1994) (noting an employee's duty under Michigan public labor relations act to bargain over the impacts of decisions even where there is no duty to bargain over the decision itself.)

collective bargaining, have an opportunity to negotiate the language that appears in the agreement, an opportunity to dispute any proposal submitted by either party, and an opportunity to ultimately reach an agreement on the language, by which each party must abide.[5]

Citizen oversight agencies, depending upon how they are structured and what authority they are given, may raise decisional or effects/ impacts bargaining issues, which must first be negotiated with the applicable police union. Alternately, where a collective bargaining agreement is already in effect, the creation of a citizen oversight agency, or the agency's practices and procedures, may violate its terms. Moreover, an employee's contractual rights and statutory rights, under the applicable labor relations statutes, to union representation during disciplinary proceedings may bleed over into the citizen oversight process.

This chapter begins with a basic overview of the labor issues often implicated by citizen oversight of law enforcement and concludes with a more in-depth survey of the experiences of municipalities in New York State, which has seen challenges by police unions over the creation of citizen oversight agencies and the authority conferred to those agencies.

C. BARGAINING, GENERALLY

Labor relations statutes or ordinances generally include within them a duty to bargain in good faith over wages, hours, and terms and conditions of employment.[6] When an issue is considered a mandatory subject of bargaining, an employer is obligated to notify the union and offer to bargain over its proposed decision and the effects or impacts of the decision.[7] Even when an issue is considered to be a permissive subject of bargaining,[8] an employer generally is obligated to first offer to bargain

---

5. Elayne G. Gold & Robert E. Smith, *Police Oversight within New York's Collective Bargaining,* 5 N.Y. St. B.A. Gov't L. & Pol'y J. 46, 48 (2003).

6. These are considered "mandatory" subjects for collective bargaining. *See* Cal. Gov't Code § 3517 (2006); Mich. Comp. Laws Ann. § 423.215 (2005); N.Y. Civ. Ser. L. § 209-a (2005).

7. *Trustees of the Calif. State University,* 28 P.E.R.C. § 169 (Cal. P.E.R.B. A.L.J. 2004); Pennsylvania State Park Officers Assoc. v. P.L.R.B., 35 P.P.E.R. § 85 (Pa. Commw. 2004).

8. *See* N.L.R.B. v. Wooster Div. of Borg-Warner Corp., 356 U.S. 342, 78 S. Ct. 718, 2 L. Ed. 2d 823 (1958).

over the effects of that decision prior to implementing it.[9] An employer who unilaterally implements a decision without first bargaining to impasse over the decision and/or effects generally commits an unfair labor practice.[10] Moreover, in the police setting, in which police unions often have the right to interest arbitration,[11] the decision (if mandatory) and its effects may be subject to compulsory interest arbitration.

D. DISCIPLINE AND DISCIPLINARY PROCEDURES

1. Bargaining Obligations

Unless excluded by statute, discipline and disciplinary procedures often are considered by labor boards to be mandatory subjects of bargain-

---

9. *City and County of San Francisco,* 28 P.E.R.C. § 139 (Cal. P.E.R.B. 2004); *Community Unit Sch. Dist. No. 4,* 2 P.E.R.I. § 1086 (I.E.L.R.B. A.L.J. 1986).

10. *Regents of the University of California,* 29 P.E.R.C. § 82 (Cal. P.E.R.B. A.L.J. 2005); *Collinsville Community Unit School Dist. No. 10,* 20 P.E.R.I. § 57 (I.E.L.R.B. Exec. Dir. 2004); *City of Highland Park,* 2004 MERC Lab Op 86 (Mich. Empl. Rels. Comm'n 2004).

11. "Interest arbitration is a process for resolving disputes over matters within the scope of negotiations. In an interest arbitration system, after the parties reach an impasse in negotiations, an arbitrator or arbitration panel (neutral, union member, and management member) has jurisdiction to hear the evidence, receive final offers from the parties, and decide the case based on the criteria and parameters defined in by statute" and the collective bargaining agreement. More than half of the states have adopted statutes governing interest arbitration, which typically will cover police and fire employees. These statutes vary considerably among the states. *See* Jeffrey Sloane, *New Developments in Municipal Law Practice: Municipal Employee Unions in California,* 188 P.L.I./ CRIM. 581 (2001).

ing.[12] Depending upon the state statute and its interpretation—and depending, of course, upon the nature and authority of the citizen oversight agency—the creation of a citizen oversight agency may well be a mandatory subject of bargaining. In *Pontiac Police Officers Ass'n v. City of Pontiac*,[13] for example, the Michigan Supreme Court found that an employer had a duty under the Michigan Public Employment Relations Act (PERA) to bargain with its police union over the provisions of a civilian trial board to review charges of police misconduct. The city, pursuant to its home rule charter, had established a civilian trial board to review charges of police misconduct and, where necessary, impose discipline. The city, therefore, claimed it was under no obligation to bargain over a grievance procedure to address employee discipline.[14] The court concluded that disciplinary procedures were a term and condition of employment and, hence, a mandatory subject of bargaining.

In contrast, in *Fraternal Order of Police, Lodge No. 5 v. Pennsylvania Labor Relations Board*,[15] a Pennsylvania court found that the City of Philadelphia's decision to institute a police advisory commission (PAC)

---

12. *Matter of Town of Greenburgh,* 94 A.D.2d 771, 462 N.Y.S.2d 718 (N.Y. Sup. Ct. App. Div. 1983) (given statute, discipline not a mandatory subject of bargaining); *Rush Township,* 35 P.P.E.R. ¶ 131 (Pa. L.R.B. Hearing Examiner's Dec. 2004) (certain disciplinary matters are mandatory, others, such as decision to investigate complaint at a higher level of management are not); *State of California (Dep't of Pers. Admin.),* 8 P.E.R.C. ¶ 15,083 (Cal. P.E.R.B. A.L.J. 1984) (disciplinary procedures found to be a mandatory subject of bargaining); *Plainwell SD,* 1989 MERC Lab Op 464, 466 (Mich. Empl. Rels. Comm'n 1989) ("disciplinary procedures" are a mandatory subject of bargaining because they affect the other terms and conditions of employment of employees covered by state employee relations statute; employee had duty to bargain over use of a trial board to determine discipline); *Medicenter, Mid-South Hosp.,* 221 N.L.R.B. 670, 675 (1975) (employer found to have duty to bargain over the method by which it investigates suspected employee misconduct).

13. 397 Mich. 674, 246 N.W.2d 831 (1976).

14. *Id.* at 677, 246 N.W.2d at 832.

15. 727 A.2d 1187, 30 P.P.E.R. ¶ 30,070 (Pa. Commw. 1999).

was not a mandatory subject of bargaining under the Pennsylvania Labor Relations Act. In 1993 the mayor, by executive order, created the PAC, which was given full discretion to investigate specific complaints of misconduct against police officers, hold public hearings, and make recommendations to the police commissioner as to discipline.[16] Full cooperation with the PAC was expected from the police officers or discipline could result. Applying a balancing test to determine whether or not the city's managerial interest in creating the PAC outweighed any impact it would have on the performance of police duties, the court upheld the Labor Board's earlier ruling that the PAC was not a mandatory subject of bargaining:

> In this case, we agree with the Board's conclusion that the City's interest in creating the PAC outweighs the interests of the police officers. The City's interest in providing public safety and providing a forum in which citizens can redress grievances against the government and its employees, as well as attempting to prevent future incidents of police misconduct and abuses of civil rights, outweighs the interests expressed by the police officers in this situation including the principal one that fears disciplinary standards have been changed by their being liable for discipline for failure to cooperate with PAC investigations. Although the establishment of the PAC was found by the examiner to add to the obligations of police to testify and otherwise cooperate in the investigations, the Board held that no change was effected in the duties the employees were previously required to do or the grounds for imposing discipline. Further, it is noted that the police will have already performed their most basic duties of law enforcement prior to the PAC investigation involving any of them. Thereafter, only the normal responsibilities of the police to cooperate and testify in an investigation of the performance of their duties to enforce the law are reviewed.[17]

---

16. *Id.* at 1189.
17. *Id.* at 1191.

As the union did not properly raise the issue of whether or not the city had a duty to bargain over the impact and effects of its decision, neither the labor board nor the court addressed that issue.[18]

Similarly, in *Berkeley Police Association v. City of Berkeley,*[19] a court found the city had no statutory duty to meet and confer with its police union before the police chief agreed: (1) to permit a member of the citizens' police review commission sit in on internal department board of review hearings at which internal affairs reports of citizen complaints were reviewed, and (2) to send a representative of the department and applicable internal affairs reports to each police review commission trial board meeting so that the representative could answer the commission's questions concerning the department's position on the complaints.[20] In *Berkeley,* the commission was empowered to investigate and make recommendations but could not intervene in disciplinary proceedings. The court, applying the public labor relations act, determined that the policies at issue were such fundamentally management-level decisions that they were not properly within the scope of union representation and collective bargaining.[21]

2. Contract Issues

Aside from possible bargaining obligations, contract issues also come into play. Many labor agreements address, in detail, how employees are to be disciplined and what rights they have during the course of a disciplinary investigation. To the extent a citizen oversight agency and its procedures conflict with a collective bargaining agreement, a municipality may face grievances and court litigation challenging the legality of

---

18. *Id.* at 1191–92.

19. 76 Cal. App. 3d 931, 143 Cal. Rptr. 255 (Cal. Ct. App. 1977).

20. *Id.* at 935, 143 Cal. Rptr. 258.

21. *Id.* at 937, 143 Cal. Rptr. 260 ("To require public officials to meet and confer with their employees regarding fundamental policy decision such as those here presented, would place an intolerable burden upon fair and efficient administration of state and local government. Such decisions cannot and should not be within the "scope of representation" by public employee associations.").

the oversight agency. Similarly, to the extent the oversight agency is a mandatory subject of bargaining, if the parties, by contract, have agreed to waive their right to midterm bargaining over mandatory subjects, the municipality may be contractually restricted from even negotiating the citizen oversight agency until such time as the contract expires.

For example, in *Jurcisin v. Cuyahoga County Board of Elections,*[22] employees and police unions sought an injunction to stop a ballot proposal by the City of Cleveland to establish a police review board on the grounds that the board, if adopted, would unlawfully conflict with the terms of their collective bargaining agreements and, thus, be void.[23] The proposed board would have the authority to receive, cause the investigation of, and recommend the resolution of complaints of police misconduct. The board could determine whether a complaint warranted no further action, recommend that it be resolved by the director of public safety, or recommend to the police chief that disciplinary action be taken.[24] If the chief and the board were in agreement, the chief would bring charges against the officer before the director of public safety, who, as before, made the ultimate determination of discipline. If the board did not agree with the chief's proposed action, it could bring a charge seeking disciplinary action directly to the director of public safety.[25]

The unions argued that, as questions of discipline fell under the grievance procedures of their contracts, the creation of a new police review board process conflicted with their contracts.[26] The contracts at issue also contained management rights provisions, which gave the city the right to suspend, discipline, demote, or discharge for just cause and the right to implement new or revise existing policies, which did not conflict with the express terms of the contracts.[27] The court rejected the unions' claims on the grounds that the proposed police review board would not affect the grievance procedures found in the contracts. As the

---

22. 35 Ohio St. 3d 137, 519 N.E.2d 347 (Ohio 1988).
23. *Id.* at 140, 519 N.E.2d at 351.
24. *Id.* at 137–39, 519 N.E.2d at 347–39.
25. *Id.*
26. *Id.* at 143, 519 N.E.2d at 353.
27. *Id.* at 143–44, 519 N.E.2d at 353.

board performed its responsibilities prior to any disciplinary action being taken by the director of public safety, any officer disciplined by the director as a result of a recommendation from the police review board would have the same right to file a grievance as the officer did prior to the creation of the board.[28] Moreover, the creation of the board, according to the court, involved the "proper exercise of management powers created by the city charter and recognized in the collective bargaining agreements."[29] In concluding, the court declared:

> We agree with the observation that a public review board that serves as a forum for allegations regarding police misconduct in the performance of their duties provides a procedure for those who are not represented at the bargaining table to raise issues with respect to police conduct. Collective bargaining does not necessarily provide an appropriate process for the full consideration of the issues raised in a complaint by a citizen against a police officer. Summers, Public Employee Bargaining: A Political Perspective (1974), 83 Yale L.J. 1156, 1197. See also Jenkins, Collective Bargaining for Public Employees: An Overview of Illinois' New Act (1983), S. Ill. U.L.J. 483, 506-507. Indeed, the issues to be resolved in a grievance proceeding initiated by a police officer would usually be different from the issues raised in a complaint filed with a public review board.
>
> We hold that, where a proposed charter amendment that would establish a police review board to investigate charges of police misconduct and recommend disciplinary action upon a finding of misconduct does not conflict with provisions of a collective bargaining agreement concerning wages, hours, and other conditions of employment, R.C. 4117.10(A), which gives collective bargaining agreements precedence over conflicting laws, does not apply.[30]

---

28. *Id.* at 144, 519 N.E.2d at 354.
29. *Id.* at 145, 519 N.E.2d at 354.
30. *Id.*

Similarly, when certain investigatory and disciplinary authority was transferred to Cleveland's police review board, the Ohio State Employment Relations Board dismissed unfair labor practice charges alleging unilateral change on the grounds that the police review board had no authority to force the city to violate the collective bargaining agreement and recommended or imposed discipline by the board was fully grievable.[31]

E. SUBPOENA POWER

When a citizen oversight agency or its procedures conflict with a collective bargaining agreement, the collective bargaining agreement in many instances will control. This conflict can arise when the citizen oversight agency is empowered to compel the participation or testimony of police officers during the citizen complaint and oversight process. For example, in *Citizen Police Review Board v. Murphy,*[32] the CPRB sought a writ of mandamus and declaratory relief against Pittsburgh's mayor, police chief, and police union to compel the direction of police officers to cooperate in review board investigations by giving interviews and testimony under threat of discipline. During the course of the proceedings, the city and union received an award from an interest arbitrator inserting into the collective bargaining agreement the provision that "no police officers shall be compelled by the city to testify before the Police Civilian Review Board."[33] The CPRB claimed the contract provisions should be deemed void as contravening public policy. The court found both that the CPRB could demonstrate no legal right to force the mayor and police chief to require officers to compel an officer to testify and that the new contract language did not undermine the CPRB's authority and was perfectly lawful.[34] It also rejected claims that the CPRB, as an agent of the city, had a right to be a party to the collective bargaining.[35]

---

31. Cleveland Police Patrolmen's Ass'n v. City of Cleveland, 17 O.P.E.R. ¶ 1255 (Oh. St. Empl. Rels. Bd. 2000).
32. 819 A.2d 1216 (Pa. Commw. 2003).
33. *Id.* at 1219.
34. *Id.* at 1221.
35. *Id.* at 1222.

F. UNION REPRESENTATION

Many states, whether expressly by statute or through case precedent, have recognized that a bargaining unit employee has a right to ask for union representation during any questioning, which he or she might reasonably believe might lead to disciplinary action. In the private sector, these rights are called *Weingarten* rights after the case in which they were recognized for private sector employees.[36] Some states provide for much broader protections than those provided for in *Weingarten*.[37] These rights often are separate and apart from rights provided in other state statutes addressing police discipline.[38] When a citizen oversight agency's investigation, whether by the oversight agency directly or by the police department after receiving input from the agency or reviewing its findings, might lead to discipline, such rights may apply to the officers who are called to testify. Labor boards have recognized that such rights apply in similar advisory board settings, for example, with internal disciplinary review boards.[39]

---

36. NLRB v. J. Weingarten, Inc., 420 U.S. 251 (1975).

37. *See, e.g., Trotwood-Madison City Sch. Dist. Bd. of Ed.,* 6 OPER § 6426 (Ohio S.E.R.B. 1989) (construing Ohio statute §4117.03(A)(3) to provide an employee with the right to have a union representative assist, accompany, or speak on his behalf in discussions with management that are relevant to the employer-employee relationship and are not routine encounters).

38. *See, e.g.,* 50 ILCS 725/1 (2005); FLA. STATS., ch. 112, § 112.532 (2005); CAL. GOV'T CODE § 3508.1 (2006).

39. *See, e.g., City of Zanesville,* 7 O.P.E.R. § 7675, 1990 O.P.E.R. (L.R.P.) LEXIS 3786 (Ohio S.E.R.B. Hearing Officer 1990) (finding employee had right under state law to have union represent him before police department disciplinary review board; representation right before civil service commission limited to that of an attorney, including a union attorney, because commission had a rule requiring that parties wishing to be represented retain an attorney); *Saginaw Township,* 3 M.P.E.R. § 21,028, 1989 M.P.E.R. (L.R.P.) LEXIS 164 (Mich. Empl. Rels. Comm'n 1989) (township unlawfully interfered with employee's exercise of protected rights by denying him the right to union representation in a police advisory board meeting at which the employee reasonably expected discipline).

G. THE NEW YORK EXPERIENCE

In New York, the Taylor Law—the public-sector labor relations statute governing all municipalities in the state,[40] except those that choose to create their own statutory scheme[41]—provides that it is an unfair labor practice for rules and regulations to be unilaterally imposed upon public-sector employees, including police officers, when those rules and/or regulations would have an effect or impact on the terms and conditions of the employees' employment with the municipality.[42] The creation of a citizen oversight agency, with the concomitant promulgation of its own set of rules, regulations, and stated obligations upon both the police department and its employees, can prove to be problematic, especially when collective bargaining and labor agreements apply and are in conflict with the agency or its processes and procedures. Below is a review of the labor issues raised as cities in New York created citizen oversight agencies.

1. New York City

In New York City, the Patrolmen's Benevolent Association (PBA) brought a Civil Practice Law and Rules, Article 78 proceeding against the city and its Civilian Complaint Review Board (CCRB) to permanently enjoin the CCRB from enforcing changes to the city charter, claiming, among other things, that the law "is ... in derogation of the contractual rights of members of the police department."[43]

The changes to the charter authorized the CCRB "to receive, investigate, hear, make findings, and recommend action upon complaints by members of the public against members of the police department that allege misconduct involving excessive use of force, abuse of authority, discourtesy, or use of offensive language, including, but not limited to, slurs relating to race, ethnicity, religion, gender, sexual orientation, and disability."[44] In addition, the charter allowed the "Board, by majority

---

40. N.Y. Civ. Serv. Law § 200–214, (2005).

41. N.Y. Civ. Serv. Law § 212(1) (2005).

42. N.Y. Civ. Serv. Law § 209-a(1)(d) (2005).

43. Caruso v. Civilian Complaint Review Bd., 158 Misc. 2d 909, 910; 602 N.Y.S.2d 487, 488 (1993).

44. *See Id.* at 911, 602 N.Y.S.2d at 489, *citing* New York, N.Y. City Charter § 440(C)(1) (1993).

vote of its members, [to] compel the attendance of witnesses and require the production of such records and other materials as are necessary for the investigation of complaints."[45] Moreover, the charter imposed "upon the Police Commissioner the obligation to ensure that officers and employees of the department appear before and respond to inquiries of the Board and its civilian investigators—provided that such inquiries are conducted in accordance with department procedures for interrogation of members."[46]

The PBA argued, in part, that the change in the city charter allowing the CCRB to interrogate police officers was a violation of their contractual rights.[47] According to the PBA, the violation "occurs ... by reason of the Board being comprised of non-police department employees, which ... conflicts with the confidentiality provisions of the collective bargaining agreement."[48]

The court, in its holding, cited the agreement's "Bill of Rights" provisions: "The 'Guidelines for Interrogation of Members of the Department' in force at the execution date of this Agreement will not be altered during the term of this Agreement, except to reflect subsequent *changes in law.*"[49] The court determined that "[a] 'change in law' is precisely what occurred here. Specifically, the City Charter 'changes the law' with respect to interrogation of officers. Therefore, there is no impairment of contractual rights."[50]

2. Syracuse

Syracuse adopted its Civilian Review Board (CRB) in 1993.[51] Subsequently, the Syracuse Police Benevolent Association (PBA) brought an improper practice charge to the state Public Employment Relations

---

45. *Id., citing* N.Y. City Charter § 440(C)(3) (1993).
46. *Id., citing* N.Y. City Charter § 440(C)(2) (1993).
47. *Id.* at 914, 602 N.Y.S.2d at 491.
48. *Id.* at 914–15, 602 N.Y.S.2d at 491.
49. *Id.* at 915 (emphasis supplied).
50. *Id.*
51. 1993 Syracuse Local Law No. 11; 1993 N.Y.C. Local Law No. 1; Rochester Resolution No. 92–4 & 95–8; Schenectady, N.Y., Ordinance No. 91–37 (City Code §§ 93–94), as amended by Ordinance Nos. 93–41, 95–07, 97–32 & 2002–09.

Board (PERB), alleging that the City of Syracuse unilaterally implemented procedures compelling PBA members to participate in hearings held before the CRB concerning citizen complaints against city police officers.[52] The PBA argued that any development of procedures, certainly those that could impact employees' terms and conditions of employment (i.e., carry the possibility of discipline if the employee fails to follow the unilaterally enacted procedure), is subject to mandatory negotiations.[53] PERB held that it lacked jurisdiction over the issue because the Syracuse police contract contained negotiated procedures for investigation and interrogation by city management, and, therefore, the matter was deferred to grievance arbitration.[54]

The Syracuse PBA filed its Demand for Arbitration[55] and, simultaneously, went to court to seek an injunction "enjoining the [City of Syracuse's CRB] from compelling the participation of [Syracuse PBA members] in hearings before the CRB while an arbitration proceeding is pending."[56] The court granted the injunction, finding that despite the city's arguments that the CRB can only recommend, and not impose, discipline (and arguably there would then be no impact upon PBA members), "[t]he issue in the arbitration is whether or not the City violated the Collective Bargaining Agreement when it unilaterally implemented the procedures set forth in Local Law No. 11 of 1993."[57] The court further stated that: "[s]ince the relief sought at the arbitration will be a ruling that the [city] cannot compel the participation of the police officer outside the procedures set forth in the Collective Bargaining Agreement, the relief will be rendered ineffectual unless ... the Court grants an injunction."[58] Currently, the injunction is still in effect, and the arbitration is pending.[59]

---

52. Syracuse PBA and City of Syracuse, 31 P.E.R.B. 3004 (1998); Rochester Police Locust Club, Inc., and City of Rochester, 26 P.E.R.B. 3049 (1993), *affirmed* 27 P.E.R.B. 7003 (1994).

53. Syracuse PBA, 31 P.E.R.B. 3004.

54. *Id.*

55. American Arbitration Association, Case No. A15 390 006 2097.

56. Piedmonte, No. 97-5241 (Sup. Ct., Onondaga Co. 1998).

57. *Id.* at 2.

58. *Id.* at 4.

59. Telephone Interview with Rocco A. DePerno, Esq., DePerno & Khanzadian, counsel to the Syracuse PBA (Feb. 3, 2003).

3. Rochester

In Rochester, the collective bargaining agreement between the City of Rochester and the Rochester Police Locust Club, Inc., provides for a disciplinary procedure, which has been part of Rochester's collective bargaining agreement since its police officers unionized.[60] Prior to the negotiated agreement on the matter, however, the city code controlled.

In 1963, the City of Rochester added Chapter 10 to its municipal code,[61] creating the Police Advisory Board (PAB) and authorizing the Board to review complaints against members of the city's police force, investigate those complaints, and provide opinions and recommendations to the police commissioner. If the Board disagreed with the police commissioner's investigative findings and proposed actions, Chapter 10 authorized the Board to hold a public hearing and make its recommendations public.[62] The city code also contained a provision authorizing the police commissioner to impose disciplinary penalties for police officer misconduct. Following the enactment of the ordinance adding Chapter 10 to the municipal code, the police union filed suit and was granted summary judgment. The summary judgment order stripped the PAB of all its functions granted by the ordinance, except the right to receive and file complaints alleging excessive or unnecessary use of force.[63]

In reversing the trial court's order, the appellate court determined that when the police commissioner and Board do not agree, the extent of the PAB's power is to make its recommendation public.[64] The court found that, "[i]n the absence of any disciplinary power vested in the Board[,] it is difficult to imagine a 'recommendation' that could exceed

---

60. *City of Rochester and the Rochester Police Locust Club, Inc.,* Article 20 (July 1, 1999 through June 30, 2001, as amd. IA 201-028; M201-104 extended through June 30, 2005). The procedure provides for investigation, interrogation, employee rights, representation, hearing procedures, document production, among other things.
61. Locust Club of Rochester, et al. v. City of Rochester, et al., 29 A.D.2d 134, 135 (4th Dept. 1968), *aff'd* 22 N.Y.2d 802 (1968).
62. *Id.* at 135–36.
63. *Id.* at 135.
64. *Id.* at 137.

one that upon the facts presented some affirmative action should be taken by the city administration."[65] According to the court, "[t]he result would be a plain difference of opinion between city officials and the Board,"[66] and held the municipal code provision, enacting a Police Advisory Board, to be valid, legal, and constitutional.[67]

In 1993, the City of Rochester and its police union were still battling over disciplinary authority. The police union brought an improper practice charge (similar to an unfair labor practice complaint) to the New York State Public Employment Relations Board (PERB).[68] The charge alleged that the city failed to negotiate in good faith when it established a civilian review board with the power and authority to review police department disciplinary investigations.[69] The union argued that its collective bargaining agreement covers the subject matter of discipline and that any change to the current procedure was to be a mandatory subject of negotiations. When PERB held that the matter, being an allegation of a breach of the collective bargaining agreement, was outside of its jurisdiction,[70] the union filed suit. The court held that:

> The contract in question contains specific details concerning disciplinary procedures for unit members. The City's action and the Club's subsequent complaint are the result of a departure from those contract terms. In this sense, there are specific contract provisions applicable and PERB may not interfere with the enforcement or lack of enforcement of those provisions. While it seems clear that the City's actions violated its contract with petitioner, that breach is not a matter within respondent's jurisdiction. The Court does not find any indication on the record submitted that negotiations were ever attempted or even demanded concerning this matter. Therefore, in the context of

65. *Id.* at 137–38.
66. *Id.* at 138.
67. *Id.* at 139.
68. P.E.R.B. Case No. U-14148; 26 P.E.R.B. 3049, 4523 (1993).
69. *Id.*
70. *Id.*

this proceeding, the Court cannot say that PERB's decision was affected by an error of law.[71]

Arguably, had the city reached the collective bargaining agreement as the court inferred, the PBA could have timely filed a grievance and persued it to arbitration to obtain its requested relief. The PBA, however, never pursued the matter. In 1995, Rochester enacted Resolution 95-8, modifying its prior creation of a review board and reestablishing the authority in the head of the police department to make final disciplinary decisions.

H. CONCLUSION

Citizen oversight agencies will continue to be created in municipalities across the country. These agencies must be considered in terms of how they fit in with the overall goal of correcting and/or overseeing allegations of police misconduct, and in creating an atmosphere of improved communication and understanding between the police department and the community at large.

Unless there is awareness and understanding of the legal and policy issues presented by collective bargaining and labor agreements, and unless the union understands and accepts the reasoning behind its creation, a citizen oversight agency will be rendered ineffectual. In municipalities where the oversight agency functions without challenge, we find that they were created in a collaborative effort between police personnel and legislative leaders. As with all matters in public-sector labor-management relations, cooperation and respect for each side's perspective will lead to a successful outcome.

---

71. 27 P.E.R.B. 7003, N.Y. Sup. Ct., Monroe Co. (March 30, 1994).

Municipal Subdivision Liability under Section 1983

8

J. Rita McNeil

A. MUNICIPAL SUBDIVISION LIABILITY UNDER SECTION 1983[1]

Section 1983. Civil Action for Deprivation of Rights

Every person who, under color of any statute, ordinance, regulation, custom, or usage, of any State or Territory or the District of Columbia, subjects, or causes to be subjected, any citizen of the United States or other person within the jurisdiction thereof to the deprivation of any rights, privileges, or immunities secured by the Constitution and

---

1. Much of the structure of this chapter was taken from SHELDON NAHMOOD'S THE SECTION 1983 PRIMA FACIE CASE AND DUE PROCESS, published as an IMLA Event Paper for the 2001 IMLA Annual Conference; the author also referred extensively to KAREN M. BLUM's paper LOCAL GOVERNMENT LIABILITY UNDER SECTION 1983, in 20th Annual Section 1983 Civil Rights Litigation Conference (March 27–28, 2003, Chicago-Kent College of Law, Chicago, Illinois).

laws, shall be liable to the party injured in an action at law, suit in equity, or other proper proceeding for redress.

1. The Prior Law: Local Governments Could Not Be Sued

A significant portion of the 42 U.S.C. 1983 (Section 1983) jurisprudence dealing with local government liability centered on what constitutes a "person" within the contemplation of Section 1983. Prior to 1978, municipal corporations were not susceptible to suit pursuant to Section 1983. This was a result of the Supreme Court's decision in *Monroe v. Pape,*[2] in which the Court, examining the legislative history of the statute, determined that a municipal corporation could not be considered a "person" for the purposes of Section 1983, and thus municipal corporations did not fall within the ambit of Section 1983. Consequently, the Court held, municipalities could not be sued under Section 1983 for either damages or injunctive relief, and local government officials could not be sued for damages in their official capacities.

2. The Current Law: Local Governments May Be Sued

Seventeen years after *Monroe,* the Court reversed itself in *Monell v. Dept. of Social Services,*[3] acknowledging that it erred in its statutory interpretation of Section 1983 in the *Monroe* decision. The Court, finding that a local government body could be considered a "person" under Section 1983, overruled *Monroe* in its finding that municipalities are completely immune from suit under Section 1983. However, the Court upheld *Monroe* insofar as it held that the doctrine of respondeat superior is not a basis for rendering local governments liable under Section 1983 for the constitutional torts of their employees. The result of *Monell* was to render local governments subject to suit at all governmental levels, including cities, counties, and special-purpose bodies. *Monell* remains the leading case in this area of the law.

---

2. Monroe v. Pape, 365 U.S. 167 (1961).
3. Monell v. Dept. of Social Services, 436 U.S. 658 (1978).

3. General Requirements for Local Government Liability under *Monell*

a. *Official Policy or Custom Requirement*

Monell requires the existence of an official policy or custom in order for a local government to be held liable under Section 1983. Respondeat superior is not enough to confer liability on the local government body; more than a mere employment relationship must be shown. The plaintiff must show that the government itself was responsible for the constitutional deprivation alleged. Liability can be premised on one of two bases: (1) the act of the government body itself, as in *Monell*; or (2) the unconstitutional conduct of a government official that is attributable to the government (the "policymaker" basis).

b. *Two Bases of Liability, in Particular, the "Policymaker" Basis*

The first of the bases is the clearer of the two. The first basis considers whether the act of the local government body is unconstitutional. If the act is unconstitutional, then the local government body can be held liable under Section 1983. For example, an ordinance from a city council that enacts a law or regulation that is clearly unconstitutional provides a basis for Section 1983 liability.

The second basis is more ambiguous and has come to be known as the "policymaker" basis of liability. The Court, albeit implicitly, addressed the "policymaker" standard for what constitutes unconstitutional conduct of a government official that is attributable to the government in *City of Canton v. Harris.*[4] Addressing a failure to train claim, the Court held that the official policy or custom itself need not be unconstitutional in order to confer liability on the government body. By implication, then, even a facially constitutional official policy or custom may, in limited circumstances, be actionable under Section 1983, if the policy or custom were executed unconstitutionally by a government official.

---

4. City of Canton v. Harris, 489 U.S. 378 (1989).

Whether a policy or custom itself, when executed by a government official, is attributable to the local government depends on whether the official is a "policymaker" for the local government body. The determination of whether an individual is a "policymaker" is expressly not a question of federal law but is strictly a question of state law, because "the States have extremely wide latitude in determining the form that local government takes, and local preferences have led to a profusion of distinct forms."[5] If a government official is, under state law, someone with final policy-making authority, then his execution or approval of the policy or custom may be attributable to the local government authority.[6] Even a single decision by a "policymaker" can render a local government body liable, although "not every decision by municipal officers automatically subjects the municipality to §1983 liability[;] [m]unicipal liability attaches only where the decisionmaker possesses final authority to establish municipal policy with respect to the action ordered."[7] Indeed, the obstacles to finding liability for a single decision can be almost insurmountable.[8]

c. *The Derivative Nature of Local Government Liability*

Leatherman v. Tarrant County[9] retracted even further whatever incremental protection *Monroe* appeared to offer to local government bodies by virtue of their status as governmental bodies. The Court in *Leatherman* held that there is no heightened pleading requirement for plaintiffs in local government liability cases. But in *City of Los Angeles v. Heller*,[10] the Court provided a measure of insulation for local government bodies by determining that local government liability is derivative in nature, finding that if a local government employee had not inflicted any injury on the plaintiff, the local government could not be liable even if its custom or policy were unconstitutional. Thus, although a municipality garners no additional protection from Section 1983 by virtue of its status as a municipality, in order to confer liability on a municipality, a plaintiff

---

5. St. Louis v. Praprotnik, 485 U.S. 112, 124 (1988).
6. *Id.* at 127.
7. Pembaur v. Cincinnati, 475 U.S. 469, 482 (1986).
8. *See* Bryan County v. Brown, 520 U.S. 397 (1997).
9. Leatherman v. Tarrant County, 113 S. Ct. 1160 (1993).
10. City of Los Angeles v. Heller, 475 U.S. 796 (1986).

must first establish an injury committed by an employee of the municipality in the exercise of the allegedly unconstitutional custom or policy.

d. *The Distinction between Official and Personal Capacity Suits*

Hafer v. Melo[11] highlighted the significant distinction between official capacity damages actions and personal capacity damages actions. Suits against officials in their official capacity should be treated as suits against the local government body because "the real party in interest in an official-capacity suit is the governmental entity and not the named official," and the local government body's policy or custom must have played a part in the violation of federal law. The only immunities available to the defendant in an official capacity action are those that the government body possesses.[12] In personal capacity suits, on the other hand, "it is enough to show that the official, acting under color of state law, caused the deprivation of a federal right."[13] Furthermore, "while the plaintiff in a personal-capacity suit need not establish a connection to governmental 'policy or custom,' officials sued in their personal capacities, unlike those sued in their official capacities, may assert personal immunity defenses such as objectively reasonable reliance on existing law."[14] When an individual city official is personally named in a Section 1983 case, it is imperative that the defendant asserts the personal defenses available. The distinction is also important because individuals may be liable for punitive damages, but the governmental entity generally is not.

4. Local Government Immunity

a. *No Qualified Immunity from Compensatory Damages: Measure of Compensatory Damages*

When a plaintiff does seek compensatory damages from a local government body for acts committed by officials in their official capacity, the

---

11. Hafer v. Melo, 502 U.S. 21 (1992).
12. *Id.* at 25.
13. *Id.*
14. *Id.*

Court has held that local governments no longer retain qualified immunity.[15] Rejecting the defendant city's assertion of the good faith of its officers as a defense that entitled it to qualified immunity, the Court reasoned: "there is no tradition of immunity for municipal corporations, and neither history nor policy supports a construction of § 1983 that would justify the qualified immunity."[16] Based on the Court's holding, lower courts have consistently allowed suits seeking compensatory damages for everything from one day's lost wages due to suspension,[17] to a denied salary increase,[18] to eliminated jobs.[19]

The Court has not addressed in any case in which a municipality was the defendant the measure of compensatory damages. However, in contexts other than suits against a municipality, the Court has addressed this question, requiring proof of actual injury.[20] Furthermore, the Court has held that mental and emotional distress, embarrassment, impairment of reputation, and similar injuries are proper components of a compensatory damages award in 42 U.S.C.S. § 1983 actions, as long as there exists a determination of an actual, provable injury.[21] The Court also has rejected the notion that a compensatory damages award under 42 U.S.C.S § 1983 may include an award for the "value" or "importance" of the constitutional rights alleged to have been violated.[22] It follows, therefore, that the same standards for the measure of compensatory damages would apply in a case in which the defendant was a municipality.

---

15. Owen v. City of Independence, 445 U.S. 622 (1980).

16. *Id.* at 638.

17. Kessler v. City of Providence, 167 F. Supp.2d 482 (D.R.I. 2001).

18. Berkley v. Common Council of City of Charleston, 63 F.3d 295 (4th Cir.1995).

19. Carver v. Foerster, 102 F.3d 96 (3d Cir.1996); *see also* Goldberg v. Town of Rocky Hill, 973 F.2d 70 (2d Cir.1992).

20. *See* Carey v. Piphus, 435 US 247 (1978), and Memphis Community School Dist. v. Stachura, 477 US 299 (1986) (both involving school districts as defendants).

21. *See id.*

22. *See id.*

b. *Absolute Immunity from Punitive Damages*

Even though, under Section 1983, punitive damages may be awarded against individual defendants,[23] municipalities retain their immunity from punitive damages.[24] The Court reasoned in *City of Newport v. Fact Concerts* that because of the wide variety of both federal statutory and constitutional law violations for which Section 1983 damages are now available, as well as the potential vulnerability of municipalities to unsympathetic juries, municipalities should remain absolutely immune from punitive damages under Section 1983.[25] However, this does not mean that a city is prohibited from paying "punitive damages when the city finds its employees to have acted without malice and when the city deems it in its own best interest to pay."[26]

5. Supervisory Liability

a. *The "Affirmative Link" Requirement for Supervisory Liability*

The determination of supervisory liability under Section 1983 presents yet another twist in Section 1983 jurisprudence. Supervisory liability runs against the individual official, is based on that official's personal responsibility for the constitutional violation, and does not require proof of official policy or custom as the "moving force"[27] behind the conduct. For a local government official to be held liable under Section 1983 for his or her acts in a supervisory capacity, the plaintiff must show an "affirmative link" between the misconduct of the subordinate and the action or inaction of the supervisor.[28] A supervisor, like a local government defendant, cannot be held liable on respondeat superior basis.[29]

---

23. *See* Smith v. Wade, 461 U.S. 30 (1983).
24. City of Newport v. Fact Concerts, 453 U.S. 247 (1981).
25. *Id.* at 270–71.
26. Cornwell v. City of Riverside, 896 F.2d 398, 399 (9th Cir. 1990), cert. denied, 497 U.S. 1026 (1990).
27. City of Oklahoma City v. Tuttle, 471 U.S. 808 (1985).
28. Rizzo v. Goode, 426 U.S. 362 (1976).
29. Monell v. Dept. of Social Services, 436 U.S. 658, 694 n.58 (1978).

b. *"State of Mind" Requirements for "Failure to Train" Supervisory Liability*

Although Section 1983 does not contain any "state of mind" requirement, lower federal courts consistently require that plaintiffs show something more than mere negligence but less than actual intent in order to support an allegation of failure to train supervisory liability.[30] The "state of mind" requirement has evolved only around supervisory liability because supervisory liability runs against the individual and does not require any proof of official policy or custom as the motive animating the conduct.[31]

In the specific context of the alleged failure of a supervisor to adequately train a subordinate, the Court has applied a "deliberate indifference" standard.[32] To hold a municipality liable under Section 1983, a plaintiff may not merely establish that the training program was inadequate or negligently administered or that a particular officer was inadequately trained.[33] Rather, "the inadequacy of training policy may serve as the basis for §1983 liability only where the failure to train amounts to deliberate indifference to the rights of persons with whom the police came into contact."[34] Deliberate indifference may be shown in either of two ways. A plaintiff may demonstrate that the municipality failed to train officials in a specific area in which there is an obvious need for training in order to avoid constitutional violations of citizens' rights.[35] Alternately, a plaintiff may show a pattern of unconstitutional conduct that was so pervasive that it implied actual or constructive knowledge on the part of the "policymakers," whose deliberate indifference was evidenced by a failure to correct once the need for training became obvious and would thus be attributable to the municipality.[36]

---

30. Blum, *supra* note 1, at 9–10.
31. *Tuttle,* 471 U.S. 808 (1985).
32. City of Canton v. Harris, 489 U.S. 378 (1989).
33. *Id.* at 390–91.
34. *Id.* at 388.
35. Blum, *supra* note 1, at 64, referring to City of Canton v. Harris, 489 U.S. 378.
36. *Id.* at 64.

B. IMMUNITIES UNDER SECTION 1983

1. Absolute Immunity for Municipal Legislators for Their Legislative Actions

In 1998, the Supreme Court extended to local legislators absolute immunity from Section 1983 suits for their legislative activities.[37] The Court previously held that "state and regional legislators are entitled to absolute immunity from liability under § 1983 for their legislative activities."[38] The Court reiterated: "We explained that legislators were entitled to absolute immunity from suit at common law and that Congress did not intend the general language of §1983 to 'impinge on a tradition so well grounded in history and reason.'"[39] In *Bogan v. Scott-Harris* the Court held: "local legislators are likewise absolutely immune from suit under §1983 for their legislative activities."[40] Absolute immunity is thus an affirmative defense that may be raised on behalf of local legislators for their legislative actions.

The determinative question then becomes whether or not the action is legislative. The Court in *Bogan* reasoned: "Whether an act is legislative turns on the nature of the act, rather than on the motive or intent of the official performing it. The privilege of absolute immunity 'would be of little value if [legislators] could be subjected to the cost and inconvenience and distractions of a trial upon a conclusion of the pleader, or to the hazard of a judgment against them based upon a jury's speculation as to motives.'"[41] The Court decided that the motive of the official in taking an action is irrelevant as long as the action can be accurately characterized as legislative. Although a local government may be liable

---

37. Bogan v. Scott-Harris, 523 U.S. 44, 49 (1998).

38. *See* Tenney v. Brandhove, 341 U.S. 367 (1951) (state legislators); Lake Country Estates, Inc. v. Tahoe Regional Planning Agency, 440 U.S. 391 (1979) (regional legislators); *see also* Kilbourn v. Thompson, 103 U.S. 168, 202–204, (1881) (interpreting the federal Speech and Debate Clause, U.S. Const., Art. I, § 6, to provide similar immunity to Members of Congress)." Bogan v. Scott Harris, 423 U.S. at 49.

39. *Bogan,* 423 U.S. at 49, citing Tenney v. Brandhove, 341 U.S. at 376.

40. *Bogan,* 423 U.S. at 49.

41. *Bogan,* 423 U.S. at 49, citing *Tenney,* 341 U.S. at 377.

for an unconstitutional ordinance, the individual legislators are immune from Section 1983 liability.

2. Qualified Immunity

a. *Introduction to Qualified Immunity*

If it is clear that an official against whom a Section 1983 suit is brought was not performing a legislative action and thus cannot assert absolute immunity, that official may still assert the affirmative defense of qualified immunity. To avail himself of the defense, the official must plead that the action alleged to have caused injury to the plaintiff was undertaken in good faith.[42] Significantly, it is not necessary for the plaintiff to have alleged that the action was in bad faith.[43] Additionally, the qualified immunity defense to Section 1983 suits is only applicable when the action is for civil damages.[44]

b. *The "Objective" Qualified Immunity Test*

i. *The Prior Two-Part Test*

The prior test for qualified immunity was articulated by the Court in *Wood v. Strickland*.[45] That test consisted of both a subjective part and an objective part. The subjective aspect foreclosed qualified immunity if the official asserting the defense "took the action with the malicious intention to cause deprivation of constitutional rights or other injury."[46] The objective aspect of the test mandated that an official could not assert immunity from liability for damages under Section 1983 "if he knew or reasonably should have known that the action he took within his sphere of official responsibility would violate the constitutional rights of the student affected."[47] An official lost his immunity if he violated either the subjective or the objective aspects of the test.[48]

---

42. Gomez v. Toledo, 446 U.S. 635, 639–40 (1980).
43. *Id.* at 640.
44. Harlow v. Fitzgerald, 457 U.S. 800, 818 (1982).
45. 420 U.S. 308 (1975).
46. *Id.* at 322.
47. *Id.*
48. *Id.*

ii. *The Court's Shift to the Objective Test Alone*

The Court modified the test in *Harlow v. Fitzgerald*,[49] eliminating the subjective part because it reasoned that as long as the subjective part of the test remained, there was no way of weeding out insubstantial claims at the summary judgment stage without substantial cost.[50] The Court explained: "substantial costs attend the litigation of the subjective good faith of government officials" including "[n]ot only ... the general costs of subjecting officials to the risks of trial—distraction of officials from their governmental duties, inhibition of discretionary action, and deterrence of able people from public service[,]" but the "special costs to 'subjective' inquiries of this kind[:] broad-ranging discovery and the deposing of numerous persons, including an official's professional colleagues ... [i]nquiries of this kind can be peculiarly disruptive of effective government."[51]

In resorting to the objective test alone, the Court explained:

> Reliance on the objective reasonableness of an official's conduct, as measured by reference to clearly established law, should avoid excessive disruption of government and permit the resolution of many insubstantial claims on summary judgment. On summary judgment, the judge appropriately may determine, not only the currently applicable law, but whether that law was clearly established at the time an action occurred.[52]

The objective part of the test was elaborated to include the crucial factor of "clearly established law" as the standard by which to gauge whether or not the official's conduct was objectively reasonable.[53] The Court characterized the newly modified test as one that would resolve the "threshold immunity question[:] ... If the law was clearly established, the immunity defense ordinarily should fail, since a reasonably competent public official should know the law governing his conduct, [but] if the law at that time was not clearly established, an official could not

---

49. Harlow v. Fitzgerald, 457 U.S. 800 (1982).
50. *Id.* at 816.
51. *Id.* at 816–17.
52. *Id.* at 818.
53. *Id.*

reasonably be expected to anticipate subsequent legal developments, nor could he fairly be said to 'know' that the law forbade conduct not previously identified as unlawful."[54] Until that threshold immunity question was decided, "discovery should not be allowed."[55] Notably, even in delineating the test for whether or not immunity would be available to an official in a Section 1983 case as a threshold question, the Court left open the avenue of "extraordinary circumstances": "Nevertheless, if the official pleading the defense claims extraordinary circumstances and can prove that he neither knew nor should have known of the relevant legal standard, the defense should be sustained. But again, the defense would turn primarily on objective factors."[56]

iii. *The Fact-Specific Inquiry Requirement*

The Court recognized in *Anderson v. Creighton*[57] that the *Harlow v. Fitzgerald* "clearly established law" standard for determining the availability of qualified immunity to a public official "depends substantially upon the level of generality at which the relevant 'legal rule' is to be identified," and attempted to clarify the level of particularity of the standard:

> The right the official is alleged to have violated must have been "clearly established" in a more particularized, and hence more relevant, sense: The contours of the right must be sufficiently clear that a reasonable official would understand that what he is doing violates that right. This is not to say that an official action is protected by qualified immunity unless the very action in question has previously been held unlawful, *see Mitchell v. Forsyth,* 472 U.S. 511, at 535 n. 12 (1985); but it is to say that in the light of pre-existing law the unlawfulness must be apparent. See, e.g., *Malley v. Briggs,* 475 U.S. 335, at 44–345 (1986); *Mitchell,* supra, at 528; *Davis v. Scherer,* 468 U.S. 183, at 191, 195 (1984).[58]

---

54. *Id.*
55. *Id.*
56. *Id.* at 819.
57. Anderson v. Creighton, 483 U.S. 635, 639 (1987).
58. *Id.* at 639–40.

Thus, the inquiry into the reasonableness of the local law at issue is to be particularized or more fact specific. The Court, realizing that this appeared to reintroduce an element of subjectivity into the inquiry, responded to this perception by stressing that whether the local law was clearly established depended not on the perception of the particular official but would be evaluated using the standard of a reasonable person in the official's position.[59]

iv. *The Roles of Judge and Jury*

The availability of qualified immunity to an official is to be determined by the judge and "ordinarily should be decided by the court long before trial."[60] Indeed:

> Unless the plaintiff's allegations state a claim of violation of clearly established law, a defendant pleading qualified immunity is entitled to dismissal before the commencement of discovery. *See Harlow,* supra, at 818. Even if the plaintiff's complaint adequately alleges the commission of acts that violated clearly established law, the defendant is entitled to summary judgment if discovery fails to uncover evidence sufficient to create a genuine issue as to whether the defendant in fact committed those acts. *Harlow* thus recognized an entitlement not to stand trial or face the other burdens of litigation, conditioned on the resolution of the essentially legal question whether the conduct of which the plaintiff complains violated clearly established law. The entitlement is an *immunity from suit* rather than a mere defense to liability; and like an absolute immunity, it is effectively lost if a case is erroneously permitted to go to trial.[61]

The Court emphasized that the availability of immunity should not be placed in the hands of the jury.[62]

---

59. *Id.* at 641.

60. Hunter v. Bryant, 502 U.S. 224, 227 (1985); citing Mitchell v. Forsyth, 472 U.S. 511, 526 (1985).

61. *Mitchell,* 472 U.S. at 526 (emphasis in original). *See also Hunter,* 502 U.S. at 227.

62. *Hunter,* 502 U.S. at 228.

3. The Relevance of State Law

An official does not lose qualified immunity if he is accused of violating a state statutory or administrative provision, as opposed to a clearly established constitutional right, unless the statute or regulation provides a basis for an action brought under Section 1983.[63] Furthermore, even a constitutional violation or a violation of a statute or provision that does provide a basis for an action brought under Section 1983 only retracts the shield of qualified immunity as to that particular violation: "officials become liable for damages only to the extent that there is a clear violation of the statutory rights that give rise to the cause of action for damages."[64] Thus, in effect, violations of state law are irrelevant in a plaintiff's attempt to hold an official liable unless the state law that an official is alleged to have violated expressly provides for a Section 1983 cause of action. The possible exception to this stricture, as raised by the dissent in *Davis v. Scherer,* is a violation of procedural due process.[65]

4. Interlocutory Appeals from Denials of Defense Motions for Summary Judgment on the Basis of Qualified Immunity

a. *The Leading Case: Mitchell v. Forsyth*

In *Mitchell v. Forsyth,*[66] the Court held that a district court's denial of petitioner's claim of qualified immunity, to the extent that it turned on an issue of law, was an appealable final decision within the meaning of 28 U.S.C. § 1291, notwithstanding the absence of a final judgment. The Court explained: "the reasoning that underlies the immediate appealability of an order denying absolute immunity indicates to us that the denial of qualified immunity should be similarly appealable: in each case, the district court's decision is effectively unreviewable on appeal from a final judgment."[67] Accordingly, the Court reasoned:

---

63. Davis v. Scherer, 468 U.S. 183, 194 (1984).

64. *Id.* at n.12.

65. *Id.* at 200. (Brennan, J., concurring in part and dissenting in part, joined by Marshall, J., Blackmun, J., and Stevens, J.)

66. *Mitchell,* 472 U.S. 511 (1985).

67. *Id.* at 526–27.

An appellate court reviewing the denial of the defendant's claim of immunity need not consider the correctness of the plaintiff's version of the facts, nor even determine whether the plaintiff's allegations actually state a claim. All it need determine is a question of law: whether the legal norms allegedly violated by the defendant were clearly established at the time of the challenged actions or, in cases where the district court has denied summary judgment for the defendant on the ground that even under the defendant's version of the facts the defendant's conduct violated clearly established law, whether the law clearly proscribed the actions the defendant claims he took. To be sure, the resolution of these legal issues will entail consideration of the factual allegations that make up the plaintiff's claim for relief.[68]

Having determined that the denial by the district court of qualified immunity for the official was a final appealable order, the Court proceeded to the *Harlow v. Fitzgerald* "clearly established law" analysis and decided that the official was afforded qualified immunity.[69]

b. *Limited Scope of Interlocutory Appeals*

The scope of an appeal from a denial of summary judgment is limited to questions of law, however. A denial of summary judgment that "determines only a question of 'evidence sufficiency,' i.e., which facts a party may, or may not, be able to prove at trial[,]"[70] is not immediately appealable as a final order under 28 U.S.C. § 1291. The Court's rationale in deciding that this was outside the scope of appealable interlocutory appeals was that the issue of evidence sufficiency is not separable from the factual, merit-based issues in a case. *Mitchell v. Forsyth,* the Court pointed out,

rested upon the view that "a claim of immunity is conceptually distinct from the merits of the plaintiff's claim." 472 U.S. at 527.

---

68. *Id.* at 528.
69. *Id.* at 530–35.
70. Johnson v. Jones, 515 U.S. 304, 313 (1995).

It held that this was so because, although sometimes practically intertwined with the merits, a claim of immunity nonetheless raises a question that is significantly different from the questions underlying plaintiff's claim on the merits (i.e., in the absence of qualified immunity).[71]

c. *Frequency of Interlocutory Appeals*

A denial of qualified immunity to an official may be appealed "at *either* the dismissal stage or the summary judgment stage is a 'final' judgment subject to immediate appeal."[72] This is so because "an unsuccessful appeal from a denial of dismissal cannot possibly render the later denial of a motion for summary judgment any less 'final.' "[73]

5. Burdens of Pleading and Proof

a. *Burden of Pleading*

As alluded to earlier, the burden of pleading qualified immunity is on the defendant in a Section 1983 action because qualified immunity is an affirmative defense. The Court reasoned that the allocation of the burden is supported by the nature of qualified immunity.

> [It] is the existence of reasonable grounds for the belief formed at the time and in light of all the circumstances, coupled with good-faith belief, that affords a basis for qualified immunity of executive officers for acts performed in the course of official conduct. *Scheuer v. Rhodes,* 416 U.S. 232, at 247–248 (1974). The applicable test focuses not only on whether the official has an objectively reasonable basis for that belief, but also on whether "[the] official himself [is] acting sincerely and with a belief that he is doing right," *Wood v. Strickland,* 420 U.S. 308, at 321 (1975). There may be no way for a plaintiff to know in advance whether the official has such a belief or, indeed, whether he will even claim that he does. The existence of a subjective

---

71. *Id.,* citing *Mitchell,* 472 U.S. at 528.
72. Behrens v. Pelletier, 516 U.S. 299, 307 (1996) (emphasis in original).
73. *Id.*

belief will frequently turn on factors, which a plaintiff cannot reasonably be expected to know. For example, the official's belief may be based on state or local law, advice of counsel, administrative practice, or some other factor of which the official alone is aware. To impose the pleading burden on the plaintiff would ignore this elementary fact and be contrary to the established practice in analogous areas of the law.[74]

It is unclear if the burden on a defendant is altered by the Court's subsequent switch to the objective test alone in *Harlow v. Fitzgerald*. Presumably the analysis remains largely unchanged, with the "reasonable grounds" for the official's conduct being evaluated by looking to the reasonable person standard rather than to the official's subjective belief.

b. *Burden of Proof*

Harlow v. Fitzgerald suggests that because the defendant bears the burden of pleading qualified immunity as an affirmative defense, the plaintiff, in order to overcome that defense, should bear the burden of proving that the defense does not apply. According to the *Harlow* test, the plaintiff in a Section 1983 action logically would have to show that the law allegedly violated by a defendant official was "clearly established law." This raises the problematic specter of a plaintiff who fails to refer to relevant or correct law and is consequently prevented from bringing suit or of a defense attorney being faced with the choice of knowingly failing to disclose a legal authority adverse to his position.[75] The Court resolved this problem by holding that "[a] court engaging in review of a qualified immunity judgment should ... use its 'full knowledge of its own [and other relevant] precedents.' "[76] In effect, then, on a defense motion for summary judgment on the basis of qualified immunity, the real burden of proving whether an official's conduct is too unreasonable to afford him qualified immunity rests with the court.

---

74.   Gomez v. Toledo, 446 U.S. 635
75.   Elder v. Holloway, 510 U.S. 510, at 515 n.3 (1994).
76.   *Id.* at 515; citing Davis v. Scherer, 468 U.S. at 192, n.9 (1984).

Los Angeles County Sheriff's Department's Risk Management and Civil Litigation Management Programs: One Law Enforcement Agency's Response to High Litigation Costs

9

Benjamin Jones
Shaun Mathers

A. INTRODUCTION

The Los Angeles County Sheriff's Department (LASD) has initiated and aggressively pursued two innovative and complementary methods for the management of its high litigation costs and personnel resources in dealing with certain types of civil claims and lawsuits. The first method, originally the Expedited Settlement Program, is the Claims and Liabilities Intervention Program, and the second method is Critical Incident Analysis. Both methods require LASD's Risk Management Bureau and a bureau component, Civil Litigation Unit, to focus its personnel's atten-

115

tion on the specific incident and allocate its resources early and effectively in the review of its procedures for identifying, investigating, settling, and litigating certain categories of civil claims and lawsuits. Each method presents opportunities for LASD and the Office of Independent Review (OIR), an independent civilian oversight group that oversees LASD, to discuss and determine if a particular incident or systemic issue requires closer scrutiny or corrective action plans. Civilian oversight and aggressive management response have resulted in positive public response, a higher degree of public safety, and a significant reduction in litigation costs for LASD and the County of Los Angeles.

A successful civil litigation program for law enforcement requires careful management and must blend a variety of competing agendas, both internal and external, into a cohesive and comprehensive strategy aimed at reducing cost, risk, and time. The underlying philosophy of such a program directly reflects upon the values of the organization and its leadership and can serve to move the institution toward positive change.

B. INTERNAL REVIEW

More than a decade ago, LASD initiated a review of its civil litigation practices, and about two years ago, in a response to OIR's input, LASD renewed that initiative to refine its existing civil litigation practices. A decade ago, LASD sought to streamline its procedures in the handling of certain categories of civil claims. In 2003, concerned about the rising costs of judgments, settlements, and defense and faced with severe fiscal shortages, LASD assigned several new supervisors to its Civil Litigation Unit and mandated that they develop a clear vision for change that would enhance efficiency and control program costs within existing resources.

At the initiation of the 2003 review, the Civil Litigation Unit consisted of 1 lieutenant, 2 sergeants, 14 deputies, and 5 professional staff members. The Civil Litigation Unit personnel investigated, processed, and managed all civil claims and lawsuits involving LASD. Before 2003, the Civil Litigation Unit received approximately 1,200 civil claims and 300 lawsuits annually. The active lawsuit caseload exceeded 420 files. Annually, LASD spent an average of $16 million in settlements and judgments.

C. EXTERNAL REVIEW

As part of its civilian oversight of LASD, OIR reviews all civil claims and LASD's responses and recommends reforms to correct specific and systemic issues and reduce, if not prevent, the recurrence of the conduct that resulted in the civil claim. Through a number of different methods, OIR monitors the conduct of LASD personnel and the agency's response to claims or allegations of misconduct. One method of monitoring specific instances and notable patterns of LASD personnel conduct and misconduct is through a review of LASD's civil claims. As a result of its review of civil claims in 2002, OIR found more than 800 civil claims that the Civil Litigation Unit had not investigated and engaged LASD in discussions about the development and implementation of better tracking and response systems to ensure prompt and proactive processing of civil claims.

D. TOWARD A STRATEGIC RISK MANAGEMENT PLAN

In response to OIR's finding on the civil claims, LASD identified three concepts that it sought to explore. Loosely defined, these were the causal, philosophical, and structural components of the strategic risk management plan. The fundamental questions were: Where and why are we spending money? Are our efforts consistent with our organization's values? Do our structures, systems, and processes meet our desired needs? LASD concluded that by studying and understanding these components, it could enhance its understanding of the processes involved in its litigation effort. LASD could then use the enhanced understanding as the foundation for implementing positive changes to its litigation and risk management efforts.

The review and interpretation of the causal component of this problem ultimately proved to be the most difficult task associated with the review process. Although LASD had more than 10 years of information regarding its litigation history, the seemingly simple questions of who, what, where, and why were quickly determined to be just the surface of a much more substantial issue. Because the causal issues ultimately affected both the philosophy and structure, the Civil Litigation Unit gave this single component the highest priority.

1. Sources of Liability

In examining the 10 years of data, a number of truths became evident. The first and foremost among these was that a small number of lawsuits represented a vastly disproportionate amount of the settlement and judgment funds spent annually. In the average year, some 15 lawsuits cost the department in excess of $100,000 each in indemnity costs. These 15 lawsuits represented only 5 percent of the litigation caseload but accounted for more than 80 percent of the funds spent annually. Because previous LASD efforts had not focused on this important concept, the Civil Litigation Unit provided the same priority and management effort to all cases, regardless of relative importance of each case. OIR attorneys and LASD managers discussed these facts and postulated that by identifying these types of cases at the earliest possible juncture and then providing an enhanced level of resources to address them, LASD could achieve its most significant gains.

Armed with this knowledge, the Civil Litigation Unit shifted its inquiry to scrutinize closely and define the similarities of high-cost cases, which were informally dubbed the "Frightening 15." With the express purpose of providing screening factors, which would assist the risk managers in rapidly identifying lawsuits and incidents that had significant cost potential, the Civil Litigation Unit conducted an extensive analysis of all cases that fell into this category. This effort resulted in the development of a screening form that flagged high-risk incidents for the litigation managers and that allowed risk managers to rapidly review and adjust investigative and organizational efforts aimed at addressing high-cost cases.

A second significant causal factor was essentially volume. LASD identified two high-volume litigation categories. Propria persona inmate lawsuits and automobile liability incidents each represented 24 percent of the litigation files handled by the Civil Litigation Unit. Low risk in terms of civil liability exposure was another similarity that these categories of cases shared. Generally, automobile liability cases had undisputed issues in terms of liability, and in these cases, the parties had documented well their respective positions and clearly established fault. The vast bulk of automobile liability incidents that progressed into lawsuits resulted from the parties' inability to agree on settlement terms, and the dispute was usually over the amount of compensation. Unlike in automobile liability cases, in propria persona lawsuits there was generally no liability, and the litigation was typically a consequence of an unhappy jailhouse resident.

A third significant source of liability was fee driven. These cases fell into the "lawsuits are not about the law" category. Usually, plaintiffs filed these lawsuits not to right a wrong or resolve a problem but rather to induce a cost-benefit analysis, which would result in LASD needlessly settling the lawsuits. These cases usually involved a lengthy and intense discovery process, and plaintiffs often sought nominal awards. A small cadre of plaintiffs' counsel, who had developed police litigation as a specialty, aggressively pursued these cases. Unfortunately, in previous cases with these attorneys, LASD had often been its own worst enemy. What LASD previously viewed as pragmatic settlements at the time spurred many of these attorneys to return for "second helpings in the buffet line."

2. Reexamining Existing Risk Management Philosophies

Armed with a better understanding of the causes of its litigation, LASD then engaged in an introspective review to determine whether or not it properly applied its underlying Core Values[1] to its risk management. Utilizing its Core Values, LASD reevaluated its existing risk management philosophies. First, after recognizing that the organization consists of human beings who would make mistakes and that a certain level of liability would attach as a simple cost of doing business, LASD concluded that in these instances it was important to resolve these civil

---

1. Upon taking office, Sheriff Leroy Baca, a progressive leader, developed and emphasized a set of Core Values. To demonstrate his personal commitment and to ensure the commitment of the organization, he required each employee to memorize the following statement, which embodied the Core Values:

As a leader in the Los Angeles County Sheriff's Department,
I commit myself to honorably perform my duties with
respect for the dignity of all people,
integrity to do right and fight wrongs,
wisdom to apply common sense and fairness in all I do
and courage to stand against racism, sexism, anti-Semitism,
homophobia and bigotry
in all its forms.

claims and lawsuits as quickly and fairly as possible. Second, LASD also acknowledged that on occasions, malice or misconduct by its employees created liability. When this type of liability was undisputed, LASD again believed that it was important to resolve these civil claims and lawsuits quickly and fairly, but perhaps more important was a commitment to make those organizational changes that would ensure these same types of activities did not reoccur in the future. Third, in those instances in which LASD viewed itself as having no liability and in which no misconduct was evidence—in the cases in which good, hardworking people had made reasonable judgments but the consequences were severe—the significant financial risk had required a weighing against the future costs of settlement.

At times, law enforcement requires the use of force that causes death or serious injury. If an organization ignores this fact and settles these cases because the cost of defense might be greater than the cost of settlement, a long line will form at the organization's door. Although this strategy might prove beneficial in the short term, the long-term harm to the checkbook and to the organization cannot be understated.

LASD's investment in its own litigation constituted the underpinning for the final management philosophy. LASD made the active management of all aspects of its litigation a stated priority, and it endeavored to partner with its attorneys to assist their defense efforts.

3. Assessing Existing Systems and Practices

Having identified the sources of liability and having developed consistent values to be applied to its litigation, LASD either refined existing practices or initiated an assessment of systems and practices to determine whether or not those systems and practices contributed to the desired results: (1) the resolution of civil claims expeditiously and fairly, consistent with LASD's Core Values; and (2) the reduction of substantial legal fees, settlements, and judgments.

OIR and LASD's Civil Litigation Unit examined the unit's work practices and determined that its investigators, rather than investigate and manage cases, had simply become document collectors. In most cases, the Civil Litigation Unit's investigators' knowledge regarding civil claims and lawsuits was limited to what defense counsel told them, and this lack of timely knowledge hampered the investigators' ability to independently access an incident, which resulted in a civil claim or lawsuit. Moreover, geography determined the assignment of each investigator's caseload, and the Civil Litigation Unit gave little or no consideration to specialization or economies of scale. Furthermore, as a whole, the Civil Litigation Unit placed a disproportionate amount of attention on filed lawsuits, and by comparison, it placed little attention on civil claims. The unfortunate results of this model were LASD was sued more frequently than necessary and ultimately paid more in legal fees to assess and resolve civil claims and lawsuits, which could have determined much earlier in the litigation process.

LASD desired to enhance efficiency and reduce costs. To reach that end, LASD concluded it necessary to identify its risk concerns at the earliest possible stage, examine those issues for liability, rapidly adjudicate those with merit, and vigorously defend those cases it viewed as having no liability. To achieve these objectives, LASD refined or initiated critical settlement programs and initiated a variety of changes within its Civil Litigation Unit.

E. STRATEGIC RISK MANAGEMENT

The first and perhaps most important alterations dealt with the early identification of risk issues. The Civil Litigation Unit shifted its focus away from waiting for lawsuits, and then handling them, to a front-loaded effort. The Civil Litigation Unit assigned a sergeant and an investigator to the civil claims process and directed them to clear the backlog, screen all civil claims for liability, and settle expeditiously those claims for which liability was clear and undisputed. This change resulted in an enhancement of the Civil Litigation Unit's expedited settlement program and in the Risk Management Bureau's initiation of an early intervention critical incident analysis program designed to settle potentially high-cost litigation, when necessary; aggressively litigate the category of cases, when necessary; and review and revise LASD policies, procedures, and practices, when necessary.

1. Expedited Settlements of Minor Civil Claims

For the past 10 years, LASD has pursued expedited settlements of a category of small monetary damage claims. Initially, under the Expedited Settlement Program (ESP), LASD authorized its Risk Management Bureau personnel to streamline procedures for settling minor property damage or physical injury matters. Prior to the introduction of ESP, a person who suffered property damage or physical injury from LASD action would file a civil claim with the County of Los Angeles Board of Supervisors for compensation for the damage or injury. Several months later, LASD would receive the civil claim. The LASD unit (e.g., custody facility or station) whose personnel's action caused the damage or injury would receive and review the civil claim and then forward the civil claim and the unit's response to that civil claim to the Civil Litigation Unit. LASD's Civil Litigation Unit would review the civil claim and the unit's response and then forward the civil claim and the response to the office of County of Los Angeles' Counsel for a determination of whether or not to settle the claim. Often, this process required several months to settle an undisputed civil claim.

ESP streamlined the civil claim process for certain categories of civil claims. Under ESP, the Board of Supervisors continued to receive the civil claims and the appropriate LASD unit continued to receive and respond to the civil claims; however, when the Risk Management Bureau received the civil claims, its personnel had the authority to settle immediately and paid undisputed civil claims for $2,500 or less. The proper exercise of this authority was contingent upon the Risk Management Bureau personnel concluding that LASD action (e.g., a deputy-involved shooting, an execution of a search warrant, or a traffic accident) clearly caused the property damage or physical injury (e.g., bullet holes in a residence's exterior or a damaged car) and the amount of compensation was $2,500 or less. Typically, there was no dispute that the property damage or physical injury resulted from LASD action. ESP permitted LASD to negotiate settlements and compensate the injured person in far less time than the traditional civil claims process. ESP eliminated processing a civil claim through a number of different LASD units and/ or County of Los Angeles agencies or outside counsel for settlement purposes and then for check-issuance purposes.

The implementation of ESP resulted in a myriad of benefits. By streamlining LASD procedures for identifying, investigating, and resolving these minor civil claims, ESP required fewer LASD and County of

Los Angeles personnel to review minor civil claims. The personnel time conserved through ESP could then be deployed in more significant matters. ESP lessened the amount of time necessary to compensate a damaged property owner or an injured person, and, as a result, ESP generated a positive response from those individuals—less frustration because of the substantial wait to have their claims recognized and resolved. Less public frustration resulted in fewer lawsuits to recover minor monetary damages. ESP substantially reduced LASD legal costs associated with settling and/or litigating these minor civil claims.

Despite these benefits, however, OIR's audit of LASD's civil claims process identified and determined that more than 800 civil claims had not been investigated. As noted earlier, OIR and LASD discussed several issues that resulted in the failure to investigate these civil claims and identified a strategic and proactive approach to enhance ESP, clear the backlog, and prevent the recurrence of such a systemic failure.

In 2004, LASD initiated the Claims and Liabilities Intervention Program (CLIP), an enhanced version of ESP. Building on the successes of ESP and seeking to avoid its failures, LASD's Risk Management Bureau devoted additional Risk Management Bureau personnel and further streamlined its approach to identifying and investigating minor civil claims and expediting the settlement process with CLIP. Under CLIP, Risk Management Bureau personnel respond more frequently to the scene of certain law enforcement incidents and, often, assess immediately the type and level of damage caused by LASD action.

In addition, CLIP personnel assess and provide preliminary processing of civil claims as they arrive at the Risk Management Bureau. Using a claimant's form and acting in the role of a "claims adjuster," CLIP personnel contact the claimant, identify the responsible LASD unit, conduct a preliminary assessment, and, if appropriate, facilitate the expedited settlement of the civil claim. At the scene or within days of the occurrence of the property damage or physical injury, LASD identifies and investigates the type of damage or injury, initiates the settlement process, and issues a check for the damage or injury. Under CLIP, the injured person often does not file a civil claim with the Board of Supervisors. Because this enhanced expedited settlement is not dependent on the injured party filing a civil claim with county officials or on an LASD unit's response, it reduces LASD and County of Los Angeles resources, including personnel hours and legal fees, devoted to processing and settling such claims. Moreover, as under ESP, CLIP has generated a favorable public response from the injured persons. CLIP has had significant success as evidenced by the identification of dozens of civil claims, immediately commencing settlement discussions, and resolving the civil claims for amounts less than $2,500.

2. Earlier Identification and Intervention of High-Risk Incidents and High-Volume and Fee-Driven Litigation

CLIP also assisted the Risk Management Bureau's identification of high-risk incidents that LASD could address early in the litigation process. Risk Management Bureau personnel employed the high-risk screening factors to identify claims that needed additional attention. Their efforts flagged some 40 cases, any one of which could become a member of the "Frightening 15." The high potential costs of these cases, compared to the costs of the remaining civil claims and lawsuits, provided significant leverage. By focusing on these cases alone, LASD could achieve substantial savings. To address these incidents, LASD initiated the Critical Incident Analysis (CIA) program.

The CIA program identifies and analyzes high-risk incidents, ideally within 60 days of occurrence. At CIA meetings, participants include representatives from County counsel; LASD's Risk Management Bureau and the involved unit, station, or jails' commander; the County's risk manager; any third party administrator; and OIR. These meetings review the incident, identify liability concerns, target areas in which additional information is needed, develop litigation strategies, and, when appropriate, recommend early settlement. This multidisciplined effort has proven extremely valuable in both the assessment and adjudication of matters. In addition, the Risk Management Bureau reassigned two investigators to focus only on the identified high-risk incidents and instructed them to partner with defense counsel and provide independent investigative efforts, which would assist in defending and reducing LASD's costs in these matters.

The Risk Management Bureau also addressed LASD's two high-volume litigation categories: propria persona and auto liability lawsuits.

The Risk Management Bureau reassigned investigators to these litigation categories. The Risk Management Bureau assigned all propria persona lawsuits to a single investigator, which allows for a greater degree of consistency in the handling of these cases. In the automobile liability cases, LASD established a similar consistency through a different resource. LASD has long possessed an extraordinary resource related to traffic investigations. LASD's Traffic Services Detail, which consists of three investigators, is responsible for intensive investigations of serious traffic accidents throughout the county. Highly trained experts in their field, these investigators are dispatched to all serious accidents involving LASD personnel. Unfortunately, upon conclusion of their investigation, these investigators were removed from the litigation process. In an effort to provide greater consistency and expertise in the automobile liability incidents, LASD folded the Traffic Services Detail into the Civil Litigation Unit and assigned them the case management responsibility for all automobile liability incidents.

To address the fee-driven litigation, LASD began to take a firm stand on all cases it viewed as having no civil liability exposure. Settlement in these matters requires LASD executive-level authorization, and LASD views each civil claim or lawsuit against the Core Values previously discussed. Although the judicial system exerted enormous pressure to move these cases off its calendars, LASD remained firm on its principles. Within the past year, LASD proceeded to trial in 19 cases and, contrary to the assertions of mediators and sometimes even its own counsel, received a defense verdict in each of those cases.

3. Corrective Action to Address Systematic Liability Issues

The final piece of change deals directly with the structural and systemic issues that revealed themselves from the careful review of the fee-driven cases. OIR and LASD thoroughly reviewed its litigation, and they detected instances for which the liability resulted from problematic policies, practices, and procedures. When appropriate, OIR ensured that the requisite internal investigations occurred at the appropriate level and consulted with Risk Management Bureau personnel regarding necessary corrective action plans. The Risk Management Bureau responded by establishing the Corrective Action Manager position, and the Corrective Action Manager monitors civil claims and lawsuits and makes appropriate recommendations and changes to ensure that systemic liability issues are addressed in a timely manner. OIR's oversight continues through its review of the implementation of these corrective action plans and their impact on LASD operations.

F. CONCLUSION: THE RESULTS

With these risk management programs in place, LASD monitored its litigation over the course of the fiscal year and reviewed its results. The results surpassed even LASD's most optimistic expectations. The Fiscal Year 2003–2004 statistics, when compared to the previous fiscal year, revealed that the active caseload decreased 17.8 percent, that new lawsuits decreased 26.9 percent, and that judgment and settlement costs decreased more than 55 percent.

Although attaining these results was not easy, it demonstrates that a well-constructed civil litigation management program that blends competing agendas, manages time and risk, and is soundly grounded in the values of an organization can prove to be effective. In the law enforcement arena, the cost reductions that a civil litigation management program generates not only enhance the bottom line but allow for significant resources to be redeployed to the public in the form of service, enhancing the safety of the entire community.

Citizen Complaints and Mediation 10

Sue Quinn

The only question about using mediation in citizen oversight is, "Why isn't there more of it?"[1]

A. INTRODUCTION

Police reform movements emerge when the social trust between communities and peace officers is damaged. Citizen oversight is a component of modern police reform. Comprehensive oversight addresses many issues and includes citizen complaint examination. Through the issues raised by breached trust in police, local jurisdictions are challenged to clearly articulate their values and put in place policies and programs congruent with those values and the law.

Historically, citizen complaints frequently received little, biased, or no attention within police agencies. Uninvestigated, belittled, or poorly investigated complaints further damage trust between citizens and police by isolating police from citizens and convincing citizens that their grievances do not matter to police.

---

1. Samuel Walker, Presentation at the NACOLE Conference (September 2003).

To address this, reformers have recommended thorough investigation and analysis of complaints. Citizen complaints are now recognized as significant sources of data that, if studied, yield information police managers can analyze and act upon. In addition to alleging individual officer misbehavior, complaint narratives help police identify problems, trends, and discrepancies. Complaint information provides police management data too valuable to be ignored.

Complaint allegations range from unnecessary lethal force to criminal or civil rights violations to real or perceived incidents of disrespect. Full and thorough investigation requires painstaking, evidence-driven, fact-finding followed by an adversarial administrative trial. Investigations are time- and labor-intensive, difficult, lengthy, and costly for the complainant, the subject officer, the department, the oversight office, and the community.

The goal of repaired community police relations is not served if complaints inappropriate for investigation are subjected to investigation. A dilemma exists, however: If citizens are to believe their concerns matter, all complaints must be handled promptly, openly, and respectfully. For certain complaints, the mediation process is a potentially satisfactory method of dealing with the citizen's grievance. As to these complaints, mediation is as able, or better able than investigation, to repair damaged trust between citizen and police.

Therefore, it is critical that communities identify complaints appropriate for full investigation from those appropriate for mediation. To fail to do so is a disservice to citizens and police.

This chapter will:

- explore why the investigation process is problematic and when the process of choice for the complaint is mediation rather than investigation,
- outline guidelines for separating complaints to mediate from complaints to investigate,
- highlight policy and legal issues,
- list resources, and
- suggest expanded uses of mediation in police oversight.

B. *MEDIATION* DEFINED

The National Conference of Commissioners on Uniform State Laws, in the Uniform Mediation Act (UMA), defines mediation as "a process in which a mediator facilitates communication and negotiation between parties to assist them in reaching a voluntary agreement regarding their dispute."[2]

Outside the legal community, but within the greater community, the term *mediation* may have one of *two similar, but not identical definitions.* It is important to use the term *mediation* precisely and be sure that all parties use the same definitions. The author refers to *informal* or *formal* mediation to make this distinction.

Informal mediation is not codified by state or federal legislation, though some governmental agencies provide conciliation services referred to as *mediation.* As such, these refer to intercession, conciliation, or a friendly intervention, usually by invitation of the parties, for settling differences or disagreements.

Formal mediation is codified by federal and state laws and by case law.

C. INVESTIGATIONS, AUDITS, AND MEDIATION: SPOKES IN THE UMBRELLA OF CITIZEN OVERSIGHT

Law enforcement is to provide fair, firm, and consistent policing to foster public trust, maintain order, investigate and prevent crime, and by doing so, maintain the social contract. Deriving authority from their communities, police must establish and maintain trust even as their work raises community tensions. When police behavior is experienced as unfair, inconsistent, or overly severe, and community tensions escalate, cities and counties move fitfully to try out reforms. Difficult for all, reforms are required when the trust-and-tension balance is disturbed.

---

2. National Conference of Commissioners on Uniform State Laws, Uniform Mediation Act § 2(1) (Adopted 2001), *at* http://www.law.upenn.edu/bll/ulc/mediat/2003finaldraft.pdf.

The public associates the notion of "citizen oversight" with investigations of *individual complaints about individual police officers' acts or omissions.* However, citizen oversight actually is a far wider umbrella. The investigation, auditing, and formal mediation models for handling citizen complaints are three spokes of the large oversight umbrella.

Where formal mediation has been incorporated into the oversight process, it has typically been in the handling of complaints about *individual* officer behaviors. This is the most obvious application of formal mediation, but it will be suggested at the end of this chapter that it need not be the only one.

D. INVESTIGATION VERSUS MEDIATION IN COMPLAINTS ABOUT INDIVIDUAL OFFICERS

In the past, complaint investigation *inside* law enforcement agencies was informal. A supervisor assessed the severity of a complaint, explained something to the citizen, and produced little, if any, documentation. Many citizens were unable to file complaints when they tried. Formal investigations occurred rarely in instances when a cursory in-house investigation was insufficient.

As police reformers recognized that citizens' grievances received short shrift inside police agencies, reforms begot more formal investigations, either external or internal. Increased formality might include:

- investigation of complaints by external oversight providers by public auditors, monitors, boards, or commissions or
- monitoring of internal investigations by public auditors, monitors, boards, or commissions.

Rules and regulations evolved as needed to establish due process, to balance between the need for confidentiality for the officer and the need for open public disclosure for the community.

Governed by civil service and state employment regulations, full and thorough investigations became, and remain, administrative, adversarial, legalistic, and lengthy. They are evidence-driven, fact-finding instruments and lead to quasi-judicial trials.

Full and thorough investigations occur so the law enforcement agency can determine what an officer did or did not do to create harm or injure the public trust, the agency, its position in the community, and created political or fiscal liability for the jurisdiction. A related question to be answered is this: What should happen to the officer who is found to have caused harm? Should the officer be terminated, suspended, demoted, administratively sanctioned, counseled, and/or retrained?

In these investigations, complaining citizens learn little to assuage their sense of insult or injury because the citizen's experience of what occurred is not the focus of the investigation. Many complaining citizens want to figure out what happened, to regain their respect, and to tell someone who will listen respectfully what the incident felt like. These complainants will not have their needs met in an investigative process. In fact, their trust in the police process may be further damaged in administrative investigation.

Although much has been written about the different experiences of citizens and police officers, it is also worth imagining the similar responses and feelings citizens, officers, and investigating supervisors may have when a complaint occurs. Consider the following perspectives.

1. To File or Not to File a Complaint: The Citizen

The citizen who complains about an officer has had a painful experience. Their experience may range from anger, astonishment, or humiliation, to outrage. They may feel victimized. If they consider filing a complaint, they may wonder if it will do any good. They may fear retaliation or ridicule. They may think it is futile. They may doubt themselves and feel paranoid. Some file anyway. Others have no self-doubt; as they file, they are fueled by a fierce sense of violation.

Complainants want their agitation recognized and responded to; they want to make sense of what happened. Some identify a specific remedy; many do not. They are shaped by and focused on what they experienced, which they replay and rehearse in memory and narrative. They may be inarticulate, but they know what they know and defend what they know. They are unlikely to consider what information about the incident they may not have.

2. To Have a Complaint Filed: The Subject Officer

The subject officer also has an emotional response to a complaint. She or he may or may not have had a difficult time with the complainant, may or may not have behaved improperly, and if she or he did behave improperly, may or may not have done it deliberately and may or may not know that the behavior offended.

Once informed of the complaint, the officer's response can range from thinking "that's what we're paid for," to being amused, angry, surprised, embarrassed, or hurt.

If the officer is well trained, she or he will be able to clearly articulate what happened. The officer may or may not want the union representative to do the articulating. Officers may dislike, fear, or disparage the complaint investigation process and may feel some paranoia. They may think it is they who should be complaining, and that there is not enough money in the paycheck to have to go through some of the bureaucratic heartburn they endure.

The officers typically want to be vindicated and want others to recognize what they have endured throughout the investigative process. They may ridicule the investigation and whatever it costs. They know what they know and defend what they know. They are unlikely to consider what information they may not have.

3. The Complaint Lands Here: The Supervisor/Manager

The supervisors/managers who receive complaints for investigation or adjudication know that the parties' responses may be highly charged and will likely include many negative emotions. They may expect one or both parties to be untruthful. They may realize that any party may give a version varnished by memory, exaggeration, retelling, or emotion. The supervisor or manager may expect that what actually happened will exist somewhere between the versions of the incident they hear.

The supervisors/managers may or may not remember their duty is to hold the conflicting narratives without making a judgment long enough to find and collect all available evidence in order to make sense of what happened, to determine what actually happened, or to state it is impossible to determine what happened. They must draw some satisfactory conclusions and articulate their reasons.

They must adequately analyze and document the complaint, evidence, and governing policies and make recommendations. If they find the allegations did occur, they must elaborate. They must suggest what remedy is in order. Is training the solution? Does policy need to be reworked? Was policy violated? If so, was it a mistake? If so, should adjudication include discipline? Was it deliberate? If so, what discipline is required? How is the complaint-finding process to be shared with the complainant and subject officer? What other internal changes are necessary?

The supervisors and managers may be irked at the requirements of the complaint process regarding time, thoroughness, and documentation. They may believe the complaint process is a futile exercise. They want the complaint resolved and closed. They know what they know and defend it. They may not consider what information about the incident they do not have.

E. MEDIATION: THE UN-INVESTIGATION

Formal mediation can provide a quicker, more respectful, empowering and cost-effective remedy for certain complaints, *particularly those that allege disrespectful, insulting, belittling, or disparaging demeanor or behavior.* For these complaints, formal mediation can better repair trust between citizenry and police than can an investigation that must fact find and adjudicate complaints through an administrative trial.

Formal mediation offers a way to take the complaint from an adversarial arena to a respectful dialogue in which all parties express what they knew and experienced and what they want. Guided by trained, neutral third parties, mediation can facilitate communication and negotiations between citizen and officer, assisting them in crafting a voluntary agreement.

F. SHIFTING FROM "EXACTLY WHAT HAPPENED" TO SHAPING THE FUTURE

Formal mediation shifts the focus from a long, usually unsatisfying, argument over "exactly what happened" to a future orientation that examines:

- what each party believed and perceived during the encounter,
- what each thought they were and now are communicating to the other and whether those attributions were accurate,
- what meaning each attributed to the other's actions,
- what law and policies governed the incident,
- what remedy or change the complainant wants,
- whether the subject officer agrees with the complainant or can offer an alternative remedy or change, and
- whether the complainant and subject officer can negotiate a mutually agreeable settlement.

Because of the inherent respect given to the parties' experience and feelings, formal mediation affords the opportunity to de-escalate both sides' reactivity to the incident. An investigation does the opposite. When a complaint is subjected to the investigation process, the complainant and officer must replay and rehearse the incident in memory and narrative. This escalates each party's reactivity and certainty about what they "know" happened and their related assumptions about why it occurred.

Perceptions, misunderstandings, and attitudes held by the citizen or the officer during the conflicted encounters create much of the "commotion" that turns an encounter into a complaint. When the commotion can be dissolved without having to prove exactly what happened and who was right, a focus on the future and problem solving can emerge.

If respectful attention is given to each version of an incident and a focus can shift from the incident to the future, both citizen and officer can experience their concerns being recognized. The citizen and officer can attempt to identify things they may have missed and consider the experience of the other party. If this occurs, the chance that they can negotiate a mutually acceptable conclusion to the complaint increases.

To the extent that communities can devise processes to help citizens and officers disclose to the other what they experienced in an incident, identify mistaken perceptions, shift attitudes, and recognize areas in which they share expectations, goals, or desires, community-police relations will be enhanced and the balance between trust and tension restored.

Formal mediation does this better than full investigation can. But formal mediation requires structured stages, skilled mediators, and adequate funding. Although it may look easy, it is not. Parties agree to attempt to mediate the issue and follow a formal multistage process. Various mediation manuals outline the structured stages of mediation, which include:

- an introduction by the mediator(s), who explains what mediation is, how it will be undertaken, what rules will govern it;
- issue(s) identification; the mediator describes the "complaint narrative" identifying its "issues"; the parties describe their versions of the issues; the mediator summarizes these and checks for accuracy;
- discussion of the issues among the parties; identification of alternatives for dealing with the issues or solving the problems described; and
- exploration and development of the alternatives; selecting among alternatives.

Like investigations, mediations must be done well to have credibility with complainants and officers. They must be adequately funded to be done well; mediators must be adequately trained and paid for their labor. It cannot be expected that untrained volunteers can be mediators nor that trained mediators will facilitate mediations as volunteers. Mediators cannot have a stake in the negotiated outcome of mediation and must be neutral third parties; they cannot be department staff.

Once a jurisdiction commits to having a formal mediation component in its oversight process and funds it, the task then is to determine which complaints are appropriate for mediation.

G. TO MEDIATE OR INVESTIGATE

Policy decisions to investigate or mediate can be built on analyses of risk management and the complaint narratives. Complaints can be grouped into four categories: (1) those that are appropriate for formal mediation, (2) those that are appropriate for full investigation, (3) those that could be mediated or investigated, and (4) those that should be neither mediated nor fully investigated, such as complaints that are clearly false or delusional complaints of an actively psychotic person.

H. COMPLAINTS MERITING MEDIATION

Complaints appropriate for mediation are those that allege: (1) disrespect of citizens (with the exception of allegations of behavior so egregious or immature that they require investigation), (2) misunderstandings of or disagreements with the law, (3) misunderstandings of or disagreements with policies or regulations, and (4) grievances in which the incident has occurred because of system limitations or error rather than individual officer error or act (i.e., jail overcrowding, deficient jail medical services, administrative errors, computer breakdowns).

In the first three types of complaints, the citizen and the officer can enter formal mediation with the goal of reaching a mutually negotiated agreement. The last category is not typically mediated at present and will be addressed in more detail at the end of this chapter.

New York City's Citizen Complaint Review Board determines what complaints are eligible for mediation in the following way:

> [A] complaint is not suitable for mediation if the officer allegedly injured someone or damaged property, if the allegations stem directly from an arrest, or if the officer has an extensive complaint history. If these conditions are met, complaints that can be mediated include those where the officer allegedly used mild physical force, made threats, refused to identify him- or herself, stopped and questioned a civilian, and used discourteous or offensive language.[3]

In Portland, Oregon, the Independent Police Monitor uses the following process:

> At the conclusion of an interview with any IPR complainant, unless a case involves an allegation of excessive use-of-force

---

3. *See New York City Civilian Complaint Review Board: Mediation, at* http://www.nyc.gov/html/ccrb/html/mediation.html.

(except in extraordinary circumstances) or an allegation of criminal conduct against an officer, the IPR Intake Investigator shall ask the complainant whether s/he would be interested in mediating the complaint.[4]

In Washington, D.C.'s Office of Police Complaints, the executive director makes the decision if a complaint is eligible for mediation:

> There are some restrictions as to which complaints may be referred to mediation. The Office of Police Complaints will not refer complaints involving allegations of the use of excessive or unnecessary force that result in physical injury. In addition, an officer may not mediate a complaint if he or she has mediated a complaint alleging similar misconduct or has had a complaint sustained by the Office of Police Complaints for similar misconduct in the past twelve months.[5]

Washington, D.C.'s policy of giving the executive director authority to mandate mediation raises the issue of whether it is really mediation if it is mandatory. In much mediation theory, mediation must be entirely voluntary. In addition, some concerned groups hold that mediation cannot be conducted on an uneven playing field and that contacts between citizens and police are never equal because the police intrinsically hold more power than the citizens. Others hold that skilled mediators can manage power imbalances and that an equitable resolution of disagreement is indeed possible between parties with unequal positions of power.

All can agree that *the degree to which one participates in mediation is voluntary and there is no requirement that the parties reach agreement by*

---

4. Independent Police Review Division, Mediation Program Protocols, PF-5.09(1) (Adopted Sept. 3, 2002), *at* http://www.portlandonline.com/auditor/index.cfm?&a=9040&c=27455.

5. *See District of Columbia Office of Police Complaints: Mediation, at* http://www.occr.dc.gov/occr/cwp/view,a,3,q,603921,occrNav,[31081].asp.

the end. If a negotiated agreement is reached, then the complaint has been successfully mediated. If no agreement is reached, the complaint has not.

1. Examples of Complaints Appropriate for Mediation

- Complainant J alleges subject officer threatened him after the complainant called the subject officer "Barney Fife."
- Complainant K alleges subject officers were rude to her when she tried to intervene in their interrogation of her adult son.
- Complainant L alleges subject officer, in an unmarked car, drove by him, flashed a badge, angrily signaled him to stop, and was discourteous when the complainant pulled over.

In summary, complaints that are candidates for mediation are complaints in which the community is better served by focusing on what each party experienced and on what could be done better in the future, rather than on determining exactly what happened and which party was right. If the allegations do not charge physical injury, legal or constitutional violation, or property damage, then mediation should be considered. If neither the community nor the police need to know "exactly what happened" and "who was right," then investigative fact-finding will not be as productive as constructing a respectful dialogue between the parties. Like thorough investigation, this is not easy, but it is possible. Consider this successful mediation from the Office of Police Complaints in Washington, D.C.[6]

> Three students at a District charter school filed complaints, alleging that a group of officers harassed them and used inappropriate language toward them while the officers stopped and searched the students after they left a convenience store near school. The police officers informed the students that they

---

6. *See District of Columbia, Office of Police Complaints: Mediation Example #1* (2003), *at* http://www.occr.dc.gov/occr/cwp/view,A,3,Q,603949.asp.

matched the description of people selling drugs. These complaints were referred to mediation, and the Office of Police Complaints and the Community Dispute Resolution Center developed a special plan for the mediation, which involved three students, school officials, and over 15 officers. The plan involved holding a number of individual meetings with the students and the officers before bringing them all together in a joint mediation session that lasted several hours.

At the start of the mediation process, the students believed that the officers should: (1) acknowledge that they have treated youth differently at the inner-city charter school than youth attending schools in more upscale neighborhoods, (2) admit to racial profiling, and (3) work with students to build a more positive relationship through a dialogue. At the outset, the officers believed that the students: (1) must do something to differentiate themselves from the neighborhood drug dealers and hoodlums because the school is located in a high-crime district with heavy drug use and frequent drive-by shootings, (2) need to work with the police to clean up the community, and (3) should follow officer instructions to defuse tensions during police stops.

The joint mediation session allowed both the students and officers to vent their frustrations and gain a better understanding of the other's perspective. The students and the sergeant in charge of the officers understood that the longstanding issues would not be resolved in one joint session. Acknowledging the need for an iterative process, the students and the sergeant agreed to set up a future meeting with the goal of forming a working group between the charter school and the police department in an effort to improve the relationship among the police, the students of the charter school, and the residents in the community surrounding the school. Satisfied with this joint commitment to cooperate in the future, the students and the sergeant signed an agreement releasing each other from any future administrative or legal claims related to the incident, and agreed that the mediation successfully resolved the issues raised in the complaints.

I. COMPLAINTS MERITING INVESTIGATION

Complaints to be investigated are those in which "exactly what happened" matters critically. They include the following: (1) excessive force with injury; (2) disregard of citizen/officer safety, which caused or could have caused death or serious injury; (3) criminal conduct; (4) civil or human rights violations; and (5) complaints of disrespectful acts so egregious or immature that they must be investigated. With such complaints, community cohesion requires evidence-driven findings of fact in order to maintain public safety, legal integrity, and the social contract. The human and fiscal costs of investigation are a necessary expense.

1. Examples of Complaints to Investigate

- Estranged wife of B calls 911 when an intoxicated B comes to her home, threatening suicide. She reports his suicide threats and asks that he be taken somewhere like a hospital to get help. Subject officer arrests B, asks B if he is going to hurt himself, and, after B says he will not, takes him to jail and does not inform jail staff of B's suicide threats. Placed alone in a drunk tank, B hangs himself two hours later.
- Decedent P, an obese man with methamphetamine in his system, died after subject officers pepper-sprayed him, hogtied him, and sat on his back before P stopped breathing. The family alleges excessive force.
- Complainant W alleges subject officers used excessive force during a search in which his shoes were removed and each of his little toes was fractured. Hospital records confirm fractures of each toe.

J. TO MEDIATE OR INVESTIGATE: VALUES, RISK MANAGEMENT, AND PUBLIC POLICY

Some complaints do not fall into either category. To deal with these, a jurisdiction can consider local values, community-police relations, and resources in order to decide how to handle the complaint. A jurisdiction must weigh the risk of doing nothing or doing something that lacks credibility and compare it with the costs, benefits, and risks of choosing to mediate or investigate. Some jurisdictions opt to avert the bureaucracy's eyes from issues raised in complaints and take no corrective action unless they are successfully sued. They conclude that civil liability for police errors or misconduct is simply an unavoidable cost of policing. The emergence of risk management tools and analyses makes this option obsolete.

Jurisdictions can conduct quantitative analyses that identify the fiscal costs of police errors or misconduct (citizen or officer deaths, injuries and disability, property damage, and civil liability) and compare them with the costs of full and thorough investigations and the costs of formal mediations. Local governments can articulate their mission and values and determine how to process citizen complaints based on their values and risk management strategies.

One jurisdiction may prohibit mediation of any allegation of racial or gender slurs, whereas another jurisdiction will consider such allegations eligible for mediation. One jurisdiction may disallow mediation for all allegations of force, and another may allow it if there is no evidence of physical injury. These sorts of local decisions dictate the complaint path. Working models exist that can be adapted to jurisdictions needing mediation components as part of their oversight process.

1. Examples of Complaints to Investigate or Mediate

- Complainant H alleges her son and a friend, both camp counselors in a rural community, were falsely arrested after a disagreement in a merchant's store. It is also alleged that the subject officers falsified the description of the incident in their report and violated juvenile detention policies.
- Complainant F alleges subject officers stopped and searched his teenage son as they played ball in a park and that the stop was based on ethnicity.
- Complainants T and W were stopped by Fish and Wildlife staff for hunting infractions. They asked for a deputy to be called. The responding officer declined to take their "citizen arrest" of

the Fish and Wildlife officer. The subject officer then allowed the Fish and Wildlife officer to confiscate T and W's clothing and left the two men to walk out of the mountains in their underwear.

- Complainant V, a man with prosthetic legs, alleges deputies harassed and ridiculed him while he was in a holding area, taking his prostheses and using their hands to "walk" the artificial legs back and forth on a counter near V.

K. LEGAL ISSUES IN THE MEDIATION OF CITIZEN COMPLAINTS

Citizen complaint mediation does not involve lawyers, so the lawyer-related issues do not arise.... Citizen complaint mediation is an alternative to a formal investigation by a police internal affairs unit or an oversight agency. Most experts in the field argue that the involvement of lawyers conflicts with the basic goals of mediation, which include building understanding and not fact-finding and determination of guilt.[7]

Formal mediation gained acceptance in the past 40 years as a way to unclog courts handing family and civil litigation in which financial settlements were a major issue. The parties' attorneys were deeply involved. This is not true in mediation of complaints about police. Complaints appropriate for mediation are not complaints in which financial remedies are at issue. If a complaint alleges acts or omissions that seriously injured person or property, the complaint requires investigation.

The National Conference of Commissioners on Uniform State Laws (NCCUSL) and the American Bar Association (ABA) Section of

---

7. Samuel Walker et al., *Mediating Citizen Complaints against Police Officers: A Guide for Police and Community Leaders* 30 (2002), *at* http://www.cops.usdoj.gov/mime/open.pdf?Item=452.

Dispute Resolution have worked jointly to establish a Uniform Mediation Act (UMA).[8] The UMA was approved by the NCCUSL in 2001 and is in the process of being introduced in state legislatures.[9]

The confidentiality of mediations is protected by federal and state law as well as professional standards for mediators.[10] To encourage candor and disclosure, information shared by the parties cannot be used in other proceedings such as a subsequent investigation. However, mandatory reporting of certain disclosure may take precedence over confidentiality requirements.

Jurisdictions preparing to adopt mediation processes must research the applicable statutes and the status of the UMA in their state. They will need to devise a confidentiality agreement for parties to a mediation. Usable models from jurisdictions conducting complaint mediation should be reviewed and adapted.

If citizen and officer agree to mediate a complaint and the process is successful, the complaint is closed without administrative adjudication. Therefore, the officer's personnel history will not record the complaint. If a complaint is unsuccessfully mediated, it may be sent for investigation; this is another policy decision for local jurisdictions to address.

L. RESOURCES

Dr. Samuel Walker, of the University of Nebraska at Omaha's Department of Criminal Justice, is recognized as the academic authority on oversight and mediation. The U.S. Department of Justice COPS program funded Dr. Walker's invaluable publication *Mediating Citizen Complaints against Police Officers: A Guide for Police and Community Leaders.* It can be found on the Internet at Dr. Walker's Web site, Best Practices in Police Accountability, at http://www.policeaccountability.

---

8. National Conference of Commissioners on Uniform State Laws, *Uniform Mediation Act* (Adopted 2001), *at* http://www.law.upenn.edu/bll/ulc/mediat/2003finaldraft.pdf.

9. *Id.*

10. Walker et al., *supra* note 14.

org/medcitzcomp.htm, or at the Department of Justice COPS' Web site at http://www.cops.usdoj.gov/mime/open.pdf?Item=452.

The fifth chapter of Dr. Walker's work, "Planning for a Successful Mediation Program," is critically important to any jurisdiction interested in building a mediation program. It identifies the critical parts of a mediation planning process. Who should become mediators and what must they know? No profession has a monopoly in the mediation of citizen complaints about police. The mediator pool is made of citizens who have invested much time developing empathic, creative listening, and reframing skills. Nationally recognized programs train mediators in the structured stages and special skills necessary for this conflict resolution process. One recognized program is the National Conflict Resolution Center, which delivers training in the United States, Europe, and Asia.[11] Other mediation training groups exist throughout the United States.

M. MODELS

Oversight offices with innovative, well-designed mediation components are models or blueprints for the rest of the country, so no local government needs to invest the time and labor to build a mediation process from scratch. Programs to review and use as models include: Washington, D.C.'s Office of Police Complaints;[12] Portland, Oregon's Independent Police Review Division;[13] Rochester, New York's Civilian Review Board;[14] and New York City's Civilian Complaint Review Board.[15]

---

11. *See National Conflict Resolution Center (NCRC), at* http://www.ncrc online.com.

12. *See District of Columbia, supra* note 9.

13. *See Portland Auditor's Office, at* http://www.portlandonline.com/auditor/index.cfm?c=29387.

14. *See Center for Dispute Settlement, at* http://www.cdsadr.org/polpro. htm#pol2.

15. *See New York City Civilian Complaint Review Board, supra* note 1.

N. OUTSIDE THE BOX: ENVISIONING OTHER USES OF MEDIATION IN CITIZEN OVERSIGHT

The use of formal mediation in citizen oversight has been limited to mediation of complaints about individual officers' behaviors. It is suggested that formal mediation has productive applications when an oversight agency identifies problem trends, flawed policies, or systemic failures as well. Mediation may be able to address these kinds of problems before they seriously disrupt public safety and trust.

In citizen oversight, the importance of clear, respectful communication is recognized as a critical component of policing and oversight. It remains of highest importance that the community and the police learn to listen to and speak with one another and that each model what they expect from the other. Mediation provides an opportunity to do exactly this. Its use to examine trends, policies, and systemic failures and to negotiate change deserves exploration.

Local government, oversight bodies, and police reformers are invited to consider the use of formal mediation to address circumstances such as these:

- trends that reflect system limitations or failures rather than individual officer actions (such as jail overcrowding, deficient jail medical services, administrative errors, computer breakdowns);
- incidents that reflect the need to reexamine policies (such as car chases leading to car crashes, force applications and weaponry, length of detentions, stop and frisk situations);
- trends that reflect the need for hiring, training, or discipline policy reviews;
- revelation of routine denial of claims following incidents of undisputed property damage due to law enforcement action.

1. Examples of Trends

- Tasers have been adopted as nonlethal weapons in the aftermath of "in policy" but preventable force deaths. Now Taser use is soaring.

- Citizens are killed or injured in crashes due to police chases. The necessity of the chases are questionable, and chase policies need to be reexamined and possibly changed.
- Over-detained citizens are in jail due to computer malfunctions or clerical errors.

O. CONCLUSION

Citizens have a duty to bear witness to and raise questions about what police do in their name. Police leaders must be ever attentive to the effect their policies and officers have on community trust. Failure to do so creates preventable damage to the public trust. The maintenance of public trust requires that citizen complaints be handled respectfully. Some complaints merit full and thorough investigation. Some merit an alternative. A respectful, cost-effective method of handling complaints is to identify which complaints should be investigated and which are appropriate for formal mediation. Models of successful complaint mediation programs are available to be emulated or adapted to other jurisdictions. It is suggested that use of formal mediation be considered for other uses in citizen oversight. It is believed that mediation between oversight professionals and police on topics such as problem trends, flawed policies, or system failures may result in conversations that lead communities and police to co-construct thoughtful, nonreactive changes.

In oversight and policing, it is often difficult adopt new paradigms. Communities and police know what they know and defend it with certainty. Mediation allows the citizenry and their police to listen, to speak, to learn from and with each other, to consider new information, and to try new agreements. It remains an underused tool.

Community Outreach and Public Education in Citizen Oversight

11

Lauri K. Stewart

A. INTRODUCTION: WHY OUTREACH?

For citizen oversight to succeed in its basic mission, outreach is not just desirable, it is essential. Citizen oversight of law enforcement is generally implemented in response to loss of public confidence in the ability of police to adequately police themselves. Citizen oversight is intended to remedy what is widely perceived as the secretive, opaque, unresponsive, and self-protective nature of many law enforcement agencies, thus bringing accountability to law enforcement. It is supposed to bring outside scrutiny to bear on the insular world of the police, on behalf of the citizenry it represents, and presumably to report back on what it finds there. If the oversight agency is not itself transparent, credible, responsive, accountable, and accessible, it is not much of a remedy. Having one opaque agency monitoring another opaque agency does not inspire a great deal of confidence.

Some of these things—transparency, credibility, responsiveness, accountability, and accessibility—are at least partially determined by how the oversight program is initially put together. If, for example, citizens are permitted to review only a few select cases, or must do so confidentially behind closed doors, then transparency, obviously, is going to be very limited by the very structure of the program.

Likewise, if no provisions ensure that those who are selected to do the oversight will be unbiased and impartial, will be selected fairly, and will be adequately trained to do the work, then credibility will obviously be an issue.

The previous section of this book has a great deal to say about the need to consider these issues when deciding how to put together an oversight program. It would be a mistake to assume, however, that just by getting the structure right to begin with, one has taken care of transparency, credibility, independence, accountability, et cetera. It simply is not so; establishing and maintaining a desired level of credibility or any of those things is a job that is never finished. Nor is it enough just to do exemplary work after the program is launched. One could have an otherwise excellent program, but what good is it if the people served either do not know about the program or do not trust it? Such awareness and trust do not happen by themselves, and that is where outreach comes in—not as a nice extra but as an integral element of the mission of oversight itself.

Fabulous outreach will not do much good if the agency is not fair, competent, and effective, but it is the means by which an agency achieves its goals of transparency and accessibility and through which the public will assess its fairness and credibility. It does not necessarily have to be formally designated "outreach" done by a formally designated "outreach person," but somehow the basic tasks of outreach need to get done, and outreach needs to be included in the planning from the beginning.

B. WHAT IS OUTREACH?

Outreach can mean different things to different people. For example, outreach can have such varied goals as promoting basic awareness of the agency to serving as a conduit of public involvement. In terms of application techniques, it can be anything from a conversation over a cup of coffee to a high-end video production. This section illustrates the range of things outreach can include in the context of citizen oversight.

1. Promoting Basic Agency Awareness

The most essential level of outreach for an oversight agency is the task of making people aware that the agency exists, what it can and can not do, and how to get in contact.

2. Reporting/Transparency

Another fundamental outreach task is providing transparency. Any oversight agency worth the name should be publicly reporting on its work and its findings, so the public can have some confidence that the watchdog is actually doing its job and have some idea of how the law enforcement agency that the oversight agency oversees is doing.

3. Networking and Relationship Building

Outreach at this very basic level means developing the relationships with key stakeholders within the community, government, and law enforcement that make it possible for an oversight agency to do the work it is charged with doing.

4. Soliciting Business

If the agency is one that can accept or handle complaints or hear appeals, then it needs to go a step beyond the goal of building basic awareness, to outreach that solicits business and encourages the public to use the agency's services. As discussed in the next chapter on stakeholders, such outreach should include special efforts to reach traditionally underserved populations.

5. Recruiting Volunteers

Some agencies include volunteer citizens, as with review board or advisory council models of oversight. Assuming these are not just noncompetitive political appointments, an agency may have the regular outreach task of recruiting a broad range of credible, representative community volunteers.

6. Soliciting Community Input and Involvement

Some agencies are specifically charged with gathering community concerns or serving a liaison role between the community and police and, thus, have a built-in outreach mandate to solicit community input and involvement. Even those not so charged would contribute to their transparency and accessibility goals—and hence, to their credibility goals—by encouraging public participation in meetings, discussion, and debates on policy or process decisions.

7. Basic Public Relations, Self-Promotion; Build, Maintain, or Restore Public Trust

This is what many people think of when they think of outreach: the effort to promote and enhance the agency's credibility and reputation in the community. Outreach is not just public relations and self-promotion—or should not be. Concentrating on the previous items will by itself contribute a great deal to an agency's image and reputation. Adding some of the following, more ambitious forms of outreach could add even more. In short, an agency promotes its own image better by being active and effective than by calculated efforts to manipulate its image.

8. Education

This is going beyond just reporting on the agency's work and evaluating the performance of the law enforcement agency. The more the agency does, the more lessons it will learn about the challenges of effective oversight, not only about the law enforcement agency it oversees but also about policing issues more generally. The greater the agency's role, the more it will see overall patterns emerging in complaints, recurring themes or problems that will suggest policy and training issues that need addressing, or gaps in citizen and police understanding of their own role in making things better or worse. Educational outreach is the attempt to share the lessons learned by the agency in its work with those stakeholders who would benefit from it.

9. Liaising between Citizens, Police; Brokering Improved Relationships

Some agencies are directly charged with improving relations between police and the community. Others find themselves stepping up to that plate as a natural extension of their efforts to share the lessons they have learned through their work. Being in a position to see both sides puts one in a unique position to try to help bring those two sides together— even to get them to realize that both are more on the same side than they may have realized.

10. Coalition Building and Problem Solving or Prevention

Reporting on what one sees is a relatively passive activity. Education is a more proactive endeavor, building on what one sees and trying to do something constructive with it. Actively working on building coalitions to solve or prevent problems is a different level entirely. Not all agencies have the resources or authority for this kind of endeavor; this is about as ambitious as outreach can get.

C. WHAT ARE YOUR OUTREACH GOALS?

To summarize broadly, outreach is the opposite of passively hoping that the public will become aware of you, understand what you do, figure out how to use your services, become involved, trust you, and recognize your accomplishments. Outreach refers to the deliberate, proactive effort to build awareness, educate, build positive and cooperative relations with stakeholders, and to solve problems.

The most fundamental purpose of outreach has already been mentioned: to make citizen oversight truly transparent, accessible, credible, and so on. Such lofty ideals do not translate directly into workable, specific goals, however.

To be practical as a guide to action, goals need to be specific, measurable, realistic, and with specific time and cost limits. Outreach goals and purposes need to be defined clearly enough that priorities can be decided on and specific plans made to accomplish those goals. In so doing, a nice by-product is that one will then have clear performance measures for outreach activities.

Having defined what outreach is, or can be, the question is what kind of outreach an agency needs, wants, and is capable of doing. This in turn depends on a number of variables.

- First, what are the structural limitations and resource limitations of the agency in terms of what kinds of outreach goals it can realistically set for itself?

- Second, look at the agency's mandate. What is it charged to do in the first place? The agency exists to accomplish what? How does one translate agency goals and mandates into specific outreach goals?
- Third, what stage of existence is the agency in? Outreach needs during the development period are very different than outreach needs for a brand new agency, which in turn are different from the outreach needs of an established agency or one in crisis.
- Fourth, consider the specific needs and challenges of the community the oversight agency serves: Portland's challenges are not the same as San Francisco's challenges. Different cities will have different needs for outreach. Local needs and circumstances will dictate what kinds and how much outreach is needed for a particular agency or city.
- Fifth, outreach needs and challenges are different for different audiences. Who are your stakeholders, and what kinds of outreach requirements can you expect for each?

These are fundamental considerations one needs to consider in defining an agency's outreach goals, and we will explore them in more detail over the next two chapters. In the final chapter we will discuss the specific tools of the outreach trade and how to use them in actually implementing an outreach strategy.

D. WHAT KIND OF AGENCY STRUCTURE AND RESOURCES DO YOU HAVE TO WORK WITH?

The most variable factor that will shape outreach requirements is the structure of the agency itself. The minimalist agency structure might be a single government worker, perhaps out of the mayor's office or the human rights office, who is working on police oversight issues in isolation and will likely have little time or energy for outreach. Likewise, an all-citizen volunteer model with no administrative staff or very limited budgets will, of necessity, have more modest outreach goals than a bigger agency with a budget and staff for more ambitious efforts.

The task of outreach may fall primarily to the director in an audit or monitor model of outreach, or it might be the shared responsibility of all members of an organization, occurring simply as a by-product of their daily work with the agency. When outreach is "accidental," being the explicit responsibility of no one, however, the danger is that no one will be thinking of it, and no one will be attending to it.

Larger agencies with dedicated outreach staff can and should be more ambitious in their outreach efforts. My position with the Independent Police Review (IPR) in Portland, Oregon, is one of the rare dedicated outreach staff positions in the field of citizen oversight.

Even in agencies with outreach staff, however, I am aware of no counterpart in the United States who is not, like me, also assigned other duties that take away from time for outreach efforts. In some agencies, the outreach person is also the staffer with the greatest responsibility for researching and writing reports, grants, and studies. In ours, I juggle outreach with complaint intake and managing a large mediation program. The reality is that even programs with outreach staff must develop strategies to make the best possible use of very limited resources.

E. WHAT DOES THE AGENCY DO?

In addition to the size, staffing, and overall resources of an agency, outreach goals will depend greatly on the nature of the agency's oversight model itself. Is the agency primarily an appellate body, the purpose and focus (and limit) of which is to hear appeals of individual complaints? Or can the agency investigate, evaluate, and go into larger policy issues? Does the agency take complaints, or does it just review occasional ones? Is the work public or behind closed doors? Are there public reports? What is the role of the community in the process (if any)? Is the agency a place people can go to vent, ask questions, get information or assistance?

To begin defining outreach goals, an agency needs to sit down and closely examine the specific elements of their mandated role, translating each into the outreach goals that logically derive from them. For example, if your oversight role is to hear cases in hearings or meetings that are closed to the public, then you clearly will not have it as an outreach goal to invite the public to your meetings. That would suggest that your role is to represent the public during those proceedings, which in turn suggests the compensatory outreach goal of finding an appropriate way to publicly report on the work you are doing and what you are learning from it.

If your agency's focus is on individual, case-by-case complaints, then you may not want to solicit public input on policy issues if you can not do anything with the input you solicit. If you are primarily an advisory body that is supposed to be representing the voice of the public, however, you will probably be soliciting a great deal of public input.

You probably do not want to promise that you will be dealing with racial profiling issues if your agency's function is purely appellate and you do not have access to enough cases or statistics to identify patterns of conduct. And you obviously would not invite people to call your agency with questions if you have no one to answer their calls.

A critical mistake of outreach is to promise more than you can deliver, which means you have set yourself up for guaranteed failure. The temptation can be strong to make such promises when you are confronted with a hostile or skeptical audience that does not believe you can make any difference or when you are dealing with overenthusiastic audiences who appear to expect too much.

In Portland, our oversight model is a hybrid of the three major models: citizen review, investigative, and auditor models. Our outreach needs are about as broad as they can be for a citizen oversight agency, so just about any size or model of outreach agency would find at least some portion of the discussion of our efforts and experiences to be applicable to their own program and needs.

First and foremost, our agency receives and tracks all complaints against the police and performs the preliminary investigations of them. The outreach goal that is derived from that function is to make people in the community aware of who we are, what we do, and how to reach us. Those outreach efforts need to include targeted outreach to groups with a history of negative contacts with police, including communities of color, low-income and homeless people, youth, et cetera.

Agencies that receive their cases from the police agencies do not *need* to do outreach to solicit complaints; indeed, it might be inappropriate for them to do so because they may not even be able to guarantee they will be accepted or acted upon, and those who do take the complaints may not have the capacity to handle any outreach-generated increase in case volume. At the very least, there should be some discussion with the agency that actually receives and handles the complaints before a significant outreach campaign is launched.

Another outreach goal derived from the complaint-receiving function of our agency is that of making the process user-friendly so it is easy and convenient to file complaints. Providing a high level of customer service is part of that goal as an important manifestation of accessibility and credibility.

We perform the initial investigations and either resolve or dismiss about half of the cases received. We then monitor those complaints that we forward to the Police Bureau's Internal Affairs department for further investigation. Even with cases that have passed out of our direct control, we are still responsible for ensuring transparency and accountability. The outreach goals that derive from that are to keep complainants informed as to the status of their cases, evaluate and publicly report on how those cases are handled, and report on the broader lessons learned from tracking and analyzing the data for trends and patterns.

Another implicit goal for an agency that monitors police investigations is the need to build a strong working relationship with Internal Affairs (IA) and command staff so that when there are problems with how cases are being handled and resolved, we can work with IA and commanders to resolve them.

We have a citizen volunteer appellate component that hears appeals of individual cases. This function inspires a number of outreach goals. First, there is the need to recruit a diverse, fair, and dedicated group of citizen volunteers. Then we need to train them, coordinate their work, publicize their meetings, invite public participation, and report on their work. We also perform or oversee audits for policy, training, investigation, and supervision issues and perform analysis on the complaint data we track. The obvious goal derived from that is to report on what we find. We also have a mediation program that needs promoting both to the public and to the police and reporting for transparency and accountability. Ultimately, we are mandated to gather community concerns and to be accessible and responsive to the public, which translates to finding ways to involve the community, to solicit their input, and find ways to make constructive use of the input received.

Appropriate outreach goals for an agency are largely a matter of honest evaluation of what the agency can and can not do, its purpose, capacity, strengths, and weaknesses. Make a detailed list of things you are supposed to do and identify the outreach goals that follow from those.

F. WHAT IS THE LIFE STAGE OF THE OVERSIGHT AGENCY?

Another important factor in anticipating outreach needs is how old and well established the agency is. Outreach goals will be different for an agency just being conceptualized than for an agency that is well known and has been around for years. The following sections discuss the kinds of outreach needs that can be anticipated for the four main life stages of an agency, from conceptualization to brand new agency, established agency to agency in crisis.

1. The Formative Phase

This is a very busy period in which fundamental choices are made about the form oversight will take, which in turn defines the potential successes and challenges to come. In many cities, citizen oversight is created as a response to some kind of high-profile controversy, sometimes a police shooting, which can open up a Pandora's box of baggage and long-simmering resentments. There is typically a lot of disagreement on what is needed for effective oversight and quite possibly strong resistance to it from some quarters.

The Independent Police Review in Portland, Oregon, for example, was the product of cumulative influences rather than a single event. Portland had already had citizen oversight for nearly 20 years, in the form of a volunteer citizen panel called the Police Internal Investigation Auditing Committee (PIIAC), but there was growing dissatisfaction with that agency as lacking in expertise, authority, and resources and concern over the increasingly negative relationship between police and portions of the community. In 2001 the mayor directed the PIIAC coordinator to establish a blue-ribbon work group of stakeholders to detail the problems with the current system and make recommendations on how to make PIIAC more effective.

As the group was studying improvements to the existing oversight system, the police response to a May Day protest in 2000 became an issue. Right before the city council was to vote on the ordinance establishing the Independent Police Review a year later, there was a controversial police shooting of a Hispanic man in a mental hospital, and, as a result, the council also mandated that the IPR would examine officer-involved shootings. Public interest and concern in oversight was high.

Cities vary greatly in terms of how they come to put together a citizen oversight program. It may be the mayor who starts the ball rolling, or it may be a project of the city council (or its equivalent). It may come as a result of a federal consent decree, or in other places it may come initially from a citizen group. Sometimes citizen oversight is proposed by the law enforcement agency itself.

Cities vary equally in terms of how much stakeholder involvement there is in the process and how much and what kind of outreach is involved. Still, as a general guide, the process of defining local problems and looking for best solutions generally involves the following steps:

a. *Identifying Stakeholders, Identifying Problems, and Evaluating Needs*

In the preliminary start-up phase, when discussion first begins about what form oversight should take, there should be an effort to identify all the stakeholders and get their input. Outreach during this period would focus on gathering public input through public meetings, public forums, and/or creation of advisory panels or committees.

Rushing this phase, bulldozing past the concerns of major stakeholders, is likely to leave an agency stuck with entire groups of people who are not buying in to the new system and with whom the agency will have difficulties in the future. Inclusion is key. Deal with them now or deal with them later, but later will almost certainly be harder.

Key stakeholders may vary for each city, but, broadly, they are the community, the administration and elected officials, and the police. The community is not a homogenous entity but includes some very distinct interest groups, including civil rights activists and members of groups who have had a history of difficulty with police, such as communities of color, immigrant populations, the homeless, and people with mental illness. Even once one has compiled what appears to be a complete list, it is advisable to allow stakeholders to self-select as well and invite any interested members of the public to become involved.

In Portland, the work group charged with redesigning the previous oversight system included nominees of each of the neighborhood coalitions in the city, police accountability activists, the League of Women Voters, the American Civil Liberties Union, the NAACP, local faith coalitions, representatives of the Hispanic community, and many others. In all, more than two dozen different interest groups were represented.

This period involves a great deal of formal and informal networking, coalition building, and gathering input and concerns from all quarters. Media can play an important role in generating interest and attention to the undertaking.

b. *Researching Models and Best Practices and Educating Stakeholders about Choices*

It is said that clever people learn from their own mistakes, but wise people learn from the mistakes of others. Once the stakeholders, issues, and needs have been identified, someone must undertake some serious research into oversight models, experiences of similar cities, and best practices. This is often done by the same group that is trying to introduce citizen oversight. Some cities hire consultants to do that research, others may assign a single staff person to this task. In still others, it is ultimately the media that does most of the research. In a few places, no one seems to have looked into best practices—or anyone else's practices.

In Portland, the blue-ribbon work group did a great deal of research on best practices; several members of that work group were knowledgeable about police oversight issues and information resources. The resulting majority report was presented to the mayor, who in turn asked the city auditor to translate those recommendations into a specific proposal for a new program. The auditor began an even more thorough and systematic round of research, including discussions with dozens of cities and visits to several programs. The resulting proposal for the Independent Police Review embodied almost all of the recommendations made in the majority report.

The prime function of outreach at this stage is to take what is learned through the research stage to educate stakeholders about citizen oversight models and best practices so that they can be as informed as possible in their decision-making processes and as realistic as possible in their expectations. At this stage, it is usual for opponents to declare citizen oversight unnecessary or downright harmful, often predicting that it will have dire consequences on the ability of police to do their jobs. By the same token, some citizens may hope for and expect more from citizen oversight than it can actually deliver—at least in the short term. Hollywood, with its fantasy depiction of officers capable of things like shooting the gun out of a bad guy's hand, has not been much help in leaving the public with realistic expectations and understandings.

c. *Selecting Solutions and Making It Happen*

The end result of this whole process is making fundamental and vital choices about the desired form of oversight. The choices made will determine the potential and limitations for the agency to come. The goal is to get as much buy-in as possible from the various stakeholders, juggling media, the public, government agencies, police, and activists.

It is not always possible or even desirable to get all parties to the same table at the same time, but each should certainly have opportunities to provide input, as should the public at large, so that the resulting oversight structure can be one that genuinely reflects the needs and values of the community it serves.

2. Hanging Your Shingle: The Brand New Agency

This is perhaps the busiest phase for outreach—scrambling to assemble a list of media outlets, making contacts with all kinds of stakeholders, community groups, and organizations. This is the period when you go to as many meetings as you can, doing dog and pony shows for your new agency, and talk to as many people as possible about what you will be doing and why. This is when you are trying to produce new business cards, brochures, presentation materials, and handouts.

This is also probably the only time besides a crisis when the media will have much interest in you. It is typically a whirlwind period of newspaper, TV, radio, and magazine interviews in between meetings with (in our case) City Council members and their staffs, city offices from the City Attorney to the Office for Neighborhood Involvement, the public defender's office, the Portland Police Association, and every roll call in every precinct.

This is also the period in which one is creating all the processes and protocols to determine how the entire work flow will go, how cases will be assigned and handled, and so on. It may be even more vital now than in the formative stage to seek the involvement of relevant stakeholders. In Portland, these processes and protocols were hammered out with the top officials of the police union, the Internal Affairs captain, citizen review committee members, city attorneys, the auditor, and others, including being open to public comment.

a. *Outreach to the Community*

As a brand new agency with almost entirely new staff, it can be a real effort to develop strategies for outreach, including building lists of stakeholder organizations, individuals, and media outlets for outreach efforts and starting the process of contacting and networking with those groups. We began with other governmental and nonprofit agencies, along with other contacts already known to us, to help identify potential contacts who were not known to us.

In addition to producing brochures, complaint forms, and other materials, we also began the equally important task of developing a distribution network for those materials to make them readily accessible throughout the city.

The first priority of outreach was to publicize the existence and mission of the IPR and to correct confusion regarding the distinction between the IPR and its predecessor, PIIAC. We produced press releases, news stories, and educational presentations; held public forums for input on policy reviews; and networked by meeting informally with individuals and community leaders to build relations with various groups and better understand their concerns.

b. *Outreach to the Portland Police Bureau*

As a new agency, the IPR was viewed by police with reasonable wariness. In order to build trust, the IPR wanted to make officers aware of how the complaint process works, the IPR philosophy, the qualifications of its staff, and what protections are in place to ensure that officers are treated fairly.

Outreach efforts to the Portland Police Bureau included meetings with the police union, commanders, rank and file officers, training staff, and various special units to educate them about IPR and the new complaint process.

Staff and citizen review members also attended or participated in police trainings, police citizen forums, and other events; went on ride-alongs with officers; and tried to balance their observation of protests and demonstrations by observing these from both sides of the police lines.

3. The Ongoing Enterprise

It is frustrating to work so hard to get the word out everywhere, visit any number of community and neighborhood groups, hold public forums, appear on TV and the front page of the paper and still hear so frequently from people, "I didn't know you existed."

One has to keep things in perspective, of course. Should we really expect everyone to know all about our little agency? People have a tendency to ignore things that are not directly relevant to them. By its nature, an oversight agency tends to be something that you do not notice until you have reason to look for it.

There is still an ongoing effort to make people aware of the agency and what it does but also to let people know what the agency is working on, how things are going, and to share what is being learned.

As experience is gained and lessons learned, oversight staff will begin to identify recurring problems and themes. For example, we noticed a theme to many of the complaints involving teens and very young adults. What should have been minor contacts quickly escalated into more serious confrontations. An officer would initiate a contact with a youth, the youth would refuse to stop or comply with requests or directions, and it would head south from there.

The common theme was that the young people had been receiving misinformation from a couple of unreliable local sources on what both they and police can and cannot legally do. Among other things, these youth were under the impression that *they* got to define *reasonable cause* for a stop, not the police. They believed that if they were unaware of having done anything illegal or suspicious, the police had no right to stop them, and not only could they refuse to comply, but they could be quite provocative about it.

As it happened, however, we found that officers in most of these cases *did* have reasonable cause. For example, in one case, a subject was unaware that he matched the broadcast description of a suspect. Accordingly we began to specifically include a more accurate discussion of stops, what directions by officers must be obeyed, and defining *reasonable cause* in literature and presentations for youth.

Likewise, the number of complaints we received about officers' use of profanity led us to a policy review that resulted in a change in police directives on the subject. When we present a segment on the complaint process at the Portland Police Bureau's Advanced Academy and other officer trainings, we routinely include discussion of the top 10 complaints against officers and how to avoid them.

There is also more time at this stage to gather feedback from the community about how the agency is doing and to hear from different segments of the public.

Customer service in general needs to be an ongoing commitment. If the agency has not been doing satisfaction surveys all along, they should probably consider doing them now. Once an agency is no longer new, there is more time to fine-tune and improve processes and services.

We continue to seek out new ways to reach special populations (particularly those with a history of conflict with police) and to increase participation and generate constructive dialogue through public meetings and meetings with community leaders.

4. Crises and Crossroads

It is advisable for every agency to give some thought to how they will respond to crises, scandals, high-profile cases and issues, demonstrations, political struggles, and attacks—preferably before the agency is in the middle of such things. For example, do you feel you need a specific policy for any volunteers and staff about when and how and in whose name they can speak to the media?

What about responding to public attacks, correcting media inaccuracies, or responding to an unfair, hostile, or damaging story? Do you turn the other cheek or go out of your way to make sure that people will not just hear the one (wrong) side? Which is worse, looking petty by getting into a public fight with critics or implying that criticism or misinformation is correct by remaining silent?

The unfortunate truth about trying to protest a critic's misinformation is that it may not help. For example, if a paper prints a mistake in a news story, even if they later apologize and print a retraction, the damage is generally done. It is the mistake the public will remember and that critics will happily repeat ever after.

What happens when a shuffling of police commanders costs you one or more of your most reliable allies in the bureau? It can undo years of effort in a day and leave you having to start all over building working relationships.

What would the agency do on the heels of a controversial shooting or a demonstration that turns ugly? In Portland, we had a high-profile shooting of an unarmed African American in what began as a traffic stop for minor violations. It was the second such shooting in less than a year. The African American community and many others were outraged; there were vigils and rallies for justice. The community was greatly divided; there were those who believed the victims brought it upon themselves, leaving police no choice. There were others who concluded the shooting was murder before any facts were even known and wanted the officer arrested immediately. There were calls to the mayor's office, the chief of police, and our agency in which callers said they had no confidence in the police investigation or the grand jury process. Everyone wanted some kind of immediate resolution or action.

Some oversight agencies are better suited than others to step into the spotlight and get into public battles.

As part of the auditor's office, the IPR response tends to be cautious, attention-avoidant, and very unsexy, following the overall auditor protocol of reaching conclusions only after thorough review of all the data. Our approach is to work for change—first discreetly behind the scenes, only going public as a last resort—as much as possible through a cooperative process rather than an adversarial one. Additionally, the IPR staff are veterans of the criminal justice system and know that things can appear very different at first glance than they do when you have all the facts.

Accordingly, we are very reticent about jumping into the middle of inflamed passions and routinely disappoint the press when they are looking for juicy quotes or sound bites, driving them to more colorful sources, which is not always a good thing. When the public wants an immediate response, an affirmation of their outrage, it is not very satisfying to hear, "It would be premature to speculate."

We stood our ground that neither we—nor the public—should jump to conclusions before all the facts were in. It did not help us in the short term, but it was honest and responsible to avoid grandstanding or making promises we could not keep, which in the long term is what credibility depends upon.

If Portland oversight was structured differently or if we had a less responsive police force and city government, there would arguably be stronger need for the oversight agency to play a more focal role in the process of responding to crisis. As it is, our feeling is generally that it would be inappropriate. Of course, we are always happy to give the sober and boring speeches about being fair, waiting for the facts, and not jumping to conclusions. We will answer whatever questions we can, express concern over an incident or situation, and convey sympathy for those who have suffered, but we will not take sides or pass judgment before we have seen all the facts.

Public attitudes toward the police, government, and oversight agencies are a fluid, constantly evolving, and quintessentially reactive phenomenon. Our director's favorite maxim is, "If people are going to be mad at you anyway, they may as well be mad at you for doing the right thing." There will be times when one is favored, times when one is disfavored. This public perception can be manipulated somewhat through outreach, but only to a degree. If an agency is not competent and not credible, no amount of outreach will make it so.

In terms of planning crisis response, the first lesson to be learned is that you must choose your battles. The second lesson is that sometimes you are going to take hits, and sometimes they will not be fair hits. This is not a profession for the thin skinned; expect slings and arrows from all sides. We have been eviscerated and praised, accused of being antipolice and of being propolice, all in the same day. The third lesson is that in the world of law enforcement and oversight, things can and do change dramatically, even overnight. One should anticipate it, be prepared for it, and never get complacent.

G. LOCAL CHALLENGES AND OUTREACH NEEDS

This brings us to looking at how outreach needs vary depending on local needs and circumstances; every city has unique outreach challenges. It is fitting that discussion comes here, between outreach in times of crisis and the following chapter on differences in outreach to various stakeholders, because what sets one community apart from another frequently comes down to crisis within or between various stakeholder groups.

These unique challenges can exist in endless variety, but some general observations can still be made. Because most oversight is born of crisis and controversy, and often the agency is specifically designed as a response to that particular crisis, a new agency is often trying to get started and operate in a community that still has open wounds. It is very likely that at least initially much of the agency's energies and outreach efforts will be directed at that reality, even perhaps to the exclusion of other issues.

For example, an agency that was created as a corrective to questionable police response to a demonstration would likely be structurally more geared to training and policy issues than an agency that was created as a corrective to discoveries of sexual abuse by officers or in response to a controversial shooting. In the former case, the agency would probably be created to have more of a focus on improving the quality of complaint investigations and supervision. In the latter case, the agency might be created to deal with the review of deadly force investigations and with a mandate to try to improve relationships between the police and the community.

But even aside from the immediate issues that may have provided the motive force for creating oversight, every community has history, old politics, and other baggage that has an impact on that community's current issues. Any of that baggage that is likely to have a heavy impact on the development and success of the oversight agency, or that has a powerful influence on key stakeholders, needs to be considered in anticipating an agency's outreach needs.

In some cities, for example, the union and police management have a relatively united front. In other places they are at open war. Some communities may have bitter resentments toward police, even if that was not an immediate factor in creating the oversight agency. These kinds of things form the reality an oversight agency must deal with, which will impact what kind of outreach they will need to focus on.

Right along with recognizing the limits of your agency's resources, right along with making a realistic list of the outreach goals that proceed from the agency's mandates, right along with considering how outreach needs will change over time should come the task of identifying some of the elephants in your community room and what kinds of outreach needs they suggest.

H. CONCLUSION

Should you wade right in to the most troubled waters and tackle the biggest challenges head on? Or is it too big to deal with at the start, taking limited resources from other outreach tasks that must be accomplished? Maybe it is better to just ignore the elephant in the room for a while until you have had time to work out a plan for dealing with it. Or maybe you try some combination of the two: a bandage for now along with a promise to get back to it as soon as you can. These are choices that any community must make for itself, but the following chapter on dealing with stakeholders may be helpful in thinking it all through.

What to Expect of Outreach: Different Strategies for Different Stakeholders

12

Lauri K. Stewart

A. INTRODUCTION

In the world of civilian oversight, there are a number of very distinct groups of people to whom outreach is directed. Each group presents a different set of challenges and requires different tactics. Because we are not directing outreach at a single, homogenous audience, we need to develop not just a single outreach strategy, but several separate ones for each of the different target audiences. These groups can be broadly divided into three sets of stakeholders: the community, other agencies, and the police.

This chapter is intended as a general discussion of the kind of issues and challenges that can be anticipated with these different groups as one begins to develop a strategic outreach plan. More detailed discussion of specific outreach tactics will come later.

B. COMMUNITY OUTREACH AND PUBLIC EDUCATION

Of all of the three groups of stakeholders, there is none as variable as the community. This group includes complainants, specific minority and special interest groups, and the public in its broadest sense.

1. Complainants

This is ultimately the portion of the public that oversight exists to serve, and its goal is to ultimately reduce their numbers. Potential complainants are the particular group we most want to ensure are aware of us, that we are easy for them to reach, that they know how to reach us, that they have enough confidence and trust in us to come to us, and that they will not regret having done so.

Toward that end, it should be a priority for any agency to provide the highest possible level of customer service and to be as accessible, convenient, and user-friendly as possible. This is as important a goal of outreach and as powerful a form of public relations as any public presentation or educational strategy.

In Portland, our efforts have ranged from simplifying and improving our complaint forms to attending 40 hours of the Portland Police Bureau's Crisis Intervention Team training to learn to deal more constructively with people who have serious mental health issues. We take complaints over the phone, off the Web site, in person, and by mail, with postage-paid complaint forms that are available in multiple languages in locations throughout the city. If complainants cannot fill out a form, we will do it for them. If they are homeless and cannot be reached for a follow-up interview, we will do the entire intake immediately. If they do not feel comfortable trying to express themselves in English or are hearing impaired, we provide translators.

We try to make sure that callers get a live and responsive person instead of our answering machine. The IPR receives many calls from people seeking information or referrals, asking questions about police procedures and policies, making comments or suggestions, or simply voicing their frustrations. Fewer than half of all calls result in formal complaints, but we believe providing this level of responsive and respectful customer service is an important service in its own right.

A continuing area of outreach has been working directly with individual complainants and appellants, guiding them through the complaint and appeals processes and addressing their concerns and questions.

Typically, when people first call us, they are very upset or angry. A large part of what they are looking for is simply an opportunity to vent to a sympathetic and concerned listener. It is our policy not to pass judgment until we have all the facts, so we have learned the fine art of being sympathetic and understanding without taking sides. When asked whether we agree that an officer was completely out of line, we demur and say—truthfully—that we really can not judge based on what we know at the moment.

We answer what questions we can, and when we know why the police took a particular action, and know that it was not misconduct (for example, not giving a Miranda warning to someone being taken into custody on a civil hold), we will generally try to explain that to the complainant. People should be able to have realistic expectations of what will happen with their complaints, how long it is likely to take, and what their options are (for example, whether their case could be mediated).

In order to get feedback and identify ways to improve, we distribute satisfaction surveys to all our complainants after their cases are closed A measure that our efforts are paying off is the steady increase in satisfaction rates we have achieved.

One of the main purposes of outreach for an oversight agency is reaching would-be complainants in the first place; that is a large part of why we reach out to the general public, minority, and other groups within the larger community, and professional groups.

2. Targeted Segments of the Community

The major focus of outreach efforts is usually not the general public but more targeted to specific groups within the community, particularly those with a history of conflict with the police.

We specifically try to target outreach to various ethnic, refugee, and immigrant communities, including the Hispanic, African American, Asian, Islamic, Native American, and Russian communities; youth agencies; sexual minorities groups, drug and alcohol treatment agencies; and service providers for the homeless and for the mentally ill.

There has been a growing understanding within the world of public communication that outreach to the general public often has little effect in reaching these specific populations. It may come as news to members of the dominant culture, but members of other groups often do not feel included when invitations are issued to the general public.

Just as it often does not occur to women to apply for traditionally male jobs or to men to apply to nursing school, for example, members of cultures outside the majority or mainstream may be prevented from participating in public meetings or making use of unfamiliar agencies out of concerns about feeling unwelcome, isolated, or out of place.

Such issues are all the stronger in the context of complaints against the police. Members of nonmainstream groups often assume they will not be believed or that it will do no good if they complain. Members of some groups, particularly immigrant and refugee groups, may have a real fear of the police and the possibility of retaliation. Some may have very real concerns about their immigration status.

Without a direct invitation to contact an agency, the presence of some members of their own group within that agency, and/or establishing some personal contact with someone inside the agency, members of groups with a nonmainstream identity often do not feel comfortable enough to contact the agency. An explicit invitation can make a great difference.

It has frequently been our experience that after making a presentation within a particular community, we almost immediately receive calls from that community, and they often ask to speak to the particular staff person that they recently met. In fact, it is not unusual for Spanish-speaking callers to ask for a bilingual member of our staff by name even if they have never met him. Clearly, he is being recommended to people within certain circles.

Similarly, effective outreach with many of these communities means going beyond the standard approach of coming in, doing a formal presentation, then immediately leaving. If one is trying to target a high level of outreach with a particular community, it is important to establish a real relationship, to provide some degree of personal connection, and to build trust.

There should be an effort to actually become familiar with and involved in the community you are trying to reach, to network by meeting informally with individuals and community leaders to build relations with various interest groups and to better understand the issues of concern to those groups, to become at least something of a familiar presence at community events, particularly during times of controversy and crisis.

As much as possible, the goal should not be outreach that is one way—from the agency to the community—nor all incoming—from the community to the agency. Ideally, the goal is to increase participation and generate constructive dialogue on issues that are relevant and helpful to the community groups in question.

Sometimes this kind of outreach is not easy or comfortable, particularly in the wake of shootings or other controversial actions. There can be tremendous pain and anger. With many groups, even when disparate treatment is not the focus of discussion, it is often the elephant in the room.

Disparate treatment and concerns about biased policing are not just racial issues, either, though there is a tendency in this culture to oversimplify such issues as confined to race. This issue of disparate treatment and disrespect on the part of police (and society more generally) has been raised not only by African Americans, Hispanics, Native Americans, and other nonwhites but also by immigrants, low-income whites, sexual minorities, people with criminal records, people who are very obese, teens and young adults, people with disabilities, people with tattoos, and people with green or spiked hair.

I am frequently asked if submitting a complaint about disparate treatment will do any good. I think it is critical to tell people the truth: It is generally very difficult to prove a disparate treatment allegation because there is very seldom any objective evidence of bias. Usually the only evidence is people's subjective perception or suspicion that they were treated differently. I explain that proving disparate treatment is generally a matter of statistics, of patterns that emerge in sheer numbers of cases.

Further, even if you can prove it, that will not stop it. There is still the challenge of finding a solution. The policies forbidding biased policing are already on the books. In many cities, the officers are already getting diversity training.

The issues are complex and they run deep, well beyond the scope of what civilian oversight can readily cure. Although it is always important for the sake of credibility not to promise more than you can deliver, I think it is especially critical with these kinds of issues to be very realistic and honest. If not, you can find both yourself and your message being quickly dismissed.

On the positive side, I also tell them that if they do not report complaints, we will not know about it or have an accurate sense of the extent of the problem. By reporting it, they contribute to the sheer numbers that allow patterns to be identified. They create a written record, a case study that can be pulled up and reviewed. We also track complaints by officer. Although it is difficult to prove any specific allegation of disparate treatment, it certainly causes concern if a particular officer keeps ending up the subject of such allegations.

By being forthright and honest about what your agency can and can not do, people may feel some frustration and disappointment. They will also have more realistic expectations, which will be less frustrating and disappointing in the long run, and you and your agency will establish and maintain a higher level of credibility, which is one of the most important overall goals of outreach.

Consistency of message is important, too. The agency should not have two faces, presenting itself opportunistically as having whatever philosophy lines up most closely with the outreach audience at hand. You cannot be propolice to police audiences, and antipolice to community groups without ultimately losing credibility. It is helpful to imagine a couple of officers in the audience any time you are talking to people in the community and to envision an activist or two in the audience when you are speaking to police.

More than once, I have had "infiltrators" in the audience or cameras or reporters I was not paying attention to, until I heard myself on the news later. It is important to remain responsible, reasonable, and fair, so no matter who is in the room, and even if you do find yourself quoted in the news, you will have no regrets over what you said.

You also must be prepared for hostile members of the audience. This group can include some of the toughest audiences to play to. You will very likely encounter some very angry, very bitter individuals and some who are unreasonable and unfair. In any case, you will always have skeptics and critics. You might one day be able to win over some of them, but not all.

For us, one source of hostile audience members is complainants who are not at all satisfied with the outcome of their complaints. There is usually (we hope!) a very good reason their complaints were dismissed or not sustained, but you may not be able to share that reason publicly (as in "it was declined because you are delusional and we know for a fact that it never happened!").

Another source of hostility for us is activists who believe our model of oversight was fatally flawed from inception and who are convinced that the only system that can possibly work is whichever one they happen to subscribe to. Or those who are convinced that we are conspiring with the cops to cover up all manner of serious misconduct because that is what government bureaucrats do (or because we are part of a vast conspiracy).

The mundane reality is that serious misconduct (at least in most agencies) is rare, and even agencies with all the powers one could dream of—subpoena power, independent investigations, disciplinary authority, and so forth—sustain about the same small fraction of all complaints as the ones without such powers. This is very disappointing to some.

More uncomfortable are those who hit closer to the mark and put their finger on real weaknesses and failings of the agency or of oversight generally. Some are simply disappointed or impatient that oversight has not been able to accomplish more and more quickly. (And those of us in oversight sometimes share that disappointment.) Unfortunately, the reality is that trying to change a social institution is a long, slow road, and getting people to understand that is itself a goal of outreach.

In the meantime, I would advise sticking to the moral high ground: Thou shalt not stoop to get angry, get ugly, get loud, or get crude. Thou shalt not attack back, condemn, or belittle, not only because it looks really bad, however justified, but also because it does not work; it only feeds the fire. Stay courteous, stay calm, stay reasonable. Instead of trying to win, follow Sun Tzu's advice, "build your opponent a golden bridge to retreat across." Look up a "verbal judo" or "Tongue Fu" book for ideas on how to disarm an opponent gracefully. If all else fails, be silent.

3. Neighborhoods and the Community-at-Large

For the most part, because this group is so enormous, outreach to them means media outreach, through neighborhood association meetings, or in conjunction with other public events, all of which will be addressed in chapter 13.

The biggest challenge I have found in outreach to the community-at-large, and many neighborhood groups, is overcoming a resounding lack of interest in police issues (unless there is some current controversy raging). When putting together forums or other public events, turnout with this largest chunk of the population is generally very light, even when there is plenty of advance promotion.

When members of this demographic are asked for input, most are positive and supportive toward police. When they have any issues about police service at all, the most common problem is traffic enforcement issues—that they wish police would crack down on young people speeding in their neighborhoods, ignoring some particular stop sign, and the like. Those who live in more troubled neighborhoods might add concerns about car prowls, burglaries, drug houses, and prostitution.

For us, the main goals of outreach to the community-at-large have been promoting general awareness of the agency, status reports on what we are doing and what we are finding, and, we hope, leaving them with a feeling of confidence in the credibility, fairness, and value of the work we do.

C. ELECTED OFFICIALS AND OTHER AGENCIES

Elected officials and other agencies will be of greater or lesser importance for outreach, depending on the particular structure of an oversight agency, but it is difficult to conceive of a structure in which they would be unimportant.

This group contains everything from the elected officials to whom the oversight agency reports to professional groups with whom police work or interact regularly, such as firefighters or mental health professionals. They are united by the fact that they have a different relation with and perspective toward the police than does the public-at-large and, thus, require both a different kind of message and a different means of outreach.

1. Administration/Government Officials

It is of course difficult to generalize about outreach to this group, as it varies so much from city to city what specific relationships exist between particular offices and officials and the oversight agency and what sort of relationship they will have.

Opposition from administration officials has not been an issue for us in Portland, but it is an issue for some agencies. Depending on how they are initially structured, agencies can be more or less protected from political vulnerability to the various agendas and political maneuverings of officials. It is also common to have strong initial resistance to oversight on the part of the police, particularly the unions, and they in turn often lobby intensively with elected officials. Those things, separately or combined, can translate to a real threat to would-be, fledgling, and even well-established agencies.

The most obvious form of opposition or sabotage by officials or administrations is through inadequate funding or loss of funding. It can take other forms, too, such as undermining the public reputation of the agency through attacks on the credibility or competence of its members; exploitation of the vulnerable at-will status of many directors and staff; attempts to render the oversight ineffective or "friendly" to particular agendas via manipulation of who is selected or hired for the agency; or finding any of a multitude of creative administrative ways to trip up the process with red tape, lack of cooperation, or creating processes or protocols that interfere with the ability of the agency to do what it is supposed to do.

This kind of opposition can involve a level of outreach that goes well beyond the usual meaning of the term, into the realm of pure politics. Ideally, early outreach efforts prevent one from ever reaching that point, though often the bitterest battles come before the agency ever even exists.

The best way to prevent significant problems with administration and elected officials is to include them as much as possible in the formation of the agency and try to maintain a good level of buy-in thereafter. Some ways of doing that include lobbying to build and maintain good relations with officials and administrators with whom the agency has a relationship and seeking their input on relevant decisions, on outreach efforts to their constituencies, and on recruiting citizen volunteers.

Outreach to this group should include making them familiar with the work of an agency, sharing the lessons learned and educating them about problems and successes, seeking their input and finding ways to partner with them, and finding ways to be useful to them.

In Portland, the IPR director is a civil service employee of the elected city auditor, completely independent of the mayor, who is commissioner of police, and the city council. The mayor is head of the city council, along with four at-large commissioners, each of whom has a portfolio of city agencies for which they are responsible.

The IPR was formed by council approval of an ordinance proposed by the city auditor. The funds for the IPR come out of the general budget for the auditor's office, so even if the IPR takes a stand the mayor or city council does not like, there is no danger of suddenly finding the IPR budget slashed or the director or staff out of a job. Thus, there is a significant political buffer between the police department, mayor's office, city council, and the IPR.

The IPR has two main connections with the city council. The first of these is in cases in which the IPR is making special ordinance or budgetary requests of the council. For example, the city council had to approve a fairly large contract for an independent review of police shootings and deaths in custody. On another occasion, the IPR sought approval of an ordinance change that would require the city attorney's office to cooperate with the IPR and Internal Affairs Division in investigating cases of alleged misconduct that come in as tort claims. Both of these required significant lobbying efforts by the IPR director and the city auditor.

The second connection is that, by ordinance, the city council is the ultimate decision-making body in the event of a disagreement between the Police Bureau and the citizen review committee on the findings of an appeal. It has only come up one time in an appeal, but on that occasion the citizen review committee voted to sustain a finding of improper arrest against some officers. The Bureau refused, and the case went before city council, who voted in favor of the Bureau.

Despite the relative independence of the IPR from the mayor's office and city council, the IPR tries to maintain a good working relationship with them. In order to achieve a measure of buy-in from council members and to take advantage of the various community connections they have formed, each council member is asked to nominate one citizen to the citizen review committee. The auditor selects the finalists of all candidates, who must then be approved by city council.

We regularly include city council members on our mailing and media lists, so they are kept informed of our activities and accomplishments. We want them to be fully aware of what we are doing and how well things are going. As mentioned before, when a decision is to be made by the city council on an issue of concern to the IPR, there may be significant meetings and other lobbying efforts. All of the council members have, at one time or another, attended citizen review committee meetings.

We also work with the various city council members on police-related issues. This usually comes up more with the mayor's office than any of the others, which is not surprising as the mayor is also police commissioner. Often, people with complaints will take them straight to the mayor's office, and staff there either refer the complainants to us or work with us directly to resolve a complaint.

2. City Attorneys

At least in Portland, this has been the group most challenging for our agency to get along with. Much of what we do and represent is anathema to city attorneys, whose primary function is to protect the city from any liability exposure. They are almost guaranteed not to be too fond of any agency that exists to investigate and publicly expose wrongdoing by city employees, particularly when it is police wrongdoing, which already generates what is often the highest level of risk exposure of any city agency.

Our relationship became particularly strained when we asserted that tort claims that allege misconduct should be reviewed like any other kind of complaint from a management and discipline perspective and that this should ultimately reduce the city's exposure.

Sometimes the most you can shoot for with outreach is to try to maintain a courteous and professional relationship. It is also not a bad idea to continue to try to cultivate what friendly contacts you do have, even in an office that is not friendly overall.

3. Allied Professionals

There are actually two fairly distinct groups under this heading: those whose work overlaps with that of our agency, sharing many of the same clients and issues, and those whose work overlaps closely with that of the police.

We wanted to make sure other agencies were aware of our services and how those services complement their respective organizational missions. For example, the City of Portland's Office for Neighborhood Involvement (ONI) overlaps with the IPR mission through their involvement with neighborhood and community groups and crime prevention efforts. They were also a valuable resource to us when identifying groups for outreach efforts, and the IPR uses the ONI e-mail notification system, in addition to a variety of media, for public notices and press releases. We began with contacts already known to us to help identify potential contacts who were not known to us. We also met with colleagues from other governmental and nonprofit agencies.

For outreach efforts, we identified other agencies that share some of the same prospective clientele with the IPR—for example, the City Office of Risk Management, the county courts, the detox center, the (then) Immigration and Naturalization Service, the Mexican embassy, and the Public Defender's and District Attorney's offices. IPR staff members have made numerous presentations to other agencies and had many formal and informal meetings with representatives, networking and developing relations that allow us to work cooperatively. Some of these agencies have become locations for the distribution of IPR information and brochures.

Another group of professionals are those most likely to interact with the police: hospital staff, criminal justice professionals, mental health workers, firefighters, paramedics, security and towing companies, transit professionals, school officials, child protective and domestic violence workers, et cetera. This is an important group, as they are in a unique position to see improper police conduct, including potentially serious misconduct. At the same time, however, they must be approached very diplomatically.

Because these allied professionals work closely with police, they also often feel considerable sympathy and loyalty toward the police. Accordingly, they are inclined to view us as the enemies of their colleagues and are often very sensitive to the impression that we are trying to get them to turn against the police. When doing outreach to this group, it is very important to stress that this is not a witch hunt, this is not cop bashing. This is just wanting them to be aware that if there are training or supervision issues that need to be addressed, neither we nor police commanders will know about it if no one speaks up. We want them to know that if they see something that concerns them, there is a place to take those concerns.

Furthermore, because these professionals have an ongoing, mutually dependent working relationship with the police, they are often very reluctant to make complaints against officers that might impact their future working relationships. When doing outreach to these groups, I let them know that we will make every effort to protect the confidentiality of the complaints, and that if that is not possible, we are able to investigate anonymous complaints so long as we have enough information to go on. (In fact, many anonymous complaints we get are from this group and other police officers.)

Ideally, one would do joint presentations to these groups with someone from the Police Bureau to lessen the appearance of oversight as the enemy of police, to "give permission" for these groups to contact us when they see problems.

I also discuss the option of mediation, which can be a very constructive way to resolve a complaint precisely because of concerns for the long-term relationship between police and allied professionals. We have done a number of mediations with complaints of this type.

4. The Police

It is not just outreach to the community that is important; so, too, is outreach to the police community. In order to be effective, an oversight agency must earn and maintain the trust of both citizens and police as a fair and impartial body.

An agency's outreach to the community will not, generally speaking, also serve as outreach to police audiences. Indeed, it may constitute anti-outreach to the police. Emphasizing the goals of greater transparency and accountability, stressing problems inherent in police policing themselves, even just singing the praises of your agency's effective work may be welcome news to the community, but to police audiences it may look like an attack on them.

It is essential for the sake of credibility not to be two-faced in the messages you deliver; consistency of message is important. You can not sweet talk the police to their face and turn around and attack them when talking to community groups that are hostile to police. We try to make it equally clear to all sides that we do not take sides at all, except in individual cases once all the evidence is in.

We knew that the police would be suspicious and distrustful of us. It is quite natural for law enforcement agencies to have serious concerns with having outsiders, who may or may not be ignorant, biased, or naive, who may or may not know anything about the norms and realities of policing and standard professional practices, passing judgment on how well officers are performing their duties.

No one likes being watched, judged, told what to do, or criticized, even if the criticisms are accurate, fair, or meant to help. Thus, one of the main goals of outreach to police is to address their concerns about whether oversight will be fair, professional, and competent and be able to tell the difference between valid complaints and those that are not.

In Portland, we also knew that failure to overcome police hostility and distrust would severely hamper our ability to accomplish our goals of long-term improvements within the Bureau. Oversight agencies that are perpetually at war with the police are often pointed to as examples of what *not* to do. As Paul Chevigny observes about civilian oversight in *Edge of the Knife,* "Without some cooperation from within, then, it is nearly impossible for the outsiders to investigate, and any policy recommendations they make are liable to be ignored."[1] Although such an adversarial relationship can make for lots of lively headlines, it does not make for mutual trust and cooperative problem solving.

So from the very beginning, we knew we had to do a lot of networking within the Bureau, meeting with commanders, union reps, internal affairs staff, and line officers to develop a functional working relationship. We made some promises, first and foremost, that we will not jump to hasty conclusions; we will study problems and make sure we have it

---

1. PAUL CHEVIGNY, EDGE OF THE KNIFE: POLICE VIOLENCE IN THE AMERICAS 267 (1995).

right before we start criticizing or telling them what to do and before we go public with it.

We agreed to give them a chance to fix the problem on their own, explain themselves, or at least to prepare for the questions and attacks they will get once it goes to press. Our ultimate goal is not to attack the police for its own sake but to ensure accountability and transparency, so this can be the best police force possible. We believe you get more progress from cooperation than from being adversarial.

The irony of outreach to the police is that if you are successful and can build a cooperative relationship with them, you will be accused by some of being too close to them, of "being on their side" and of selling out. Even though it has been clearly demonstrated that you can not be effective in oversight *without* the cooperation of the police, some in the community believe that the more adversarial the relationship is between the oversight agency and the police, the more effective the oversight agency is.

5. The Unions

The position of the union is generally that many, if not most, complaints are false or unfair attacks or retaliation by bad people against good officers who are just doing their jobs. The loyalty of unions in fighting for their members produces a nearly obligatory defensiveness.

Police unions exist to promote the best interests of their officers. Sometimes, however, the best interests of the officers are at odds with the best interests of the community they serve, with police management and the interests of effective management practices, with the requirements of fair and timely discipline, and with goals of overall improvements to the agency.

In many cities, the union is one of the bigger thorns in the side of civilian oversight, fighting them every step of the way. This also underscores the potential benefit of getting along reasonably well with the union.

In Portland, we are fortunate enough to have a relatively good relationship with our unions. Perhaps it was just luck at having personalities that worked together or maybe the result of having done a lot of early outreach to the union, to include them from the start in developing processes, protocols, and outreach to the rest of the department.

For example, as we were putting together the mediation program, we consulted with the union from the beginning about what kinds of cases would be eligible, who we would use to conduct the mediations, what records would be kept, and what kinds of incentives there would be for officers to participate in the mediation program.

It was not always sunshine and sweetness; they had many concerns, grilled us with very pointed questions, and many were initially openly scornful of mediation as nothing but "Kumbayah" sessions with unreasonable citizens. In the end, however, they saw the mediation program as offering a real benefit to their officers.

The go-ahead officers got from the union was crucial to the early success of the mediation program. Where officers initially were very hesitant to agree to mediation and wanted days to think it over so they could talk to their union representatives, now they typically pick up the telephone to agree to mediation within minutes of getting the requests.

We have tried, where reasonable, to address their concerns, to get them to see and know us, and to get them used to working with us. Although we were not willing to compromise on best practices, we still wanted to get as much buy-in from the union as possible. If we did one thing right, that may well be it.

6. Command Staff

Police commanders are often crusty, tough, old school, old boys. Many are more used to giving orders than to negotiating or compromising. They often resent being ordered around, told what to do, or having their authority usurped, especially by a bunch of civilians. They are often skeptical of new paradigms.

Of course, there are exceptions. Some of our strongest allies have been (and continue to be) commanders in the department who early were willing to give us a chance to prove ourselves. They saw us as potentially useful for information on trends or problems in their precincts or divisions and identifying problem officers. Some request reports, even suggestions, or ask us to set up mediations for Bureau cases. We have been asked to participate in interviews, to attend or present police trainings, and to observe protests or marches. I think most see the benefits of an independent agency now.

Although one might occasionally want to meet with commanders in group meetings, most outreach to this group is accomplished informally, through individual contacts, one on one. Over time it is possible to build a relationship of mutual trust and respect, in part by trying to find ways to be genuinely useful to them, through meetings to discuss issues or problems, calls to give or get information, and accepting invitations to do ride-alongs. (Of course, it helps that some are very likeable.)

7. Internal Affairs

Depending on one's oversight model, this may well be the most critical relationship to build in terms of an oversight agency's overall capacity to be effective. An agency at war with internal affairs (IA) may have a very difficult road ahead. In most oversight models, IA retains primary or sole investigative authority. They are the ones many oversight agencies are trying to work with and make recommendations to.

Internal Affairs may be the gatekeepers of which cases an oversight agency has access or exposure to (never mind if the city code says they have to cooperate; if people want to, they can be very uncooperative about cooperating). Even if the oversight agency has real authority to make findings, investigate on their own, subpoena officers, recommend discipline, and access and review files, a bad relationship with IA can make their job much more difficult.

In Portland, we were fortunate to have an IA captain who saw civilian oversight as more than just a necessary evil but as even a potentially positive thing. He worked closely with us to develop formal written policies, procedures, and protocols. When he opposed a proposed action, he always had a thoughtful reason for doing so.

IA were the first ones in the Bureau who began to trust and appreciate us. By prescreening complaints, sifting those that required investigation from those that did not, and by doing the preliminary investigation with our own investigators, we cut their workload dramatically so they could concentrate their efforts on the cases that needed the most attention.

Before, they had to look into every complaint that came in the door, no matter what. Like most cities, about a third of all our complaints do not allege any misconduct. We get complaints from arrested drug addicts who want their methamphetamine back. Or the man who thinks police are beaming rays into his head while he sleeps. Or the guy who admits speeding through a school zone but feels that getting a ticket is still unfair. Or the woman complaining because police would not arrest a neighbor for calling her an unflattering name.

In partnership with IA, we developed a triage system for cases and means of resolving them that are not only more efficient but are also more in tune with how complainants tell us they want their complaints resolved: as service complaints, mediations, and referrals to precinct commanders, in addition to the older options of administrative declines, investigation, and discipline.

We brought in a database system that made effective case management possible, that could not only track the progress of individual cases but could also analyze the data and efficiently identify problem trends and problem officers—all things that were not possible before.

There was not always agreement—there were battles—but they were professional and respectful. Because of the degree of cooperation we enjoyed from the beginning, we never had to do much outreach to IA.

In many places, however, there might be a need to do so. Outreach to IA would probably follow the same general form as outreach to police command staff, relying primarily on informal, individual relationship building. The general objective would be wanting to have them see and recognize that: (1) you are not biased, unfair, ignorant, or naive; (2) you value constructive input from them; and (3) you may even be useful.

8. Rank-and-File Officers

Beyond unions, commanders, and internal affairs, the major targets for outreach to police are the rank-and-file officers. Beyond the same general distrust of civilian oversight that is normal for any police audience, there is little homogeneity to this group. Officers range from baby-faced recruits to grizzled grandparents, idealists to burned-out cynics, those who manage problems with words to those who favor force.

The only other common thing to keep in mind about rank-and-file officers is the speed with which rumors fly and how little it can take to trash the reputation of your agency among them. As mentioned before, a positive relationship with the union makes a big difference in building a positive relationship with the rank and file.

In our agency's first few months of existence, the director spoke personally at every roll call for each shift in each precinct in the city. Even their own chief had never done that.

When launching the mediation program, the Bureau's in-house videographers helped us to produce a roll call video introducing it. The process of case development and scheduling mediation cases has itself been a useful way to reach out and build connections to the rank-and-file officers and build a positive reputation within the Bureau.

Other means of contact include regular presentations at the police academy and in-service trainings and having staff and citizen review members attend some police trainings, go on ride-alongs, and attend police meetings.

In the course of taking complaints, we sometimes see situations that can be easily resolved to everyone's satisfaction simply by calling the officer or supervisor to see what is going on—for example, if citizens just want a question answered, or have their property returned, or when there is a neighbor dispute. In such cases we make those calls, and over time have built a good working relationship with some officers. For all the successes, however, there is still plenty to do. It is an ongoing process.

9. Special Units

One should consider other units within a department for outreach as well. In our Bureau there are other units with whom we have considerable contact, with whom we work directly, or simply where we are trying to address patterns of complaints we receive. As such, we go to some effort to build good working relations with these units.

Our relationship with the staff of the Training Division has been very helpful in developing training sessions for our staff and citizen review committee members. They are receptive when we go to them for general questions about police training as well as more specific questions about whether or not an officer's action was within policy and training parameters. They have also been open to suggestions about things to add or do differently in their training of officers. They regularly invite us to do presentations for new and continuing officers on how the complaint process works and how to avoid getting complaints against themselves in the first place.

We have also worked with the Crisis Intervention Team (CIT) officers (who are trained in crisis intervention techniques and how to work with the mentally disturbed). We have been pushing for some time to expand the scope of the program so that all officers receive this valuable training in de-escalation.

We are currently working with the School Police division to create a new brochure and expand presentations to youth on what their rights are and how to avoid problems with the police.

Other examples of outreach to special units include sharing the lessons learned from complaints about traffic enforcement, property/evidence holding and release, and the handling of family violence cases.

As with other outreach to the police, this kind of relationship building does not employ many of the slick PR tools more commonly associated with outreach. Instead, it depends primarily on the kind of relationship that is built slowly over time, one phone call or meeting at a time. It is not the product of clever methodology but rather depends on genuine goodwill and mutual respect.

Nuts and Bolts: Using the Tools of the Outreach Trade

13

Lauri K. Stewart

A. INTRODUCTION

This chapter does not pretend to be a definitive manual for how to conduct outreach, but it does discuss some of the basic tools of the outreach trade that are most likely to be relevant to oversight agencies of differing sizes and levels of resources.

It is roughly divided into two sections: tools that aid communication from the outreach agency to those outside (outbound) and tools that aid communication from those outside to the oversight and/or law enforcement agency (inbound). The first section has three parts: (1) written outreach tools, (2) nonwritten outreach tools, and (3) a separate discussion of media outreach. We will then look at inbound and miscellaneous outreach efforts. For easier reference, a table is included in appendix H (available on CD Rom supplement) that allows for comparison, at a glance, of the principal strengths and limitations of the different techniques.

B. OUTBOUND OUTREACH: FROM THE AGENCY TO THE PUBLIC

1. Written Communication

Written communication is an attractive medium for outreach because it cannot only carry a lot of information but can also deliver a standardized, consistent message that can potentially reach large numbers of people. There are basically two forms print outreach can take: standardized literature that is available on an as-needed basis over time (e.g., brochures) and special, time-limited products that may be released only once or for a short time (e.g., an advertisement, article, or newsletter). Although it takes time and skill to put together an effective initial product and it generally costs money to print and mail or publish, print outreach is still one of the most efficient and cost-effective forms of outreach.

The caveat is that written forms of outreach are ultimately only as good as their distribution. They need to be accessible, which means not only having them in representative languages but also finding reasonable ways to get the written material to their intended audience. This means really thinking about the audiences you are trying to reach, where they are most likely to go, and what services they are most likely to use. Those are the places to try to distribute your literature. In Portland, we produce brochures in multiple languages and have regular distribution sites that we keep stocked across the city, including the precincts, community centers, public libraries, and agencies that serve those most likely to have contacts with the police. In addition to the sites that we commit to keeping stocked, we supply brochures to any groups that request them.

Outreach in written form also has weaknesses. Standardized messages can be a good thing, but there are times when it is helpful to customize the message so that it will be useful and relevant to the audience in question; one size can not be assumed to fit all. Written messages also cannot take the place of personal contact and face-to-face outreach and networking. It should be kept in mind that written communication is a medium that favors the middle and privileged classes, who are not always the audience you most need to reach. Written communication depends largely on the vocabularies, literacy level, and language skills of the audience, which can be problematic when you are trying to reach those who do not have such skills.

Beyond these general observations about written forms of outreach, the following section describes some of the different forms of written outreach, with observations specific to each.

a. *Agency Literature: Brochures and So Forth*

Brochures and business cards are the most basic level of outreach necessary just to be fully functional as an agency. It is also one of the quickest and easiest forms of outreach. Brochures are relatively inexpensive to produce and can be quite effective if there is a strong distribution network that makes the literature produced readily available to the public. Aside from updating and revising, the only ongoing commitments it requires are paying for new printings and effectively monitoring and improving the distribution system.

One of our first tasks of outreach in Portland was generating brochures explaining what our agency does and how it does it and production of the complaint/commendation forms in multiple languages. We thought we had obeyed the prime directive of brochure writing: KISS— keep it short and simple. As we gathered feedback and suggestions from various quarters, however, we realized this material was a work in progress.

We had started with two separate documents: one informative and one complaint/commendation form, which we eventually merged into a single document. Ruthless editing and reediting carved away more than half the original text, so both brochures would fit mostly on a single legal-size page. We also edited out the "ten-dollar words" in favor of a more informal, everyday vocabulary. We were ultimately able to use a larger font and have more "white space" in the brochure without sacrificing any essential information. Our goal was to make the brochure less overwhelming to those with limited literacy, language skills, or simply limited time and patience.

Our brochure is a four-fold that is divided by a perforated line into two halves: the complaint form and the description of the process. The complaint form portion of our brochure is also a postage-paid mailer.

This enables the brochure to do double duty as a means of outbound communication about the agency but also allowing for input from the public; they can mail in their complaint or comments and keep the contact and process information for reference.

It is, of course, desirable to have brochures and business cards created by design professionals, with an effective, memorable logo and color photos and graphics on good-quality paper. It is easy to equate a primitive, amateurish brochure with an amateurish, insignificant agency. It is possible to go too far the other way, however. An overly slick look may smack of self-promotion and is probably more appropriate for commercial businesses than for oversight agencies.

We have a larger budget than most agencies, yet we err on the side of being overly humble in our brochures. They are black ink on colored paper, and the only graphic or logo is the Portland city seal on the cover. About the only splurging we did was on paper with a "granite" texture thick enough that the text does not bleed through to the reverse side. We use different colors for different brochures, so we can tell at a glance if it is a mediation brochure (pale green) or a complaint form in English (light blue), Spanish (gold), Russian (gray), et cetera.

In deciding on the content, it helps to simply list the essential information the brochure needs to contain, including a list of the agency's primary functions or mandates, as discussed in chapter 11. At a minimum, the brochure needs to describe the agency, what authority it has, and what it can do (and at least by implication, what it cannot do). It should describe how the public can lodge complaints about police, the agency's role within that complaint or oversight process, and how the public can obtain the services of the agency (including contact information).

Once you think you have it right, run it past at least a few representatives of different segments of the community you most want to reach—just be sure they are people you can trust to tell you what they *really* think, rather than what they think you want to hear.

b. *Web Pages*

Even though they are electronic rather than print, I would include Web pages at this point in the discussion, as they are still written communication, and most of the same strengths and weaknesses of print forms apply equally to them. In the case of Web pages, the most obvious limitation is that not everyone has access to them, and they favor the middle and upper classes even more than print formats. Unless one translates them into other languages, Web pages also greatly favor those with the requisite literacy and language skills. For example, this is not the best medium to reach the homeless or the non-English-speaking immigrant/refugee population.

In the last 10 years, however, Web pages have become as basic to doing business for an agency as business cards and brochures. Ever-growing numbers of people use the Internet, and it has the advantage of being accessible from just about anywhere, any time. It can also contain a very large quantity of information, far more than could ever be put in a brochure or even in an annual report. This can be a very important tool for education and transparency, reporting on the work of the agency, the law enforcement agency it oversees, and the lessons learned in the process. A Web site, however, is only as good as what is on it, how many people know about it, and how easy it is to use. A Web site cannot do outreach without some outreach to let people know it is there for them to use.

Web pages can be one of the cheapest, fastest ways to provide agency information because it does not even involve printing costs, but it does require someone who can put it together properly, either a staff member, a volunteer, or (if one can afford it) a contracted professional. As a city agency, we had access to skilled staff in putting together our Web pages. Of course, the downside is that the city has a standard format to which we must conform, which limits our capacity to customize our pages as we might like.

At a bare minimum, an agency's Web pages should contain all the information found in the brochure. But it can provide much more. Our Web site includes an online complaint/commendation form, and about 12 percent of all our complaints come in this way. We also provide a means of sending comments or questions, thereby allowing the Web site to serve double duty, not only for out-bound outreach but for in-bound outreach as well. There are pages on the mediation program and a schedule of upcoming meetings and events. All Independent Police

Review (IPR) policy reviews and reports and the annual reports are available online. Our Web site contains information on the history of our agency, including the ordinance that established the IPR and defined its structure and powers, and all of the protocols that describe how we do our work. We have a FAQs page of frequently asked questions. We are currently developing a newsletter that will also be available online.

c. *Newsletters*

Newsletters are labor intensive for the person responsible for producing them but can be a very effective tool for ongoing education, reporting, and awareness building. They are cost-effective and allow for a significant amount of standardized information but in a format that can be more accessible, community oriented, and widely read than technical or annual reports. As with any other produced information, it depends on the literacy level of its readers, and it cannot be any more effective than its distribution network.

The key to producing a successful newsletter is to include items that are relevant and interesting to the target audiences. Given the inherently interesting nature of oversight work and the public's generally high level of interest in police and crime issues, it should not be difficult to find good topics. Keep a running list of possible topics, things that you find interesting or that you think might be useful or interesting to others. To maintain credibility, it is important not to let it be overly or obviously self-serving.

Newsletter items might include monthly or quarterly statistical reports on current or recent cases or complaint activity; discussion of current or recent projects, reports or policy reviews; recent police actions or issues; selected recent local or national articles on topics of interest (e.g., Taser policies or recent legal decisions on search and seizure); profiles of staff or volunteers; recent accomplishments or activities of the agency; relevant accomplishments of individuals or organizations in the community; and perhaps short columns by various stakeholders or government, police, and/or community partners in oversight.

Oversight is a fascinating field, and there are few opportunities for outsiders to glimpse or really get a flavor of the day-to-day work and issues of an oversight agency or to understand some of the more complex issues and concerns. Newsletters can provide that glimpse.

d. *Agency Reports*

It is difficult for an oversight agency to contribute to greater transparency if it does not report on its oversight work and make these reports available to the public. There are two main kinds of reports: regular reports on the agency's work and reports on special topics, such as policy reviews, formal recommendations, or other research or activities. It is reasonable to expect that these will be adequately detailed to give a good picture of the subject matter and how well the oversight agency and law enforcement agency are performing their respective mandates.

C. REGULAR REPORTS

At a minimum, quarterly or annual reports should discuss the agency's performance on each of the main functions the agency is mandated to perform (or has undertaken to perform). As discussed in chapter 11, determining what needs to go into an annual report is largely a matter of honest evaluation of what the agency can and cannot do, its accomplishments, and its strengths and weaknesses. The more an agency does, the more it has to report.

Portland produces exhaustively detailed and thorough reports on all complaints received, their disposition, all policy reviews, outreach efforts—virtually all our activities. Unfortunately, these reports are often almost as exhausting to read as they are to produce.

Herein lies the negative aspects of technical reports: to be thorough and well done, they are labor intensive. Not all agencies have the resources to produce them. Like other forms of written outreach, they depend on the literacy skills of the audience. Because they are highly technical, statistical, and often overloaded with detail, the level of literacy required is particularly high. This is a self-flattering way of saying that they are deadly dull and few people will ever read them. As such, although they are still important as a full accounting of what we have done and what we have found and an assessment of our own performance as well as that of the Police Bureau, reports of this kind cannot be relied upon as the sole or primary mechanism to provide meaningful levels of transparency—or credibility—for an agency.

One should try to make them as relevant and user friendly as possible, though if they go too far in that direction, they run the risk of becoming too short or too superficial to be thorough. It is also advisable to produce short summaries of larger reports; they are far more likely to actually be read and allow people to get general answers to their most general questions and concerns without having to wade through the whole thing. They are much less unwieldy (and expensive) to mail or hand out to large numbers of people at meetings, presentations, and other occasions out in the community. They can also serve double duty by providing much of the text for press releases when the reports are publicly released.

D. SPECIAL REPORTS

The second category of reports is the special, one-time projects. These might include one-time technical reports (e.g., policy reviews, formal evaluations, and recommendations) or reports of events, activities, case studies, or audits. Some of our reports of this type have included an investigation of whether police were inappropriately taking people to the local drunk tank as a form of retaliation, a review of the Bureau's policies on officer use of profanity, and an evaluation of the handling of tort claims alleging police misconduct. Reports of this type are frequently considerably shorter and more interesting to read than the regular reports because they (we hope) deal with topics of greater interest to the average reader. Even with these it can be a good idea to produce a short, one-page summary for wider distribution than the reports will get.

These one-time publications can also include more informal projects, however, such as information sheets on how to get property released, how to appeal a towing charge, correcting widespread misconceptions about when police are required to Mirandize people, or why they will not take stolen car reports in civil disputes. They could include information on how to prevent escalation in police-citizen encounters, what teens need to know about their rights and how to prevent trouble with police, or how officers can prevent complaints from citizens.

To do oversight work is to encounter patterns of problems, to learn valuable lessons, to invent wheels, and to find solutions to problems. Any time you find yourself wishing more people in the community (or the police department, or city government, etc.) knew about or better understood something, that something is probably a good candidate for such an information sheet, theoretical paper, popular or professional article, or inclusion in a newsletter. These kinds of informational/educational projects can be a powerful outreach tool, of high interest and relevance to their audience, and valuable for creating and maintaining public awareness, interest, and credibility.

E. NONWRITTEN FORMS OF OUTBOUND OUTREACH

1. Informal Discussion and Networking with Individuals

Outreach can involve quite an array of sophisticated outreach methods and tools, some of which depend on technology, some on training, and some that are splashy and impressive. I strongly believe, however, that even though it is humble, low tech, and old as dust, informal discussion and networking with stakeholders is still one of the most vital kinds of outreach an oversight agency does. As mentioned in chapter 12's discussion of outreach to different stakeholders, some groups are a harder sell, more frustrated, or suspicious than others. When trying to do outreach with these groups, it is helpful to keep in mind that at least in the beginning, people are won over one at a time, generally through a personal connection.

There is no substitute for direct conversation with individuals to learn about their perceptions and frustrations and the issues that concern them, and no better way to build alliances, partnerships, and collaborative working relationships. Informal discussion is where the problem-solving process generally begins, where the more sophisticated strategies are worked out along with the enlistment of the assistance and cooperation of those you will need to make those strategies work. For agencies with very limited staff or resources, this may well be the principal tool of outreach, not by a single "outreach person," but by all the staff and/or volunteers the agency has.

Networking will not serve one well unless, first and foremost, it is well done. Such a task should not be given to someone who lacks the interpersonal skills to do it well. Such networking is also time-consuming and difficult to plan because the best connections are often ad hoc, which means the staff needs to be out encountering people. Although the impact of outreach efforts is obviously limited when speaking to individuals one on one rather than in groups, it is sometimes possible to accomplish more lasting good out of one conversation with a key figure of a particular community or agency than in a half-dozen more formal presentations to that same group.

I have listed informal networking as an outbound technique, but obviously this kind of networking is two-way, interactive communication.

2. Speaker's Bureau: Dog and Pony Show

After networking with individuals, this is probably the most basic form of nonwritten outreach for oversight agencies: the time-honored dog and pony show presented at all kinds of community gatherings. This can be as low tech as you and a handful of brochures or as sophisticated as a presentation software product with animation and sound clips.

The advantage to presentations is that once you have prepared one, it is easily repeated, easily customized for different kinds of audiences, and offers considerable flexibility. Although there is some standardization of information, presentations can also be adjusted on the fly, depending on the facilities, time constraints, and audience interests and needs.

Making presentations to community groups is a significant opportunity not only to network, build goodwill, and increase credibility, but it can also be interactive. I always try to use such presentations as an occasion to engage in real dialogue, answer any questions community members have, discuss local concerns, and informally get a sense of their views about police and our agency's work.

The disadvantage to these presentations is that the audiences are generally small and very specialized, so one does not get broad reach from this type of outreach. Also, it takes considerable sustained effort and many individual calls to wrangle invitations to make presentations. In my experience, if you wait for groups to come to you with a request, you will wait a long time.

By the same token, however, this is one of the principal means of doing outreach to very targeted audiences. At some point early in the life stage of an agency, it is important to borrow and/or develop a list or, better yet, a directory of community contacts for all kinds of outreach efforts. The list should be very broad: neighborhood groups; schools and colleges; business associations; ethnic and religious communities; immigrant and refugee communities; sexual minority communities; activists and advocates for various causes, including youth, social justice, the homeless, and the mentally ill; health and social service agencies, including emergency rooms, service providers to domestic violence and sexual assault victims; criminal justice professionals, from the police you oversee to the courts, prosecutors, public defenders, probation and parole and jails; various community service providers; and social groups such as Optimists, Rotary, and so on. Keep adding to the list as you learn of new groups. It has become almost reflexive to offer myself as a speaker any time I am speaking with someone from a group that has meetings.

The effectiveness of this type of outreach depends in part on the content of the presentation and the skill of the presenter; above all, make sure that your message is consistently fair, responsible, and absolutely honest, or you will undermine credibility instead of build it.

It is also important to avoid the boring. In addition to presenting relevant information in an interesting way, it helps to make it clear how it is relevant—not just the "what" but also the "why" and the "so what?" If you begin to notice that at a certain point you are seeing a lot of glazed or wandering eyes, fidgets, yawns, or snores, it is definitely time to consider an overhaul and revision of the presentation or to recruit a presenter who is more animated or engaging. Likewise, if no one has any questions at the end, that is generally a sign that the presentation has failed the interest and relevance tests. A perfunctory presentation is not good enough. If nothing else, get someone who is a good, engaging speaker to edit or rework the presentation to make it more appealing.

3. Public Meetings and Case Hearings or Appeals

Holding meetings in public—preferably regularly scheduled meetings— is one very simple way to provide basic levels of transparency, to educate the public and the media on the agency's work on oversight and law enforcement issues more generally, and to improve community perceptions of credibility.

Obviously, how well public meetings serve those goals depends first and foremost on if the structure of one's oversight agency even permits discussion of cases or findings in public or does its work confidentially behind closed doors. Accomplishing those outreach goals through public meetings depends, second, on how accessible the meetings are, how well attended they are, if they really address issues of interest, and if there is any meaningful role for the public who do attend.

If an agency does not regularly hold public meetings to do their work, it is advisable that they hold at least some regular public meetings to report on their work, to discuss issues of substance, and to allow for input and interaction with the community.

In Portland, almost all of the work of the Citizen Review Committee, including appeals of complaint findings, is conducted in monthly public sessions, held in locations throughout the city. Work not conducted in public must be, at least, reported on in public; public comment is taken after all agenda items of substance and before decisions are made. We are currently discussing ways to allow for an even higher level of public involvement.

4. Educational Presentations, Workshops, Seminars, Conferences

This category of outreach is not used for general public relations purposes so much as for targeted educational efforts; however, the best public relations often happens when that is not the primary goal. This category of techniques is very much like those discussed in the written outreach part of this chapter and is often undertaken as a way to introduce written educational products.

At the most modest level, this might involve being a presenter at a community group's meeting or at a conference on topics related to the oversight agency's work. For example, I have done presentations for mediation and dispute resolution professionals on police-citizen mediation, for youth groups on knowing your rights in dealing with law enforcement, for criminal justice professionals on the roles of emotions and "face" in the criminal justice process, for both citizens and police officers on how to prevent police-citizen conflict, and so on.

Other examples of outreach of this type is doing guest lectures, seminars, or even teaching classes at local high schools or colleges. More ambitious projects, with or without other stakeholder partners, might include putting together your own conferences, seminars, or training programs.

This kind of outreach is time intensive to develop, prepare, and organize, and to do well it requires some talent as a teacher or presenter. One could fairly argue that it is also peripheral to an agency's primary outreach needs, and one must guard against diverting too many resources away from those primary goals. Educational presentations can increase the agency's visibility, reputation, and credibility, however, and they typically have social value in and of themselves and allow the agency to share the lessons learned.

5. Public Inquiries and Expert Panels: "Meet the Press"

These kinds of outreach techniques are part public meeting and part extended press conference. There are different ways to conduct public inquiries, some very formal quasi-judicial processes, some more informal postmortems of actions, with public presentation of evidence to provide a complete portrait of an incident, action, or problem. Although I have attended many such events sponsored by community groups, activist groups, the mayor, the district attorney, and even the Police Bureau itself, we have never had occasion to sponsor one ourselves.

In the expert panel format, various experts or representatives are invited to participate in a panel discussion of a particular problem or issue via questions directed through a moderator.

The purpose of both panels and inquiries is primarily educational, and they usually address topics at the center of some current controversy. The intent is generally to educate the media and the public, to allow for balanced presentation and debate of different perspectives on an issue. If done well, it can help reduce public tensions.

Therein lies the challenge of panels and inquiries; although they can be educational and promote constructive dialogue and healing, they are labor intensive to put together, and public response will depend greatly on the topic. The effectiveness of panels depends on the quality and balance of the panelists and having a skilled, effective moderator. Absent those crucial requirements, such panels may be counterproductive and further inflame an already volatile community.

F. OUTBOUND OUTREACH THROUGH THE MEDIA

Going to the media is generally the first solution suggested when people are trying to come up with the best way to reach the largest number of people in a community. Indeed, when you talk about outreach to "the public" as a whole, you are, for the most part, really talking about outreach via print, television, and radio news media.

When talking about outreach through the media, it is important to have realistic expectations. You cannot count on the media to do your outreach for you because you cannot count on media interest or cooperation. They have their own priorities and concerns that may have nothing to do with yours. Although the media are supposed to cover matters of public interest, they retain the right to judge whether a particular bit of news *is* of public interest or not.

I cannot count the number of times I have heard people propose to "go to the media" to bring attention to a problem or issue, as if one can simply order a front-page story the way one might order a burger and fries. Unless there is some kind of very high profile situation happening, only presidents and other cultural superstars can hold a press conference or put out a press release and expect the media to come running.

So, having dampened unrealistic expectations of the media, how can you use the media for outreach? There are basically four ways to try get the media to do outreach for you. Ordered from most passive to least, they are as follows:

(a) Hope the media will notice you.
(b) Send press releases to invite the media to notice you.
(c) Actively pursue media coverage.
(d) Generate or tap into current controversy or heightened emotions.

1. Wait for the Media to Notice You or Decide to Pay Attention to You

First, you may wait a long time for the media to decide to pay attention to you. Second, be careful what you wish for; you just might get it. If media attention does come your way, there is no guarantee it will be favorable or flattering, even if you are doing a wonderful job. Sooner or later most agencies will have at least one unpleasant experience of being on the wrong end of media coverage.

The reality of media outreach is that the media are constrained by standards of newsworthiness. Bad news is intrinsically more interesting than good news, failures are often more compelling than successes, and conflict is more compelling than accord. For all the popular condemnation of the media as ambulance chasers, this all-too-human tendency seems to be very basic to us all. Ongoing, benign situations are nice but not particularly compelling. They do not trigger sharp interest or concern—or even notice, oftentimes.

Related to this, the media are constrained by limitations on what is timely. Ongoing situations or processes often do not meet the criteria of timeliness and newsworthiness. I once had an editor who used to say that if we could run a story any time, it is probably neither timely nor newsworthy. News stories need to be news: something new, something different, something important or at least interesting, something happening now. You generally need to be able to tack a "today" or "tomorrow" or at least a "yesterday" into the lead to meet the timeliness test or be able to tie it to some current story or issue.

The exception to that general rule is the feature story, which is more flexible than news stories, being more narrative, subjective, human interest, and "soft" stories. For example, our city paper did a feature article on our citizen-police mediation program, built around a dramatic retelling of one case. It should be noted they did not come up with the idea for that story on their own, however. There is more information later in this chapter on the art of pitching stories.

2. Press Releases

The most usual way to try to get media coverage is through the press release, and the first consideration is your media list itself. Because your press releases will not go any farther than the list of media you are using, it is important to develop a good media list that includes not only the larger mainstream print, television, and radio outlets but also the smaller, alternative, specialized-audience, and neighborhood media.

My media list, for example, contains everyone from the Associated Press to local business publications; Asian, Hispanic, and African

American papers; publications for the gay and lesbian community; regional and neighborhood papers and newsletters; and weekly and alternative papers. Unless I am targeting a very limited audience or a particular geographical region, the press releases I send out are e-mailed to the entire list.

In Portland, we were fortunate in being able to inherit the core of our media list from the City of Portland's Office of Neighborhood Involvement, rather than having to create it entirely from scratch. Anyone trying to create a media list would be well advised to try to borrow one from another office or agency that does broad outreach to a similar audience.

Once you have a media list that can reach the populations you want to reach, the main issue is what you send to the media on your list.

Sometimes a press release is issued almost as a formality; for example, because public meeting laws demand public notification. If you do not care what happens to it after you send it or whether it gets published or not, then the only requirement for the press release is that it should contain all the information required for adequate public notification: usually who, what, when, where, and maybe even why.

Producing a press release that might actually get media coverage is harder. Most media outlets are staffed by very busy people who are deluged with press releases, many of which may not strike a reporter or editor as worthy of reading, let alone publishing. To actually get your press releases covered (or even read) it is advisable to keep them as short as you can while still saying everything you need to say. They should be written to answer the editors' (and ultimately the readers') main question: "Why should I be the least bit interested?"

In addition to being succinct and well organized, press releases should have a hook that is at least mildly interesting. The hook is the particular fact, angle, perspective, or detail that the story is built around, the element that can generate enough interest to make a person pay attention to the story in the first place. There is a fine art to recognizing and picking out the bits of a report or event that will be the most interesting or relevant to people or finding a compelling way to present the information you most want people to know, whether they are interested or not.

What this means is that merely providing information in a press release is generally not enough; you must also provide at least some interpretation or elaboration to answer the ever-present question, "So what?" For example, instead of writing, "X agency released their annual report today," write something like "Agency X reports complaints of police rudeness increased in 2005."

One method to identify the best hook is to literally ask and answer questions about the implications of the basic information, chiefly, "Why should people care about this information?" "What problem does it suggest or solve?" "What new questions or concerns does it raise?"

It is customary to start with the hook in the first sentence or paragraph, if not in the title itself. Press releases, like many news stories, are usually written in the so-called inverted pyramid form, with the most important information (i.e., the main point) at the very beginning and the elaboration and less critical details following. The idea is that if the article (or press release) is too long to fit the available space, it will still be complete and make sense even if an editor amputates from the tail up until the piece fits the space (rather than expecting the reporter or editor to spend a lot of time rewriting to make it shorter).

For example, in a press release announcing a public forum, I started with the most critical information up front (e.g., the what, when, and where) and the longer background or explanatory detail in decreasing order of importance (e.g., that we were seeking public input as part of a policy review on officers' use of profanity, followed by some background on the issue). Some outlets completely ignored the press release. Some just posted the first paragraph to their bulletin boards of upcoming public meetings; a couple ran pieces of varying lengths, using more or less of the detail I had provided (or calling for more).

Generally, the goal of a press release is not simply to be published but to generate enough media interest to result in reporters calling for more information and using the press release as the springboard for creating a longer, more informative story.

That said, I do not think it is entirely possible to predict what will generate media interest, even if you are a veteran. I have sent out press releases I thought were interesting that did not generate a single call for more information, and others I thought were pretty dull ended up on the TV news an hour later. Go figure.

3. The Active Pursuit of Media Attention

Beyond passively awaiting decisions by the media as to whether or not to pay attention to you—with or without a press release—there is the strategy of actively pursuing media coverage. This can be done in a variety of ways, including asking for it, demanding it, producing your own, and/or buying the coverage you want.

Some of these may depend on how well you cultivate reasonably good relations with reporters and editors in your area. The cultivation of such relationships is itself an important part of outreach. By cultivating good relations with the media, or at least a few good reporters, you increase the odds that they will seek you out for comment on relevant stories and be receptive when you ask them for anything. You increase the odds that you will be treated fairly in the press, given a chance to respond to critics, and be less likely to receive hostile coverage.

A hostile reporter is more than capable of coloring a story to reflect negatively on you, to choose unflattering photos, quotations, and to make your critics look good. For example, we have one local reporter with an agenda who uses every story he does on our agency as an opportunity to repeat what he knows to be misinformation.

Much more common than overt sabotage by a reporter are ignorance and misunderstanding. The structure and functions of the average oversight agency are rather complicated to describe. More generally, there is also a fairly steep learning curve about civilian oversight of police. It is relatively rare for reporters (or anyone else) to take the time to understand and get it all correct.

The best way to ensure that a reporter gets it right is to be willing to take the time to explain it all. That is, after all, one of the goals of oversight: to get people to know and understand who you are and what you do. This is another reason to cultivate good relationships with the media, so that, over time, most of the regulars who write about police and oversight issues will have a good understanding of the structures, history, and issues, so they can get it right.

Assuming you have a good working relationship with the media, the most direct way to pursue media coverage is to ask for it. You can always approach reporters or editors directly with a story idea to see if they are interested, as long as it is genuinely newsworthy and there is enough meat to it to make it worth a story. It should be well thought out before you try to pitch it, and all the caveats about newsworthiness and timeliness apply here. If you have background information or know of other sources that should be included, it is helpful to have all that information close at hand. There are not many editors or reporters who will turn down a good story that arrives on their desks practically gift wrapped.

Generating media interest in your story is also partly a matter of luck, of how much and what kind of other news your news is competing with. For example, the feature story on our mediation program was originally supposed to run in early summer 2004 but was preempted by a controversial police shooting. To have run the mediation story at that point would have created the impression of strong propolice bias on the part of the paper and insensitivity toward members of the community who were very upset. It would have been generally inappropriate in a manner similar to running a cheerful breakfast cereal ad during a televised special on people dying of famine. Our story ended up being bumped back a few months.

You may also want to target smaller local publications. Rather than relying on reporters and editors to produce the stories you want, you can always try to produce them yourself if you have the staff, skill, and time for it. Smaller papers and newsletters often depend largely or entirely on outside submissions for their content. This can be an important tool in the larger process of outreach to specific community and neighborhood groups. The editors and coordinators of such publications should be on your contact lists, anyway, and generally you can just call them up and offer them your story.

Even larger papers will sometimes accept freelance stories if they are well-written, interesting, not overtly biased, or self-enhancing. If nothing else, there are guest editorials or even letters to the editor.

a. *Television*

Television is a slightly different animal from print media. Although the same caveats about newsworthiness and timeliness still apply, if you want to successfully request attention from mainstream television stations, it helps enormously if there is some interesting visual element to the story. If the story is interesting enough, however, they can usually find ways to add some visual element, such as filming the director in front of the office. I have even seen TV reporters desperate enough to rely on a shot of someone pulling a file out of a filing cabinet or answering a phone.

Another thing to keep in mind about television stories, though, is that although more people watch TV than read newspapers, television stories are extremely brief, to the point of being so superficial they may do more harm than good. I used to write television news stories; our average story was about three fairly short sentences. A full "investigative story" was three to five minutes and maybe 20 sentences. It is very difficult to do any kind of justice to a complex topic with stories that are effectively just photo captions. If it is a very simple idea or piece of information you need to get across, that might be adequate, but I would certainly advise caution if it is something more complex or if it is important to have background understanding. A little information, just like a little knowledge, can be a dangerous thing.

An approach that is even more active is either trying to land a spot as a guest on a local TV talk show or putting together your own program for airing on a local cable station. This kind of format allows a great deal more depth and complexity in the information shared, compared to TV news. With talk shows, though, one is largely at the mercy of the host. If the hosts are fluffy lightweights who ask inane questions or adversarial types who would rather attack than learn, it is difficult to convey the information that needs to be conveyed in the way it needs to be presented.

In many areas, there is also the option of producing one's own program for showing on public service or private cable stations, though this requires skilled production to produce a decent program, and unless you can find volunteers, this can get expensive. With both types of programming, there is the distinct disadvantage that they are likely to be watched by very small numbers of people.

b. *Radio*

Radio talk or interview shows are another alternative, less abbreviated than TV news, though more limited that TV programs. They are often more in need of story ideas than TV. Any given station generally only reaches a narrow audience, however. Although this is a problem if you are trying to reach the entire community, it can be ideal if you are trying to reach a targeted group. If TV is biased toward stories with a strong visual element, however, radio favors those with a strong audio element. They prefer doing interviews with people who are articulate (in a colloquial way), animated, and preferably have a little warmth and humor. The nightmare radio guest is long-winded, very slow speaking, deadly dull, and/or uses overly specialized, technical, or pompous vocabulary.

c. *Videos*

Another tool that is multimedia, but not quite the same as TV or other media, is producing educational videos for the general public, targeted audiences, or the police. This is generally not for self-promotion efforts so much as for problem solving through education—most likely some variation on how to avoid escalating citizen-police contacts or how some process (such as appeals or mediation) works. Videos are more compelling than print and can be very powerful, but there are two main challenges: It is demanding and generally expensive to do videos well, which is required for them to be effective; perhaps more frustrating, it is only effective if it is viewed by the people who need to see it, which means its effectiveness depends largely on its distribution. Distribution can take a lot of time and effort, so much so that it is not unusual for even very well-done videos to sit unused in boxes or on shelves.

d. *Purchasing Media Attention*

Another entire realm of media outreach is buying time or space to get your message out, the most obvious of which is through advertising. This can range from messages on anything from refrigerator magnets to billboards or the sides of buses. It could be print, television, or ads soliciting business ("X Police—How are we doing?" or "Racial profiling—Has it happened to you?"), to an insert in the local paper.

If you have a modest amount of information that needs wide exposure, you might consider producing or commissioning a newspaper insert, a separate section of the newspaper all your own (or in collaboration with various agency partners). These can be very effective for introducing complex information to large numbers of people in the community and to ensure you get the amount, depth, and breadth of coverage an issue requires.

The problem may be trying to find enough different articles and columns on the chosen subject to justify an entire insert, which is typically at least six full newspaper pages. With some topics—use of Tasers, police shootings, racial profiling issues, the history and range of civilian oversight, and so forth—that should not be too difficult. Otherwise, it might be worth making it a collaborative effort with relevant partners.

Generally, advertising is likely to be most useful to an oversight agency that is just starting up, trying to get the word out that they are in business. They can also be useful to solicit community input for a particular, limited purpose, such as a study of disparate treatment or recruiting volunteers. Advertisements can carry only a very limited amount of information—generally just a slogan, statement, or question, maybe a line of detail, and the agency name and contact information. Still, depending on the media, how much, and how long you advertise, this can have about as broad a reach as you are ever likely to get (outside of some big crisis or controversy).

It can also contribute powerfully to perceptions of credibility among certain sections of the community, but one must consider the effects on *all* the stakeholders. For example, if not handled diplomatically and fairly, an advertising campaign that encourages people to make complaints against police could easily be perceived as hostile to police and alienate both officers and those citizens who support them.

The last thing to keep in mind is that advertising costs increase in direct proportion to how much, how broadly, how long, and how impressively you advertise. It can be very expensive.

e. *Information Flyers/Bill Stuffers*

Another way to get word out to a community about your agency, current projects, or problem-solving efforts that is somewhere between other forms of written outreach and advertising is by piggybacking your message with an existing distribution network to those you want to reach. It is possible to get creative in identifying existing, ongoing distribution networks that reach those you want to reach, and you might be able to hitch a ride for your message.

One of the easier and generally cheaper ways to do this is to try to talk a local utility company into allowing you to include a one-page flyer (bill stuffer) with their customer's bills one month. This gives you wide distribution, though it needs to be well done to be effective or even to get read. It can look pretty illogical to recipients, however, a non sequitur that inspires the question, "Why is this in my gas bill?"

More aggressive pursuit of media attention begins to take one into the realm of trying to stage media events or publicity stunts. This class of activities is limited only by the imagination. It could consist of anything from riding naked through the city, sponsoring a benefit concert, bringing in a prominent figure as a speaker or trainer, or staging a demonstration. Although there are creative ways of doing such things that are ethical and appropriate, it is a range of tactics with which I would advise caution. Such tactics should not serve one set of stakeholders yet alienate another. They must pass the test of fairness, objectivity, responsibility, and credibility.

4. Generate or Tap into Current Controversy or Heightened Emotions

If I am inclined to be suspicious of media events and publicity stunts, I would certainly advise against anything that smacks of grandstanding, sensationalism, generating controversy, or exploiting tragedy or outrage as a way to get one's face or words in the press. The most common context for such things is making judgmental public statements on the heels of a scandal or controversial police action, such as a shooting.

In my experience with public controversy, the higher the passion, the fewer the facts. One lesson that is very clear in handling, reviewing, and investigating complaints—and even more starkly in mediating them—is that there are always at least two sides to every story, and the truth is very seldom what it appears at first glance. Simply put, people in the field of civilian oversight should know better than to pass judgment before they have seen all the evidence.

Aside from ethical issues, taking advantage of controversy or outrage is likely to be counterproductive as an outreach strategy. Although such tactics might play well to some audiences, it might strongly alienate others. It could mean sacrificing any pretense of fairness and objectivity and, hence, credibility.

This is not to say that one should maintain a policy of remaining silent during periods of crisis or controversy. Quite the contrary, it may be extremely important to speak up, but it must be done responsibly, from a perspective that is fair and objective and that encourages the same from others. It is possible to express concern, sympathy, and compassion without simultaneously passing judgment on a specific case or controversy.

If you have done your outreach work well with the media—made sure your agency is visible, accessible, credible, and a good source of information or perspective—the odds are that no grandstanding will be required to get the media to come to you in times of crisis and controversy.

G. INBOUND OUTREACH: LISTENING TO AND ENGAGING THE PUBLIC

Not all agencies do inbound outreach, in which the goal is to encourage public input and involvement. Some limit inbound outreach efforts to the preliminary development phase in an agency's life stage or as part of policy reviews or research on specific issues. Agencies with citizen volunteers generally do outreach to recruit volunteers, which is a slightly different form of inbound outreach.

Some of the means of generating public input have already been discussed as part of the outbound outreach discussion. For example, complaint forms and Web pages can be designed to allow for and invite public comments and suggestions. Meetings can be opportunities to listen to people and discuss concerns, not just to talk at them. This section will not repeat those discussions but will limit itself to those forms of inbound outreach that have not yet been discussed elsewhere.

What is ironic is that it takes so much outbound outreach to accomplish inbound outreach goals and reach the people you are trying to involve. And some methods do not come cheap.

1. Advisory Committees, Councils, Task Forces, Panels

One of the easier ways to ensure citizen input is to recruit a bunch of citizens for that purpose. This could be a panel, committee, or task force for a specific project, such as making recommendations on what kind of civilian oversight to establish. It could also be a standing body that meets on a regular basis, such as an advisory committee or council.

Either format can allow for input from a greater variety of perspectives than one is likely to get into one room at one time in any other way, which in turn can allow for increased mutual understanding. Although such an approach excludes the general public from participation or input, in terms of citizen input it is better than nothing. It also has the advantage of being much more manageable than trying to include anyone and everyone.

Such groups can serve to bridge gaps in the community, dispel misinformation, and are more likely to generate media attention than some back-office gathering of officials. These groups generally enhance the credibility of an agency or problem-solving effort, depending on the following factors:

- how credible and representative its members are,
- how credible and clear the process is, and
- whether or not good use is made of the citizen input obtained.

On the negative side, these groups can be time- and labor-intensive to recruit and coordinate and generally only work as well as their members. Also, there is the real possibility that you might end up with the advisory group equivalent of a runaway jury or have a rebellion on your hands that would do more harm than good. It is a delicate balance to put together and maintain a group that is effective, versus merely window dressing or lip service to public involvement, and a group that will devolve into proud but ineffective turf warriors.

2. Public Forums

I was amused recently to see in a guide to public involvement the following succinct advice on public forums: "Avoid if possible. Not a constructive format."[1] For all that public forums are often spoken of as the holi-

---

1. Internatinal Association for Public Participation, Toolbox, Practioner Tools, *at* http://www.iap2.org/associations/4748/files/toolbox.pdf, p. 7 (2000–2004).

est of holy forms of inbound outreach, outreach professionals and officials often groan at the mere thought of them.

It is not a reluctance to engage and listen to the public that inspires this lack of enthusiasm, it is the simple reality that it is so difficult to make them constructive, so they will improve instead of worsen the relationship with the community. Public forums are wonderful stages for the disgruntled to vent, but they are not always the best formats for increasing mutual understanding and respect.

Although forums give people a chance to speak, they do not easily lend themselves to dialogue or even affirmation of people's views. They are often not only polarized and adversarial but also tend to heighten that polarization and antagonism. The audiences are generally self-selected and do not necessarily include all the people one is hoping to hear from. Unless there is some significant controversy currently brewing, it can be difficult to get a decent turnout. Never pick a really sensitive topic for a forum just as a way to get people to come. In general, you want to be careful about opening up cans of worms unless you have some plans on what to do with them after you open them.

In planning forums, it is important to be clear on what kind of input you want to make possible and what you hope to do with it. Unless the whole point of the forum is just to hear people's stories, the "serial griper" model of noninteractive forums should be avoided, in which people wait their turn to walk up to a microphone, speak for however many minutes they are allowed, and get no more response than a "Thank you. Next?" Expect to get some folks who have had one or more bad experiences with police, often years prior, and they will not rest until everyone knows the story of what happened to them.

In Portland, we have a man on a decade-long crusade to get police to stop enforcing laws regarding vehicle registration and driver's licenses because, according to his interpretation of the law, it is unconstitutional. Every city has individuals who blame police for ruining their lives by arresting them, towing their car, getting their concealed weapons permit revoked, or failing to investigate the use of satellite signals in a vast conspiracy to control people's minds.

All of that said, there is still a time and place for public forums. Before making important decisions that will have an impact on the community, one should hear what that community has to say on the subject. A case in point is making decisions about what kind of civilian oversight a city should adopt or what it should include, address, or avoid in order to maintain credibility.

Another type of situation in which public forums or hearings can be very important is to determine the scope of an undocumented problem or to put a human face or story to otherwise cold statistics. A case in point would be a forum to educate public officials on the realities of racial profiling as experienced by people in the community. Recently, Portland had some public forums to listen to the views and experiences of inner-city youth in their dealings with police. These can be powerful experiences.

It is always easier to attack than to improve. The challenge is to try to create an interactive forum that allows for genuine dialogue and constructive problem solving. Consider looking for other, more targeted ways to get what you need accomplished, such as going to the people you want to hear from, instead of trying to get them to come to you, or considering more constructive discussion formats, as the next section discusses briefly.

3. Focused Discussion Formats

There are a number of different formats besides forums for generating public discussion. I recently saw a list that included formats I had never even heard of before. Among the more familiar are dialogue circles, talking circles, roundtable discussions, community facilitations, and group mediations.

The basic idea is that they are all interactive dialogues in which people have time to fully hear and be heard, and they generally involve some involvement by moderators, facilitators, or mediators to try to keep the focus on constructive, problem-solving dialogue rather than critical, adversarial attacks. Generally, these formats all recognize that feelings, not just facts or ideas, are a central part of what needs to be addressed and resolved because it is people's feelings that make these kinds of issues so powerful in the first place. Anything that does not address people's emotional issues is almost guaranteed to leave participants frustrated and dissatisfied, even if you are dealing with tough types who scoff at talk about feelings.

These kinds of dialogue formats are best suited to problem solving, prioritization, or thorough discussion of sensitive or volatile issues. For example, if you are trying to get a neighborhood group to prioritize the policing issues of greatest importance to them, you might use a round-table format, dividing the group into smaller groups led by your citizen volunteers or staff members, to talk over and decide on the top three issues and why those are important or what the possible solutions might be. After a specified time, representatives from each smaller group share with the whole group what they came up with until the group reaches a degree of consensus on what the final number of priorities are.

The advantage to these kinds of formats is that they can foster open and constructive communication and maximize feedback from all participants. (Some more hostile or dominating participants may perceive that as an unfair attempt to silence them or to "divide and conquer." There is some truth to that; it is generally not desirable to allow a few individuals to dominate and hijack the entire discussion.) These formats can build credibility and foster a real sense of community ownership of the issues and the solutions. To make these kinds of formats successful, they need to be focused. The first requirement is to have a clear purpose for gathering people's views and definite questions to answer. People need to understand—preferably before they even make the decision of whether or not to attend—what they are being asked to do.

The second requirement is a good chief moderator, facilitator, or person directing the show. Anyone who has ever seen a poorly conducted meeting of this type will understand how critical it is to find the right person, and it is not a common gift. It can also be rather expensive to engage someone with the necessary interpersonal skills or to train volunteers to do it well. It takes technical skill and experience, great energy, enthusiasm, tact, humor, toughness tempered by genuine warmth, and compassion; someone who can both command and convey genuine respect. Should you find the perfect person, please clone him or her for me.

The chief drawback to this type of outreach—beyond the problem of finding the right person to conduct it—is the time it takes to fully discuss these issues. Some formats—such as dialogue circles or mediations—are not even expected to be concluded in a single session.

It is not just the time for the actual session, though; it takes a great deal of time and work to put such events together, to do the outreach to bring the people to the table in the first place, to conduct the session, and then to put the final product into usable form (e.g., as a report or set of recommendations). It is not unheard of for project managers to spend a year or more of full-time effort on the more ambitious efforts of this type; they are often contractors or temporary employees engaged just for that purpose.

Which brings us to the second drawback: This kind of outreach can be very costly. For very serious, long-term issues like trying to improve race relations, it might be worth it. For more casual purposes—or very limited budgets—one might have to improvise.

4. Methods to Get at Very Specific Input

Sometimes you just want to hear whatever is on people's minds, but sometimes you need to have their minds on very specific issues. For example, you might need to know whether or not they trust you, what their attitude is toward police, whether or not they have ever experienced disparate treatment, or which of several policy issues they think is a priority.

5. Hotlines

One technique for determining the prevalence of a problem is to invite people to call and tell you about it, and you must make it as easy and convenient as possible for them to do so. This is particularly useful when you are dealing with a problem that people are unlikely to report, such as disparate treatment, mistreatment of illegal immigrants, or misconduct witnessed by other police officers or allied professionals or others who fear retribution. Hotlines are an efficient way to gather information and serve to increase an agency's visibility while also conveying accessibility.

If your agency already receives complaints by phone, it would be a simple matter to take those calls along with the regular ones or set the phones up so one can select reports of that kind as a menu option, with the capacity to record them. Otherwise, it is expensive to create and staff a dedicated hotline, particularly if it is a 24-hour line. Even if you record responses or collect them in written form, there is still the labor of monitoring and analyzing them afterward. It is not generally worth the expense and effort unless you are pretty sure you can count on a high volume of calls and/or if it is going to be a clearly time-limited project (e.g., for 60 days after a television report on the topic).

Such a hotline was established in California to collect accounts of racial profiling, but that was a statewide project that ran for months, not the undertaking of a single oversight agency. Also, because such lines are typically anonymous and the cases will not be fully investigated, there is the certainty that you will only be hearing one side of the story and the possibility that side is not entirely accurate. If there is one lesson learned by investigating lots of complaints, it is that there is almost always more than one side to a story, even when everyone involved is well-intentioned and sincere.

Nonetheless, hotlines can be a way to understand the prevalence of a problem that otherwise might never be reported. Certainly a lot of smoke suggests there may be a fire.

6. Employing Research Methodologies in Outreach

Surveys and questionnaires, focus groups, interviews, and telephone surveys are all methods developed by polling experts and academic researchers to get answers to very specific questions. In general, it is researchers and analysts who work with these methodologies more than outreach staff do. Sometimes it is a fine line between outreach and research. If one needs answers to specific questions, these are ways to get them.

If outreach does employ these methods, those using them should understand how to conduct them properly or know when to hire or consult with someone who does. This is not the time or place for a crash course in research methodology, though certainly an agency should engage those with such expertise before trying to produce statistically meaningful research, particularly on highly sensitive topics.

a. *Surveys/Questionnaires*

Sometimes the easiest way to find out what the community, or some segment of it, thinks about an issue is simply to ask them. This can yield credible, statistically significant results, and it can include people not usually heard. Researchers everywhere struggle with the frustration of typically very low return rates (as in 30 percent or less), however. Also, the results can be no better than the quality of the sampling and the quality of the questions: It is as easy to be too leading in questions as it is to be not leading enough.

b. *Focus Groups*

Focus groups are a variation on the theme of focused discussion formats, discussed earlier, though typically much smaller than facilitated public dialogues. Another difference is that focus groups assemble a random sample of a particular population that, it is hoped, will be statistically representative of the population from which they are drawn. The point is not problem solving or building bridges so much as finding out what is a typical way of looking at a particular issue. It allows for an in-depth exchange of information. In sum, it is really more a testing or research method than a format for public input in the usual sense, but it can be a valuable way to find out what people think or believe about an issue or how the community is likely to react to proposed policies, actions, or products.

c. *Telephone Surveys*

Telephone surveys allow for more questions and more depth than written surveys and generally have a higher response rate, though they are also significantly more labor- and dollar-intensive than mailed surveys.

d. *Face-to-Face Interviews*

Interviews allow for more questions and much more depth than written or telephone surveys or, potentially, even focus groups. They are also the most time- and staff-intensive, however, and effective interviewing takes significant skill. It could conceivably be a useful technique for outreach staff if you are working on an article, educational product, or perhaps supplementing general public input with a few very detailed case studies about a particular issue or recommendation. Finding and recruiting subjects can be a challenge.

In general, the most important rule to keep in mind with all of these formal research methodologies is that you will not have statistically reliable results unless your sample of respondents is both large enough and representative enough to allow you to generalize from it. If the sampling is seriously skewed, the conclusions you draw from it all will be equally seriously skewed, and the agency's credibility could—and should—suffer as a result.

The second most important rule is that research is no better than the questions it asks, and the ability to ask the right questions is much more difficult than it seems. Questions must be tightly focused, though not overly limiting or leading. This is generally not a task for amateurs, particularly if you are dealing with topics as visible and volatile as police-citizen conflict. Credibility is critical and depends on research being done right.

That brings us to the last important consideration for any of these methodologies: If you want a good, credible product, you need skilled people to put them together, administer them, and analyze the results. And that is generally both labor- and cost-intensive.

H. CONCLUSION: PULLING IT ALL TOGETHER

I have tried to assemble here all the advice and information I wish I had had access to when I first started doing this work. Parts may go well beyond the needs and resources of some agencies, but I hope every agency will find at least some portion that is relevant and useful. Even in agencies with greater resources, those resources are still limited, and hard choices have to be made about priorities.

Now comes the more difficult work of weaving all the separate pieces together into a customized outreach plan, as each agency ultimately must do for itself. What do you most need to accomplish, and how will you do that?

An agency's plan must be based on the unique challenges of each jurisdiction, based on the agency's resources and structures and a realistic assessment of what the agency can and cannot do. It should recognize that outreach goals and tactics will change as the agency matures and vary depending on the stakeholders one is trying to reach.

Once the goals are clear, the task is to decide how to accomplish them; which tools will serve best and how one can avoid the pitfalls and maximize the benefits of each.

Without outreach, civilian oversight is opaque, silent, and invisible to the public. Although, obviously, it helps if an agency has a formally designated staff person to put the considerable time and energy into effective outreach, it is never only one person's job, but a team effort. Everyone in the agency is part of that team and needs to be very aware of the fact that the agency's credibility and public image do not just depend on their work product. Everyone on that team is shaping the image and credibility of the agency with every phone call they answer, every meeting they attend, every report they write, and every comment they make to stakeholders as well as to the press.

No matter how good a job an agency might do, it cannot accomplish its primary mission—providing greater transparency and accountability of law enforcement agencies and, ultimately, increasing public confidence in law enforcement—without effective outreach.

Appendix A:
Selected Bibliography

LAW REVIEWS AND LAW JOURNALS

Barbara E. Amacost, *Organizational Culture and Police Misconduct,* Geo. Wash. L. Rev. 72, 453 (2004)

Hazel Glenn Beh, *Municipal Liability for Failure to Investigate Citizen Complaints against Police,* Fordham Urb. L.J. 25, 209 (1998)

Merrick Bobb, *Civilian Oversight of the Police in the United States,* St. Louis U. Pub. L. Rev. 22, 151 (2003)

Justina R. Cintrón Perino, *Developments in Citizen Oversight of Law Enforcement,* Urban Law. 36, 387 (2004)

Annette Gordon-Reed, *Watching the Protectors: Independent Oversight of Municipal Law Enforcement,* 40 N.Y.L. Sch. L. Rev. 87 (1995)

Sean Hecker, *Race and Pretextual Traffic Stops: An Expanded Role for Civilian Review Board,* Colum. Hum. Rts. L. Rev. 28, 551 (1997)

Richard Jones, *Processing Civilian Complaints: A Study of the Milwaukee Fire and Police Commission,* Marq. L. Rev. 77, 505 (1994)

Kevin M. Keenan and Samuel Walker, *An Impediment of Police Accountability?: An Analysis of Statutory Law Enforcement Officers' Bills of Rights,* 14 B.U. Pub. Interest Law Journal 185 (2005)

Reenah Kim, *Legitimizing Community Consent to Local Policing: The Need for Democratically Negotiated Community Representation on Civilian Advisory Councils,* 36 Harv. C.R.–C.L. L. Rev. 461 (2001)

Debra Livingston, *The Unfulfilled Promise of Citizen Review,* Ohio St. J. Crim. L. 1, 653 (2004)

Eileen M. Luna, *Law Enforcement Oversight in the American Indian Community,* Geo. Pub. Pol'y Rev. 4, 149 (1999)

Erik Luna, *Transparent Policing,* Iowa L. Rev. 85, 1107 (2000)

Shannon McNulty, *Building Trust in Northern Ireland: The Role of Civilian Review of the Police,* Ind. Int'l & Comp. L. Rev. 12, 219 (2002)

Stephen Rosenbaum, *Keeping an Eye on the I.N.S.: A Case for Civilian Review of Uncivil Conduct,* La Raza L.J. 7, 1 (1994)

Samuel Walker, *The New Paradigm of Police Accountability: The U.S. Justice Department "Pattern or Practice" Suits in Context,* St. Louis U. Pub. L. Rev. 22, 3 (2003)

PERIODICALS AND PUBLICATIONS

Justina R. Cintrón, *The New York Experience: A Comparison of Existing Models of Citizen Oversight of Law Enforcement,* N.Y. St. B.A. Gov't L. & Pol'y J. 5, 11 (fall 2003)

Ralph Crawshaw, *Civilian Oversight of Policing: Governance, Democracy and Human Rights,* Brit. J. Criminology 42, 215 (2002)

Peter Finn, *Getting Along with Citizen Oversight,* FBI L. Enforcement Bull. 69(8), 22 (2000) http://www.fbi.gov/publications/leb/2000/aug00leb.pdf

Robert J. Freeman, *Police Review Boards Meet the Public Right to Know: Balancing Public Trust and Personal Privacy,* N.Y. St. B.A. Gov't L. & Pol'y J. 5, 51 (fall 2003)

Elayne G. Gold and Robert E. Smith, *Police Oversight within New York's Collective Bargaining,* N.Y. St. B.A. Gov't L. & Pol'y J. 5, 46 (fall 2003)

International Association of Chiefs of Police, *Police Accountability and Citizen Review: A Leadership Opportunity for Police Chiefs* (2002) http://www.theiacp.org/documents/pdfs/Publications/police |accountability.pdf

Iris Jones, *Racial Profiling and Traffic Stop Data: Is it Reliable?,* N.Y. St. B.A. Gov't L. & Pol'y J. 5, 41 (fall 2003)

Kim Michelle Lersch, *Police Misconduct and Malpractice: A Critical Analysis of Citizens' Complaints,* Policing 21, 80 (1998)

Kim Michelle Lersch and Tom Mieczkowski, *Who Are the Problem-Prone Officers? An Analysis of Citizen Complaints,* Am. J. Police 15, 23 (1996)

Debra Livingston, *Maximizing the Value of Citizen Review: Lessons from New York City,* N.Y. St. B.A. Gov't L. & Pol'y J. 5, 27 (fall 2003)

Max T. Raterman, *Police Disciplinary Procedures and Civilian Review Boards,* Police Department Disciplinary Bulletin 2–6 (June 2001)

Todd R. Samolis, *Mediating Disputes between Citizens and Police,* N.Y. St. B.A. Gov't L. & Pol'y J. 5, 34 (fall 2003)

Graham Smith, *Rethinking Police Complaints,* Brit. J. Criminology 44, 15 (2004)

Richard J. Terrill, *Alternative Perceptions of Independence in Civilian Oversight,* 17 J. Pol. Sci. & Admin. Volume 17, No. 2, 77 (1990)

Samuel Walker, *Citizen Oversight, 2003: Developments and Prospects,* N.Y. St. B.A. Gov't L. & Pol'y J. 5, 5 (fall 2003)

Samuel Walker, *Civilian Review: Facing the New Reality,* Police Union News 1 (December 1991)

Samuel Walker, *Civilian Review of the Police in Los Angeles: What, Why, and How,* Open Forum 4 (May/June 1991)

Samuel Walker, *Answers to 10 Key Questions About Civilian Review,* Law Enforce. News (March 31, 1992)

Samuel Walker, *Complaints against the Police: A Focus Group Study of Citizen Perceptions, Goals, and Expectations,* Crim. Just. Review 207–226 (1997)

Samuel Walker, *A Primer on Police Complaint Data,* Subject to Debate (March 1998)

Samuel Walker and Carol Archbold, *Mediating Citizen Complaints against the Police: An Exploratory Study,* J. Disp. Res. 231 (2000)

Samuel Walker and Vic Bumphus, *The Effectiveness of Civilian Review: Observations on Recent Trends and New Issues Regarding Civilian Review of the Police,* Am. J. Police 1–26 (1992)

Samuel Walker and Nanette Graham. *Civilian Complaints in Response to Police Misconduct: The Results of a Victimization Survey,* Police Quarterly 65–89 (1998)

Samuel Walker and Betsy Kreisel, *Varieties of Citizen Review: The Implications of Structure, Mission and Policies for Police Accountability,* Am. J. Police 65–88 (1996)

STUDIES AND REPORTS

Americans for Effective Law Enforcement, *Police Civilian Review Boards* (1982)

Merrick Bobb, *Civilian Oversight of the Police in the United States,* Global Meeting on Civilian Oversight of Police, Rio de Janeiro (September 2002) http://www.parc.info/pubs/pdf/Bobbpresentation. pdf

Allyson Collins, *Shielded from Justice: Police Brutality and Accountability in the United States,* Human Rights Watch (1998) http://www. hrw.org/reports98/police/index.htm

Peter Finn, *Citizen Review of Police: Approaches and Implementation,* Unites States Department of Justice (March 2001) http://www.ncjrs. org/pdffiles1/nij/184430.pdf

Joel Miller, with assistance from Cybele Merrick, *Civilian Oversight of Policing: Lessons from the Literature,* Global Meeting on Civilian Oversight of Police (May 5–8, 2002) http://www.vera.org/publication_ pdf/178_338.pdf

Douglas Perez, *Police Review Systems,* MIS Report, NCJRS 24 (August 1992)

Emma Phillips and Jennifer Trone, *Building Public Confidence in Police through Civilian Oversight,* Vera Institute of Justice (September 2002) http://www.parc.info/pubs/pdf/verapaper.pdf

Police Accountability Resource Center, *Review of National Police Oversight Models for the Eugene Police Commission* (February 2005) http://www.parc.info/pubs/pdf/PARC%20Eugene%20Police%20 Commission%20Report.pdf

Christopher Stone and Merrick Bobb, *Civilian Oversight of the Police in Democratic Societies,* Global Meeting on Civilian Oversight of Police (May 5–8, 2002) http://www.vera.org/publication_pdf/179_ 325.pdf

U.S. Commission on Civil Rights, *Revisiting Who Is Guarding the Guardians? A Report on Police Practices and Civil Rights in America* (2000), No. 005-901-00074-0 http://www.usccr.gov/pubs/guard/main.htm

U.S. Department of Justice, *Principles for Promoting Police Integrity: Examples of Promising Police Practices and Policies* (2001) http://www.ncjrs.org/pdffiles1/ojp/186189.pdf

Samuel Walker, *Achieving Police Accountability: New Directions in Citizen Review of Complaints,* Omaha, Neb.: Open Society Institute (1998)

Samuel Walker, *Citizen Review of the Police—1998 Update,* Omaha: University of Nebraska at Omaha (1998)

Samuel Walker, *Citizen Review Resource Manual,* Washington, D.C.: Police Executive Research Forum (1995)

Samuel Walker, Carol Archbold, and Leigh Herbst, *Mediating Citizen Complaints against Police Officers: A Guide for Police and Community Leaders* (2002) http://www.cops.usdoj.gov/mime/open.pdf?Item=452

Samuel Walker and Vic Bumphus, *Civilian Review of the Police: A National Survey,* Omaha: University of Nebraska at Omaha (1991)

Samuel Walker and Eileen Luna, *A Report on the Oversight Mechanisms of the Albuquerque Police Department* (1997) prepared for the Albuquerque, New Mexico, City Council. Available at http://www.cabq.gov/council/abqrpt.html

Samuel Walker and Betsy Wright, *Citizen Review of the Police 1994: A National Survey,* Washington, D.C.: Police Executive Research Forum (1995)

Maya Harris West, *Community-Centered Policing: A Force for Change,* PolicyLink in partnership with the Advancement Project (May 2001) http://www.policylink.org/pdfs/ForceForChange.pdf

BOOKS AND TREATISES

Carol A. Archbold, *Police Accountability, Risk Management, and Legal Advising* LFB Scholarly Publishing, LLC, New York (2004)

Paul Chevigny, *Edge of the Knife: Police Violence in the Americas* The New Press, New York (1995)

Ronald M. Fletcher, *Civilian Oversight of Police Behavior,* in Michael J. Palmiotto, ed., *Police Misconduct: A reader for the 21st century* Prentice Hall, Saddle River, New Jersey (2001)

Andrew J. Goldsmith, *Complaints against the Police: The Trend to External Review* Clarendon Press, Oxford, England; Oxford University Press, New York (1991)

Andrew Goldsmith and Colleen Lewis, eds., *Civilian Oversight of Policing: Governance, Democracy and Human Rights* Hart Publishing Co. New York (2000)

Anne Grant and Tara O'Connor Shelley, eds., *Problem-Oriented Policing* Police Executive Research Forum, Washington, DC (1998)

Douglas W. Perez, *Common Sense about Police Review* Temple University Press, Philadelphia (1994)

Samuel Walker, *New Directions in Citizen Oversight: The Auditor Approach to Handling Citizen Complaints,* in *Problem-Oriented Policing* Police Executive Research Forum, Washington, DC (1998), 161–78

Samuel Walker, *The New World of Police Accountability* Sage Publications, Inc., Thousand Oaks, California (2005)

Samuel Walker, *Police Accountability: The Role of Citizen Oversight* Wadsworth/Thomson Learning, Belmont, California (2001)

Samuel Walker, *Setting the Standards: The Efforts and Impact of Blue Ribbon Commissions on the Police,* in William A. Geller, ed., *Police Leadership in America: Crisis and Opportunity* Praeger Publishers, New York (1985), 354–70

Paul Winters, *Policing the Police* Greenhave Press, San Diego (1995)

Samuel Walker and Eileen Luna, *Institutional Structure vs. Political Will: Albuquerque as a Case Study in the Effectiveness of Citizen Oversight of the Police* in Andrew Goldsmith and Colleen Lewis, eds., *Civilian Oversight of Policing: Governance, Democracy and Human Rights* Hart Publishing, Oxford, England (2000), 83–104

PRACTITIONER MATERIALS

The Citizen-Police Mediation Program of the Independent Police Review Division, Independent Police Review Division, Auditor's Office, Portland, Oregon http://www.portlandonline.com/auditor/index.cfm?c=29387

Mediation, Office of Police Complaints, Washington, D.C. http://www.policecomplaints.dc.gov/occr/cwp/view,a,3,q,603921,occrNav,|31081|.asp

National Association for Civilian Oversight of Law Enforcement, *Investigation, Monitoring and Review of Complaints: A Practitioner's Case Study Guidelines* (Annual Conference, October 5–8, 1999) http://www.nacole.org/investigative%20guidelines2.html

National Association for Civilian Oversight of Law Enforcement, *Recommended Minimum Training for a New Civilian Oversight Board or for New Members to a Board* http://www.nacole.org/training.htm

Sue Quinn, *Varieties of Civilian Oversight: Similarities, Differences, and Expectations,* National Association for Civilian Oversight of Law Enforcement (revised Dec. 2004) http://www.nacole.org/Models CivOversight_1204.pdf

WEB SITES OF INTEREST

Organizations and Associations

Americans for Effective Law Enforcement
http://www.aele.org

Canadian Association of Civilian Oversight of Law Enforcement (CACOLE) http://www.cacole.ca

Commission on Accreditation for Law Enforcement Agencies
http://www.calea.org

National Association of Civilian Oversight of Law Enforcement
http://www.nacole.org

Police Associations

Fraternal Order of Police
http://www.grandlodgefop.org

Hispanic American Police Command Officer's Association
http://www.hapcoa.org

International Association of Chiefs of Police
http://www.theiacp.org

National Association of Police Organizations
http://www.napo.org

National Association of Women Law Enforcement Executives
http://www.nawlee.com

National Black Police Association
http://www.blackpolice.org

National Center for Women and Policing
http://www.womenandpolicing.org

National Latino Peace Officers Association
http://www.nlpoa.org

National Organization of Black Law Enforcement Executives
http://www.noblenatl.org

National Sheriffs' Association
http://www.sheriffs.org

The Police Foundation
http://www.policefoundation.org

Public Interest Groups

American Civil Liberties Union (ACLU)
http://www.aclu.org

Civilrights.org
http://www.civilrights.org

Human Rights Watch
http://www.hrw.org

Macarthur Justice Center
http://macarthur.uchicago.edu

National Association for the Advancement of Colored People (NAACP)
http://www.naacp.org

National Urban League
http://www.nul.org

Government

National Institute of Justice
http://www.ojp.usdoj.gov/nij

Office of Community Oriented Policing (COPS)
http://www.cops.usdoj.gov

Special Litigation, Department of Justice
http://www.usdoj.gov/crt/split

U.S. Department of Justice
http://www.usdoj.gov

Oversight and Police Practices

Management and Assessment of Hi-Risk Police Tactics
http://www.deadlyforce.com

Police Assessment Resource Center (PARC)
http://www.parc.info

Police Center
http://www.policecenter.com

Police Executive Research Forum
http://www.policeforum.org

Police Professionalism Initiative at University of Nebraska
http://www.policeaccountability.org

Police Training.net
   http://www.policetraining.net

Policing.com
   http://www.policing.com

Vera Institute of Justice
   http://www.vera.org

Appendix B:
Listing of Citizen Oversight Agencies in the United States

ARIZONA

Tucson

Office of Independent Police Auditor
100 North Stone, Suite 610
Tucson, AZ 85701
Telephone: (520) 791-4593
Fax: (520) 791-5140
Web site: http://www.ci.tucson.az.us/ia

Citizen Police Advisory Review Board
c/o Tucson City Clerk's Office
P.O. Box 27210
Tucson, AZ 85726-7210
Telephone (messages): (520) 791-4121
Web site: http://www.ci.tucson.az.us/cparb

CALIFORNIA

Berkeley

Police Review Commission
1947 Center Street, Third Floor
Berkeley, CA 94704
Telephone: (510) 981-4950
TDD: (510) 981-6903
Fax: (510) 981-4955
Web site: http://www.ci.berkeley.ca.us/prc

Berkeley Police Review Board
University of California, Berkeley
Office of the Vice Chancellor
200 California Hall, #1500
Berkeley, CA 94720-1500
Telephone: (510) 643-0680/642-3100
Fax: (510) 642-9483
Web site: http://bas.berkeley.edu/Resources/PoliceReview.htm

Claremont

Police Commission
c/o City of Claremont
P.O. Box 880
207 Harvard Avenue
Claremont, CA 91711-0880
Telephone (City Hall): (909) 399-5460
Telephone (Citizen Facilitator): (909) 240-6628
Fax: (909) 399-5492
Web site: http://www.claremontpd.org/community/police_commission/
poco.htm.

Long Beach

Citizen Police Complaint Commission
211 East Ocean Boulevard, Suite 410
Long Beach, CA 90802
Telephone: (562) 570-6891
Fax: (562) 570-7613
Web site: http://www.longbeach.gov/cpcc

Los Angeles

Office of the Inspector General
Los Angeles Police Department
201 North Figueroa Street, Suite 610
Los Angeles, CA 90012

Telephone: (213) 202-5866
Fax: (213) 482-1247
Web site: http://www.lacity.org/oig

Los Angeles County

Department of Ombudsman
510 South Vermont Avenue, Suite 215
Los Angeles, CA 90020
Telephone: (213) 738-2003
Telephone: 800-801-0030 (inquiries)
Fax: (213) 637-8662
Web site: http://ombudsman.lacounty.info

Office of Independent Review
4900 South Eastern Avenue, Suite 204
Commerce, CA 90040
Telephone: (323) 890-5425
Fax: (323) 415-7549
Web site: www.laoir.com

Special Counsel to Board of Supervisors
Merrick Bobb, Police Assessment Resource Center
Biltmore Court
520 South Grand Avenue, Suite 1070
Los Angeles, CA 90071
Telephone: (213) 623-5757
Fax: (213) 623-5959
Web site: http://lacounty.info/bobb.htm and www.parc.info

Novato

Police Advisory and Review Board
75 Rowland Drive
Novato, CA 94945
Telephone: (415) 897-0985
Fax: (415) 892-8126

Oakland

Citizens' Police Review Board
One Frank H. Ogawa Plaza, 11th Floor
Oakland, CA 94612
Telephone: (510) 238-3159
TTY: (510) 238-2007
Fax: (510) 238-7084
Web site: http://www.oaklandnet.com/government/citizens/homepage.
html

Richmond

Police Commission
P.O. Box 4046
330 Twenty-Fifth Street, Room 301
Richmond, CA 94804
Telephone: (510) 307-8007
Fax: (510) 231-3061
Web site: http://www.ci.richmond.ca.us/Public/police_commission.htm

Riverside

Community Police Review Commission
3900 Main Street, 6th Floor
Riverside, CA 92522
Telephone: (951) 826-5509
Fax: (909) 826-2568
Web site: http://www.riversideca.gov/CPRC/

Sacramento

Office of Public Safety Accountability
915 I Street, Fifth Floor
Sacramento, CA 95814
Telephone: (916) 808-5704
Fax: (916) 808-7618
Web site: http://www.cityofsacramento.org/cityman/t_monitor.html

San Diego

Citizens' Review Board on Police Practices
Civic Center Plaza
1200 Third Avenue, Suite 916
San Diego, CA 92101
Telephone: (619) 236-6296
Fax: (619) 236-6423
Web site: http://www.sandiego.gov/citizensreviewboard

San Diego County

Citizens' Law Enforcement Review Board
1168 Union Street, Suite 400
San Diego, CA 92101-3819
Telephone: (619) 515-6029
Fax: (619) 238-6775
Web site: http://www.sdcounty.ca.gov/clerb

San Francisco

Office of Citizen Complaints
480 Second Street, Suite 100
San Francisco, CA 94107
Telephone: (415) 597-7711
TYY: (415) 597-6770
Fax: (415) 597-7733
Web site: http://www.sfgov.org/site/occ

San Jose

Office of the Independent Police Auditor
2 North Second Street, Suite 93
San Jose, CA 95113
Telephone: (408) 794-6226
Fax: (408) 977-1053
Web site: http://www.ci.san-jose.ca.us/ipa

Santa Cruz

Independent Police Auditor
915 Cedar Street
Santa Cruz, CA 95060
Telephone: (831) 420-6295
Fax: (831) 420-5011
Web site: http://www.ci.santa-cruz.ca.us/cm/ipa.html

COLORADO

Denver

Office of the Independent Monitor
Wellington Web Municipal Office Building
201 West Colfax Avenue, Department 1201
Denver, CO 80202
Telephone: (720) 913-3306
Fax: (720) 913-3305
Web site: www.denvergov.org/oim

CONNECTICUT

Hartford

Civilian Police Review Board
c/o Hartford Office of Human Relations
550 Main Street
Hartford, CT 06103
Telephone: (860) 543-8595
Fax: (860) 543-8595
Web site: http://www.hartford.gov/human_relations/

New Haven

Civilian Review Board
New Haven City Hall

165 Church Street, Floor 3R
New Haven, CT 06510
Telephone: (203) 946-7904
Fax: (203) 946-7911

FLORIDA

Fort Lauderdale

Citizens' Police Review Board
c/o Fort Lauderdale City Clerk's Office
City Hall, Seventh Floor
100 North Andrews Avenue
Fort Lauderdale, FL 33301
Telephone: (954) 828-5002
Fax: (954) 828-5017
Web site: http://ci.ftlaud.fl.us/documents/crb/crb_agenda.htm

Key West

Citizen Review Board
417 Eaton Street
Key West, FL 33040
P.O. Box 1946
Key West, FL 33041
Telephone: (305) 293-9835
Fax: (305) 293-9827
Web site: http://www.keywestcity.com/agenda/CRB/crb.asp

Miami

Civilian Investigative Panel
155 South Miami Avenue, PH 1-B
Miami, FL 33130
Telephone: (305) 579-2444
Fax: (305) 579-2436/400-5028
Web site: http://www.ci.miami.fl.us/cip

Miami-Dade County

Independent Review Panel
140 West Flagler Street, Suite 1101
Miami, FL 33130
Telephone: (305) 375-4880
Fax: (305) 375-4879
Web site: http://www.miamidade.gov/irp

Orange County

Citizen Review Board
c/o County Attorney's Office
Administration Building, 3rd Floor
201 South Rosalind Avenue
Orlando, FL 32801
Telephone: (407) 836-7355
Fax: (407) 836-5888
Web site: http://www.orangecountyfl.net/aware/advisory/board_details.
asp?id=66

Orlando

Citizens Police Review Board
c/o City of Orlando—City Clerk's Office
400 South Orange Avenue, 2nd Floor
P.O. Box 4990
Orlando, FL 32802-4990
Telephone: (407) 246-2251
Fax: (407) 246-3613
Web site: http://www.cityoforlando.net/cityclerk/boards/cityboards.htm

Seminole County

Civilian Review Board
100 Bush Boulevard
Sanford, FL 32773
Telephone: (407) 665-6600
Telephone (Professional Standards Division): (407) 665-6611
Web site: http://www.seminolesheriff.org/advisories/civ_review.php

St. Petersburg

Civilian Police Review Committee
P.O. Box 2842
St. Petersburg, FL 33731-2842
City Hall, First Floor
175 Fifth Street, North
St. Petersburg, FL 33701
Telephone: (727) 893-7229
TDD/TTY: (727) 892-5259
Fax: (727) 551-3379
Web site: http://www.stpete.org/cprc.htm

Stuart

Independent Review Board
c/o City of Stuart—City Clerk's Office
121 S.W. Flagler Avenue
Stuart, FL 34994
Telephone: (772) 288-5306
Telephone (City Manager): (772) 288-5312
Telephone (City Attorney): (772) 288-5386
Fax: (772) 288-5305
Web site: http://cityofstuart.com/clerk/boards.html#STUART%20
INDEPENDENT%20REVIEW%20BOARD

HAWAII

Hawaii County

Police Commission
25 Aupuni Street, Room 200
Hilo, HI 96720
Telephone: (808) 961-8412
Fax: (808) 961-8563
Web site: http://www.hawaii-county.com/police_commission/police_
commission.htm

Honolulu

Police Commission
1061 Richards Street, Suite 170
Honolulu, HI 96813
Telephone: (808) 547-7580
Web site: http://www.honolulupd.org/main/hpc.htm

Kauai

Police Commission
c/o Office of the Mayor
4444 Rice Street, Suite 235
Lihue, HI 96766
Telephone: (808) 241-6300
Fax: (808) 241-6877
Web site: http://www.kauai.gov/Default.aspx?tabid=272

Maui County

Police Commission
55 Mahalani Street
Wailuku, HI 96793
Telephone: (808) 244-6440
Web site: http://www.co.maui.hi.us/boards/bDetail.php?BoardID=28

IDAHO

Boise

Office of the Community Ombudsman
150 North Capitol Boulevard
Boise City Hall, 3rd Floor
P.O. Box 500
Boise, ID 83701-0500
Telephone: (208) 395-7859
TTY: 1 800 377 3529
Fax: (208) 395-7878
Web site: www.boiseombudsman.org

ILLINOIS

Chicago

Police Board
30 North LaSalle Street, Suite 1220
Chicago, IL 60602
Telephone: (312) 742-4194
Fax: (312)742-4193
Web site: http://egov.cityofchicago.org/city/webportal/portalEntity
HomeAction.do?BV_SessionID=@@@@0279702812.1129217947@@
@@&BV_EngineID=ccccaddfmfdjgefcefecelldffhdfgm.0&entityName
=Chicago+Police+Board&entityNameEnumValue=156

INDIANA

Indianapolis

Citizen Police Complaint Board and Citizen Police Complaint Office
148 East Market Street, Suite 508
Indianapolis, IN 46204
Telephone: (317) 327-3440
Fax: (317) 327-4380
Web site: http://www.indygov.org/eGov/City/DPS/CPCO/home.htm

IOWA

Iowa City

Police Citizens' Review Board
410 East Washington Street
Iowa City, IA 52240-1826
Telephone: (319) 356-5041
Web site: http://www.icgov.org/pcrb.htm

KENTUCKY

Louisville

Metro Human Relations Commission
410 West Chestnut Street, Suite 300A

Louisville, KY 40202
Telephone (Citizen's Advocate): (502) 574-4357
Telephone: (502) 574-3631
Fax: (502) 574-3190

MAINE

Portland

Police Citizen Review Subcommittee
Portland City Hall
389 Congress Street
Portland, ME 04101
Telephone: (207) 874-8480
Web site: http://www.ci.portland.me.us/police.htm

MARYLAND

Baltimore

Civilian Review Board
Equitable Building
10 North Calvert Street, Suite 915
Baltimore, MD 21202
Telephone: (443) 984-2654
Fax: (410) 244-0176
Web site: www.baltimorecity.gov/government/crb/

Prince George's County

Citizen Complaint Oversight Panel
Largo Government Center
9201 Basil Court, Suite 466
Largo, MD 20774
Telephone: (301) 883-5042
TDD: (301) 952-5167
Fax: (301) 883-2655
Web site: http://www.goprincegeorgescounty.com/Government/boards
commissions/CCOP/index.asp

MASSACHUSETTS

Cambridge

Police Review and Advisory Board
51 Inman Street, 2nd Floor
Cambridge, MA 02139
Telephone: (617) 349-4396
TDD: (617) 349-6112
Fax: (617) 349-4766
Web site: http://www.ci.cambridge.ma.us/~PRAB/

MICHIGAN

Detroit

Office of the Chief Investigator
2111 Woodward Avenue, 8th Floor
Detroit, MI 48201
Telephone: (313) 596-2499
Fax: (313) 596-2482
Web site: http://www.ci.detroit.mi.us/police_commissioners/office_
chief_investigator.htm

Flint

Ombudsman Office
Flint Municipal Center North Building
20 East Fifth Street, Second Floor
Flint, MI 48502
Telephone: (810) 766-7335
Fax: (810) 766-7262
Web site: http://www.ci.flint.mi.us/ombuds-old/ombuds.html

Grand Rapids

Civilian Appeal Board
c/o City of Grand Rapids
City Hall
300 Monroe Avenue, Northwest

Grand Rapids, MI 49503
Telephone: (616) 456-4023
Web site: http://www.ci.grand-rapids.mi.us/index.pl?page_id=540&
board=Grand%20Rapids%20Police%20Civilian%20Appeal%20Board

MINNESOTA

Minneapolis

Civilian Police Review Authority
400 South Fourth Street, Room 1004
Minneapolis, MN 55415-1424
Telephone: (612) 673-5500
Fax: (612) 673-5510
Web site: http://www.ci.minneapolis.mn.us/cra/

St. Paul

Police-Civilian Internal Affairs Review Commission
100 East Eleventh Street
St. Paul, MN 55101
Telephone: (651) 292-3583
Web site: http://www.stpaul.gov/depts/police/iau_pciarc.html

MISSOURI

Kansas City

Office of Community Complaints
Century Towers
635 Woodland Avenue, Suite 2102
Kansas City, MO 64106
Telephone: (816) 889-6640
Fax: (816) 889-6649
Web site: http://www.kcpd.org/kcpd2004/OCC.htm

NEBRASKA

Lincoln

Citizen Police Advisory Board
555 South Tenth Street, Room 208
Lincoln, NE 68508
Telephone: (402) 441-7511
Fax: (402) 441-7120
Web site: http://www.lincoln.ne.gov/city/mayor/boards/ab_other.
htm#ot_cpa

Omaha

Public Safety Auditor
1905 Harney Street, Suite 530
Omaha, NE 68102
Telephone: (402) 546-1704
Fax: (402) 996-8361
Web site: http://www.ci.omaha.ne.us/departments/public_safety_
auditor/default.htm

NEVADA

Las Vegas

Citizen Review Board
310 South Third Street, Suite 319
Las Vegas, NV 89155
Telephone: (702) 455-6322
Fax: (702) 382-7426
Web site: www.citizenreviewboard.com

NEW JERSEY

Teaneck

Civilian Complaint Review Board
c/o Teaneck Municipal Clerk's Office
Municipal Building

818 Teaneck Road
Teaneck, NJ 07666
Telephone: (201) 837-4811
Fax: (201) 837-1222
Web site: www.teanecknjgov.org

NEW MEXICO

Albuquerque

Independent Review Office of the Police Oversight Commission
P.O. Box 1293
Albuquerque, NM 87103
Plaza del Sol Building
600 Second Street, Northwest
Eighth Floor, Room 813
Albuquerque, NM 87103
Telephone: (505) 924-3770
Fax: (505) 924-3775
Web site: http://www.cabq.gov/iro/

NEW YORK

Albany

Citizens' Police Review Board
80 New Scotland Avenue
Albany, NY 12208
Telephone: (518) 445-2329
Fax: (518) 445-2303
Web site: http://www2.als.edu/glc/cprb

New York City

Civilian Complaint Review Board
40 Rector Street, 2nd Floor
New York, NY 10006
Telephone: (212) 442-8833
Fax: (212) 442-8800
Web site: http://www.ci.nyc.ny.us/html/ccrb/home.html

Village of Ossining

Civilian Police Complaint Review Board
c/o Ossining Village
Clerk's Office
16 Croton Avenue
Ossining, NY 10562
Telephone: (914) 941-4099
Fax: (914) 941-1580
Web site: http://www.villageofossining.org/cit-e-Access/webpage.
cfm?TID=24&TPID=3527

Rochester

Civilian Review Board
Center for Dispute Settlement
300 State Street, Suite 301
Rochester, NY 14614
Telephone: (585) 546-5110
Fax: (585) 546-4391
Web site: http://www.cdsadr.org

Syracuse

Citizen Review Board
201 East Washington Street
City Hall Commons, Room 705
Syracuse, NY 13202
Telephone: (315) 448-8750
Fax: (315) 448-8768

NORTH CAROLINA

Charlotte

Citizens Review Board
c/o Office of the City Clerk
600 East Fourth Street, 7th Floor
Charlotte, NC 28202

Telephone: (704) 336-7493
Fax: (704) 336-7588
Web site: www.charmeck.nc.us/Departments/City+Clerk?Boards+and
+Commissions/Boards.htm

Winston-Salem

Citizen Police Review Board
c/o City Winston-Salem Secretary's Office
City Hall, Suite 140
101 North Main Street
Winston-Salem, NC 27102
Telephone: (336) 727-2224
Fax: (336) 727-2880
Web site: http://www.cityofws.org/Departments/City_Secretary/Staff/
staff.html

OHIO

Cincinnati

Citizens Complaint Authority
805 Central Avenue, Suite 610
Cincinnati, OH 45202
Telephone: (513) 352-1600
Fax: (513) 352-3158
Web site: http://www.cincinnati-oh.gov/cca/pages/-5509-

Cleveland

Police Review Board
c/o Cleveland Department of Public Safety
Public Safety Administration
601 Lakeside Avenue, Room 230
Cleveland, OH 44114
Telephone: (216) 664-3736
Fax: (216) 664-3734
Web site: http://city.cleveland.oh.us/government/departments/
pubsafety/diroff/adminind.html

Dayton

Citizen's Appeal Board
c/o City of Dayton
101 West Third Street
Dayton, OH 45402
Telephone: (937) 333-5200
Fax: (937) 333-4293

OREGON

Eugene

Police Commission
777 Pearl Street, Room 106
Eugene, OR 97401
Telephone: (541) 682-5852
Fax: (541) 682-8395
Web site: http://www.eugene-or.gov/portal/server.pt?space=
CommunityPage&cached=true&parentname=CommunityPage&
parentid=0&in_hi_userid=2&control=SetCommunity&CommunityID
=339&PageID=0

Portland

Independent Police Review Division
1221 S.W. 4th Avenue, Room 320
Portland, OR 97204
Telephone: (503) 823-0146
Fax: (503) 823-3530
Web site: http://www.portlandonline.com/auditor/index.cfm?c=26646&

Salem

Community Police Review Board
c/o Salem City Manager's Office
555 Liberty Street Southeast, Room 220
Salem, OR 97301
Telephone: (503) 588-6255

Telephone (Staff Liaison): 588-6219
Fax: (503) 588-6354
Web site: http://www.cityofsalem.net/~citygov/bds_comms/bclist.htm#cprb

PENNSYLVANIA

Philadelphia

Integrity and Accountability Office
1401 J.F.K. Boulevard, Tenth Floor
Municipal Services Building, Room 1002
Philadelphia, PA 19102
Telephone: (215) 686-4594
Fax: (215) 686-4426

Police Advisory Commission
34 South 11th Street, 6th Floor
Philadelphia, PA 19105
Telephone: (215) 686-3991
Web site: http://www.phila.gov/pac

Pittsburgh

Citizen Police Review Board
816 Fifth Avenue, Suite 400
Pittsburgh, PA 15219
Telephone: (412) 765-8023
Fax: (412) 765-8059
Web site: http://www.city.pittsburgh.pa.us/cprb

RHODE ISLAND

Providence

External Review Authority
550 Broad Street
Providence, RI 02907

Telephone: (401) 228-6989
Fax: (401) 228-6998
Web site: http://www.blue-orange.org/pera/index.php

TENNESSEE

Knoxville

Police Advisory and Review Committee
City County Building
400 Main Street, Suite 537
Knoxville, TN 37902
Telephone: (865) 215-3869
Fax: (865) 215-2211
Web site: www.ci.knoxville.tn.us/boards/parc

Memphis

Civilian Law Enforcement Review Board
125 North Main Street, Suite 200
Memphis, TN 38103-2017
Telephone: (901) 576-6840
Fax: (901) 576-6259
Web site: www.cityofmemphis.org/framework.aspx?page = 85

TEXAS

Austin

Office of the Police Monitor
P.O. Box 1088
Austin, TX 78767
1106 Clayton Lane, Suite 100E
Austin, TX 78723
Telephone: (512) 974-9090
Fax: (512) 974-6306
Web site: http://www.ci.austin.tx.us/opm

Dallas

Citizens Police Review Board
City Manager's Office
Dallas City Hall
1500 Marilla Street, Room 4CN
Dallas, TX 75201
Telephone: (214) 670-3246
Fax: (214) 670-4965
Web site: http://www.dallascityhall.com/dallas/eng/html/citizens_police
_review_board_a.html

Houston

Citizens' Review Committee
1200 Travis, Suite 2001
Houston, TX 77002-6006
Telephone: (713) 308-8939
Web site: http://www.houstontx.gov/police/iad.htm

UTAH

Salt Lake

Police Civilian Review Board
451 South State Street, Room 512
Salt Lake City, UT 84111
Telephone: (801) 535-7230
Web site: http://www.ci.slc.ut.us/civilianreview/

WASHINGTON

King County

Office of Citizen Complaints—Ombudsman
400 Yesler Way, Room 240
Seattle, WA 98104
Telephone: (206) 296-3452
Fax: (206) 296-0948
Web site: www.metrokc.gov/ombuds

Seattle

Office of Professional Accountability
Police Headquarters
610 Fifth Avenue
P.O. Box 34986
Seattle, WA 98124-4986
Telephone: (206) 615-1566
Telephone (Internal Investigation Section): (206) 684-8797
Fax: (206) 233-5139
Web site: www.ci.seattle.wa.us/police/opa

Office of Professional Accountability Review Board
c/o City of Seattle
P.O. Box 34025
Seattle, WA 98124-4025
City Hall
600 Fourth Avenue, Floor 2
P.O. Box 34025
Seattle, WA 98124
Telephone: (206) 684-8888
Fax: (206) 684-8587
Web site: www.cityofseattle.net/council/oparb

WASHINGTON, D.C.

Office of Police Complaints
1400 I Street, North West, Suite 700
Washington, DC 20005
Telephone: (202) 727-3838
Fax: (202) 727-7638
Web site: http://www.policecomplaints.dc.gov

Office of the Independent Monitor
1001 Pennsylvania Avenue, N.W., Suite 800
Washington, DC 20004
Telephone: (202) 639-7472
Web site: www.policemonitor.org

WISCONSIN

Milwaukee

Fire and Police Commission
City Hall
200 East Wells Street, Room 706
Milwaukee, WI 53202
Telephone: (414) 286-5072
Fax: (414) 286-5059
Web site: http://www.city.milwaukee.gov/display/router.asp?docid=312

Table of Cases

Anderson v. Creighton, 483 U.S. 635, 639 (1987), 108

Berkeley Police Association v. City of Berkeley, 85

Bogan v. Scott-Harris, 523 U.S. 44, 49 (1998), 105

Citizen Police Review Board v. Murphy, 88

City of Canton v. Harris, 489 U.S. 378 (1989), 99

City of Los Angeles v. Heller, 475 U.S. 796 (1986), 100

City of Newport v. Fact Concerts, 453 U.S. 247 (1981), 103

Davis v. Sherer, 468 U.S. 183 at 191, 195 (1984), 108, 110

Fraternal Order of Police, Lodge No. 5 v. Pennsylvania Labor Relations Board, 83

Hafer v. Melo, 502 U.S. 21 (1992), 101

Harlow v. Fitzgerald, 457 U.S. 800 (1982), 107, 108, 111, 113

Jurcisin v. Cuyahoga County Board of Elections, 86

Leatherman v. Tarrant County, 113 S. Ct 1160 (1993), 100

Malley v. Briggs, 475 U.S. 335, at 44-345 (1986), 108

Mitchell v. Forsyth, 472 U.S. 511 (1985), 110–12

Mitchell v. Fortune, 472 U.S. at 511 n.12 (1985), 108

Monell v. Dept. of Social Services, 436 U.S. 658 (1978), 98–99

Monroe v. Pape, 365 U.S. 167 (1961), 98

Scheuer v. Rhodes, 416 U.S. 232, at 247–248 (1974), 112

Wood v. Strickland, 420 U.S. 308, 321 (1975), 106, 112

Index

ACLU (American Civil Liberties Union), 28, 30, 158
Administrative Procedure Act, 74
Albany Citizens' Police Review Board, 249
Albuquerque
    Independent Counsel, 7
    Police Oversight Commission, 26, 249
    Public Safety Advisory Board, 7
American Bar Association, 143
American Civil Liberties Union. *See* ACLU
appointment process, for oversight agencies, 25–29
Arizona
    Tucson Citizen Advisory Review Board, 235
    Tucson Office of Independent Police Auditor, 235
Armacost, Barbara, 19
Austin Office of Police Monitor, 254

Baca, Sheriff Lee, 5, 119n
backlogs
    for citizen oversight groups, 68
    in complaint investigations, 41
    funding for, 65
Baltimore Civilian Review Board, 26, 30, 245
bargaining. *See* collective bargaining; decisional bargaining; effects/impacts bargaining
Berkeley, information-gathering ordinance in, 72
Berkeley Police Review Board, 236
Berkeley Police Review Commission, 4, 235

Best Practices in Police Accountability, 144
bias, in law enforcement, 173
Bobb, Merrick, 5, 15
Boise Community Ombudsman, 14, 17, 243
Brechner Center, 76
burden of proof, in local government immunity, 113

California
    Berkeley Police Review Board, 236
    Berkeley Police Review Commission, 4, 235
    Claremont Police Advisory Commission, 236
    Long Beach Citizen Police Complaint Commission, 236
    Los Angeles County Department of Ombudsman, 237
    Los Angeles County Office of Independent Review, 237
    Los Angeles County Special Counsel on Kolts Commission, 237
    Los Angeles Office of the Inspector General, 236
    Novato Police Advisory and Review Board, 237
    Oakland Citizen's Review Board, 237
    Orange County Citizen Review Board, 241
    Richmond Police Commission, 238
    Riverside Community Review Commission, 237
    Sacramento Office of Public Safety Accountability, 238

San Diego Citizens Review Board
on Police Practices, 238
San Diego County Citizens' Law
Enforcement Review Board,
239
San Francisco Office of Citizen
Complaints, 239
San Jose Office of Independent
Police Auditor, 239
Santa Cruz Independent Police
Auditor, 239
Cambridge Police Review and Advisory
Board (PRAB), 7, 40, 245
caseloads, for citizen oversight
groups, 64–65
Charlotte Citizens' Review Board, 250
Chevigny, Paul, 182
Chicago Police Board, 244
Chief Investigator Office, Detroit,
Michigan, 246
Christopher Commission 1991, 12, 14
Cincinnati
Citizens Complaint Authority, 26,
29, 43–44, 251
Collaborative Agreement, 43
U.S. Department of Justice and, 43
citizen authority
in Detroit Police Board, 23n
in Los Angeles Police Commission,
23n
Citizen Complaint Commission, Long
Beach, California, 236
Citizen Complaint Oversight Panel,
Prince George's County, Maryland,
245
Citizen Complaint Review Board
(CCRB), Washington, D.C., 3, 7, 26,
41
citizen complaints
categories of, 128, 136
confidentiality of, 181
as data sources, 128
due process in, 130
effectiveness of, 17–10
evaluation criteria for, 6
experiences of complainants in,
131–32

experiences of police officers in, 132
failings of, 12–13
fair investigation of, 17
initial investigation of, 36
investigation eligibility of, 140–42
investigation process in, 128, 132
law enforcement internal investigation of, 130
mediation eligibility of, 136–37, 138
mediation legal issues of, 142–44
mediation of, 6, 128, 181
mediation v. investigation for, 133–
36
oversight umbrella for, 130
police agency attention to, 127
by police departments, 14
police union involvement in, 132
prescreening of, 185–86
prevention of, 196
problems in, 15
process evaluation of, 17–18
process requirements for, 133
public expectation for, 171
staffing for, 6
supervisor/manager role in, 132–33
timely action in, 41
tracking of, 174
citizen involvement, in complaints
process, 2
citizen oversight
federal consent decree for, 157
law enforcement call for, 157
in Portland, Oregon, 156–59
citizen oversight experts, for law
enforcement agency monitoring, 57
citizen oversight groups. See also citizen
review boards; oversight agencies;
police auditor
from 1920s through late 1940s, 2–3
1970s revival of, 4
access to police records by, 77
advocates of, 7
alternative models of, 17
authority of, 23
backlogs for, 41, 65, 68
caseloads, 64–65, 68
challenges to, 21–23

civil rights movement impact on, 3
collective bargaining challenge to, 79–80, 88–90
communication in, 145
community perceptions of, 24
compensation of, 61–62
competing interests impact on, 48, 51
consolidation and development in, 5–6
credibility of, 21, 24, 66, 68, 135, 148, 164
decisional bargaining in, 80
definition of, 2
effectiveness of, 19
enabling laws for, 72
expectations for, 34, 159, 174
formative phase of, 156–57
freedom of information laws impact on, 72–77
funding of, 6–7, 21, 40, 59–60, 62–65
government mandate for, 60
as governmental policy-making body, 71
growth of, 1, 4–5
hearings before, 37
history of, 2–10
impartiality of, 23, 51
independence of, 42, 63
information technology for, 68
internal/external training for, 56–57
International Association of Chiefs of Police opposition to, 9
investigative skills of, 57–58
investigators for, 63
judgments by, 211–12
labor agreements and, 88–90
labor issues implicated by, 81
of large law enforcement agencies, 64–65
law enforcement agency knowledge of, 67
with law enforcement internal investigation, 61
law enforcement opposition to, 50–51
law enforcement orientation of, 52
law enforcement process in, 52
legality of, 85–87
legitimacy struggle for, 4–5, 9–10, 18
limits to, 173
major goals of, 17
mandates for, 152, 154, 166
member qualifications in, 25, 29–30, 67, 148
operational expenses for, 65
opponents to, 9, 50–51, 79
outreach by, 147
outside United States, 1–2, 9
performance measures in, 20
police activity review by, 42
police commissions impact on, 15
police contract issues impact on, 85–87
police cooperation with, 71, 73
police department relations with, 77
police discipline power by, 23
police unions and, 7–9, 32–33, 50–51, 62, 80–82, 85–87, 132, 183–84
political process in, 7
powers of, 35
public acceptance of, 22
public forum of, 24
public outreach by, 23
public recommendations of, 66
reporting requirements for, 68–69
research on, 20
setbacks to, 6–7
of sheriff's departments, 1
sources of change in, 7–9
staffing for, 6, 59–61, 63, 66–68
stakeholders for, 158
success factors for, 22–23
sustain rate for, 18
time commitment of, 61–62
training for, 47–48, 51–52, 58, 66
types of, 22
citizen oversight groups outreach. *See* outreach
citizen oversight movement, maturity of, 5, 20

citizen oversight outreach. *See* outreach
citizen police academies
    focus of, 54–55
    time constraint impact on, 54–55
    usefulness of, 53–54
Citizen Police Advisory Board, Lincoln,
    Nebraska, 247
Citizen Police Complaint Board,
    Indianapolis, Indiana, 244
Citizen Police Review Board
    Pittsburgh, Pennsylvania, 253
    Winston-Salem, North Carolina,
      250
citizen review. *See also* citizen oversight
    groups; citizen review boards
    National Institute of Justice study
      of, 35
    of police department internal
      process, 38
    policy issue recommendation
      through, 39
citizen review boards. *See also* citizen
    oversight groups
    advocates of, 13
    appointment methods for, 25–27
    Baltimore, Maryland, 245
    Charlotte, North Carolina, 250
    civil rights demand for, 3, 12
    composition of, 12
    diversity on, 31
    as executive agency, 25
    Fort Lauderdale, Florida, 240
    without independent power, 13, 13n
    Key West, Florida, 240
    Las Vegas, Nevada, 248
    mayor's selection of, 25
    New Haven, Connecticut, 240
    Oakland, California, 5, 237
    Orange County, California, 241
    oversight agencies and, 11
    police auditors v., 15–16
    Portland, Oregon, 200
    Rochester, New York, 250
    Seminole County, Florida, 242
    St. Louis, Missouri, 27n
    Syracuse, New York, 91, 250
    training for, 37

Citizens' Appeal Board, Dayton, Ohio,
    251
Citizens' Complaint Authority, Cincin-
    nati, Ohio, 251
Citizens Complaints, King County,
    Washington, 255
Citizens' Law Enforcement Review
    Board, San Diego County, Califor-
    nia, 239
Citizens Police Review Board
    Albany, New York, 249
    Dallas, Texas, 254
    Orlando, Florida, 241
    of Santa Cruz, 6–7
Citizens Review Board on Police
    Practices, San Diego, California, 238
Citizens' Review Committee, Houston,
    Texas, 254
citizens rights, constitutional violation
    of, 104
civil damages, qualified immunity for,
    106
civil litigation. *See* litigation
Civil Litigation Unit - LASD, 115–17,
    125
    claim review by, 122
    investigator caseload of, 120–21
civil rights activists, citizen review board
    demand of, 12
civil rights movement, 3
Civilian Appeal Board, Grand Rapids,
    Michigan, 246
Civilian Complaint Review Board,
    Teaneck, New Jersey, 248
Civilian Investigative Board, Miami,
    Florida, 241
Civilian Law Enforcement Review
    Board, Memphis, Tennessee, 253
civilian oversight, criminal trial model
    of, 13
Civilian Police Complaint Review
    Board, New York City, New York,
    249
Civilian Police Review Committee, St.
    Petersburg, Florida, 242
Civilian Review Authority, Minneapolis,
    Minnesota, 247

Claims and Liabilities Intervention
Program - LASD, 115, 123
Claremont Police Advisory Commission,
236
Cleveland Police Review Board, 86, 251
collective bargaining. *See also* decisional
bargaining; effects/impacts bargaining
  citizen oversight groups challenge
    of, 79–80
  citizen oversight groups conflict
    with, 85–87
  defined, 80–81
  legal, policy issues of, 95
  mandatory subjects of, 82–83
  in Rochester, New York, 92–94
  in Syracuse, New York, 92
  union representation in, 85
Colorado, Denver Office of Independent
Monitor, 249
Committee on Constitutional Rights, of
Los Angeles Bar Association, 3
Community. *See also* public attitudes
community
  activists, 33
  advocates, 32
  outreach, 150, 151, 160–61, 170,
    172, 175–76, 198
  police relations and, 1, 24, 44, 146,
    166
  policing programs, 2
Community Complaints Office, Kansas
City, Missouri, 247
Community Dispute Resolution Center,
Washington, D.C., 139
Community Ombudsman Office, Boise,
Idaho, 243
Community Police Review Board,
Salem, Oregon, 252
community policing programs, police
policy in, 2
Community Review Commission,
Riverside, Californian, 237
compensation, of citizen oversight
members, 61–62
compensatory damages, 102
complainants, 131–32, 170–71, 174

complaint investigation, citizen involvement in, 2
Complaint Review Board (CRB), in
Washington, D.C., 3
Connecticut, New Haven Civilian
Review Board, 240
consultants
  for citizen oversight groups, 158
  for law enforcement agency
    monitoring, 57
control of law enforcement, 2
Core Values, 125
  in LASD risk management, 119
credibility, of citizen oversight groups,
  21, 24, 66, 68, 135, 148, 164
criminal trial model, of civilian oversight, 13
Critical Incident Analysis (CIA) of
LASD, 115, 124

Dallas Citizens' Police Review Board,
254
Dayton Citizens' Appeal Board, 251
decisional bargaining, in citizen
  oversight groups, 80
democracy, law enforcement control in,
2
Denver Independent Monitor Office, 249
Denver Office of Independent Monitor,
249
Denver police auditor, 14
Detroit Board of Police Commissioners
(BPC), 4
Detroit Office of Chief Investigator, 246
Detroit Police Board, citizen authority
in, 23n
disparate treatment, 176
  by police, 173
diversity, on citizen review boards, 31
diversity training, for law enforcement,
173
due process, in citizen complaints, 130

Edge of the Knife, 182
effects/impacts bargaining, for citizen
  oversight groups, 80
Eugene Police Commission, 252

evaluation criteria, for complaint investigation, 6
Expedited Settlement Program (ESP), of LASD, 115, 122
expert witnesses, 66
external training seminars, for citizen oversight members, 56–57

Federal Freedom of Information Act. *See* FOIA
Fire and Police Commission, Milwaukee, Wisconsin, 256
Flint Ombudsman Office, 246
Florida
  Fort Lauderdale Citizen Review Board, 240
  Key West Citizen Review Board, 240
  Miami Civilian Investigative Board, 241
  Miami-Dade Independent Review Panel, 241
  Orlando Citizens Review Board, 241
  public-records legislation in, 76
  Seminole County Sheriff's Office Civilian Review Board, 242
  St. Petersburg Civilian Police Review Committee, 242
  Stuart Independent Review Board, 242
FOIA (Federal Freedom of Information Act), 74
  exemptions to, 74
  investigation process and, 75
  police department impact of, 74–75
Fort Lauderdale Citizen Review Board, 240
42 U.S.C. 1983 (Section 1983). See Section 1983 Civil Action
Freedom of Information Act. *See* FOIA
freedom of information laws
  for citizen oversight groups, 73
  exemptions to, 75
  presumption of access in, 77
  for states, 75

funding
  for backlogs, 65
  for expert witnesses, 66
  of mediation, 135
  for oversight agencies, 6–7, 21, 40, 59–60, 62–65

Gennaco, Mike, 16
government agencies
  citizen oversight mandate from, 60
  law suites against, 98
  oversight of, 8
government officials
  opposition to oversight agencies by, 177
  oversight agency outreach to, 176–79
Grand Rapids Civilian Appeal Board, 246

Hawaii
  Hawaii County Police Commission, 242
  Honolulu Police Commission, 243
  Kauai Police Commission, 243
  Maui County Police Commission, 243
Hawaii County Police Commission, 242
high-profile incidents, citizen oversight groups from, 32, 35, 48
Honolulu Police Commission, 243
Houston Citizens' Review Committee, 254

IA. *See* Internal Affairs
IACOLE (International Association of Citizen Oversight of Law Enforcement), 4
IACP (International Association of Chiefs of Police), citizen oversight opposition of, 9
Idaho, Boise Office of Community Ombudsman, 243
Illinois, Chicago Police Board, 244

immunity
    affirmative defense of, 112
    for local governments, 105
independent investigators, for citizen
    oversight groups, 67
Independent Monitor Office, Denver,
    Colorado, 249
Independent Police Auditor (IPA)
    San Jose, California, 5, 239
    Santa Cruz, California, 239
    Tucson, Arizona, 235
Independent Police Monitor, Portland,
    Oregon, 137
Independent Police Review Division
    (IPR), Portland, Oregon, 145, 153,
    156, 178–79, 252
Independent Review Board, Stuart,
    Florida, 242
Independent Review Office, Los Angeles
    County, California, 237
Independent Review Office of Police
    Oversight Commission, Albuquer-
    que, New Mexico, 249
Independent Review Panel, Miami-
    Dade, Florida, 241
Indiana, Indianapolis Citizen Police
    Complaint Board, 244
Indianapolis Citizen Police Complaint
    Board, 244
information gathering
    in Berkeley, California, 72
    for citizen oversight groups, 72–78
    from law enforcement, 73
information technology, for citizen
    oversight groups, 68
Inspector General Act of 1978, 8
Inspector General Office, Los Angeles,
    California, 236
Integrity and Accountability Office,
    Philadelphia, Pennsylvania, 252
interest arbitration, 82n
Internal Affairs (IA)
    investigative authority of, 185
    outreach to, 185–86
    oversight agencies relationship with,
    155, 185–86
    workload of, 186
internal affairs investigations
    citizen oversight with, 61
    of police misconduct, 48–49
internal disciplinary review boards,
    Weingarten rights in, 89
internal police complaint procedures, 12.
    See also complaint investigation
internal training seminars. *See also*
    training
    for citizen oversight members, 56
International Association of Chiefs of
    Police. *See* IACP
International Association of Citizen
    Oversight of Law Enforcement. *See*
    IACOLE
investigation process
    of citizen complaints, 36, 140–42
    FOIA and, 75
Iowa City Police Citizens' Review Board,
    244
IPA. *See* Independent Police Auditor
IPR. *See* Independent Police Review
    Division

Kansas City Office of Community
    Complaints (OCC), 4, 13, 247
Kauai Police Commission, 243
Kerner Commission 1968, 12, 14
Key West Citizen Review Board, 29n,
    240
King County, Washington, Office of
    Citizens Complaints, 255
Knoxville Police Advisory and Review
    Committee, 253

labor agreements, citizen oversight
    groups and, 88–90
LaGuaurdia, Mayor Fiorello, 3
Las Vegas Citizen Review Board,
    248
LASD (Los Angeles County Sheriff's
    Department), 14–16, 20
    civil claims external review, 117
    civil claims risk management plan
    of, 117

Civil Litigation Unit of, 115–17, 120–21, 122
Claims and Liabilities Intervention Program of, 115, 123
Corrective Action Manager and, 126
Critical Incident Analysis method of, 115
Expedited Settlement Program, 115, 122–23
expedited settlements by, 121–24
lawsuit caseload of, 116
liability from policies, practices, 125
litigation cost management by, 115–16, 120–26
litigation history of, 117
Office of Independent Review and, 5, 116, 120
Office of Internal Review, 17
police monitor, 39
Risk Management Bureau of, 122
risk management philosophy of, 119
Special Counsel creation of, 5
Traffic Services Detail of, 125
law enforcement. *See also* police officers
accountability of, 59
citizen oversight group's knowledge of, 52–53
citizen oversight opposition of, 50–51
citizen oversight request by, 157
control of, 2
in democracy, 2
diversity training for, 173
information gathering from, 73
internal training programs in, 56
litigation programs for, 115–16
outreach to, 181–83
oversight agencies relations with, 182–83
public confidence in, 50, 58, 69, 131
social contract of, 129
transparency in, 47, 59–60, 69, 182
Lawlessness in Law Enforcement, Wickersham Commission report on, 3
lawsuits, official v. personal capacity, 101

League of Women Voters, 158
liability. *See also* policymaker liability
from policies, procedures, 125–26
Lincoln, Nebraska Citizen Police Advisory Board, 247
Lindsay, Mayor John, 3
litigation categories, 124–25
litigation costs, 116
LASD management of, 115–16
settlement v., 120
use of force and, 120
local government(s). *See also* government agencies
absolute immunity for, 105
compensatory damages and, 101–3
derivative liability for, 100–101
immunity for, 101–3, 105
liability under *Monell* for, 99–101
"objective" qualified immunity test for, 106–9
qualified immunity for, 101–2, 106
local government immunity, 101–9
burden of pleading in, 112
burden of proof in, 113
fact-specific requirement for, 108
interlocutory appeals and, 111–12
judge, jury roles in, 109
state law and, 110
Long Beach Citizen Police Complaint Commission, 236
Los Angeles Bar Association, Committee on Constitutional Rights, 3
Los Angeles County
Office of Independent Review, 237
Ombudsman Department, 237
Special Council to Board of Supervisors on Kolts Commission, 237
Special Council to Sheriff's Department - LASD, 5
Los Angeles County Sheriff's Department. *See* LASD
Los Angeles Inspector General Office, 236
Los Angeles Police Commission, 15
citizen authority in, 23n

Maine, Portland Police Citizen Review
    Subcommittee, 245
Maryland
    Baltimore Civilian Review Board,
        245
    Prince George's County Citizen
        Complaint Oversight Panel,
        245
Massachusetts, Cambridge Police
    Review and Advisory Board, 245
Maui County Police Commission, 243
mayor, city council, oversight agency
    support by, 34–35
media
    active pursuit of, 206–7, 211
    constraints on, 203
    coverage by, 203
    outreach through, 159–60, 175,
        202–12
    oversight agencies relationships
        with, 163, 202–3
    press releases and, 203–6
*Mediating Citizen Complaints against
    Police Officers,* 144
mediation
    acceptance of, 143
    additional uses in citizen oversight
        for, 145
    applications of, 145
    of citizen complaints, 128
    complaint de-escalation through,
        134
    complaints appropriate for, 133, 138
    confidentiality of, 143
    credibility in, 135
    defined, 129
    dialogue in, 133–34
    disclosure in, 143
    examination process during, 134
    formal, 129
    funding of, 135
    future orientation in, 134
    informal, 129
    lawyer involvement in, 142
    legal issues in, 142–44
    mandatory v. voluntary, 137–38
    models of, 145–45

negotiated agreement from, 138
    planning process for, 144
    police unions and, 184
    risk management with, 136
    structured stages of, 135
    training groups for, 144
    trends for, 145–46
mediation v. investigation, 133–36
    cost benefit analysis in, 141
    for individual officer behaviors,
        130–33
    values, risk management, public
        policy, 141–42
mediators, outcome stake of, 136
Memphis Civilian Law Enforcement
    Review Board, 253
Miami Civilian Investigative Panel, 241
Miami Independent Review Panel (IRP),
    28
Miami-Dade County Independent
    Review Panel, 241
Michigan
    Detroit Office of Chief Investigator,
        246
    Flint Ombudsman Office, 246
    Grand Rapids Civilian Appeal
        Board, 246
Michigan Public Employment Relations
    Act (PERA), 83
Milwaukee Fire and Police Commission,
    256
Minneapolis, mediation programs in, 6
Minneapolis Civilian Review Authority
    (CRA), 6, 247
Minnesota, St. Paul Police-Civilian
    Internal Affairs Review Commission,
    247
Miranda, 171
misconduct
    by oversight agencies, 175
    by police, 8, 48–49
    public attitudes towards, 8
Missouri, Kansas City Office of
    Community Complaints, 247
municipal subdivision liability, under
    Section 1983 Civil Action, 97–104
municipality. *See* local government(s)

NAACP, 158

National Association for Citizen Oversight of Law Enforcement (NACOLE), 4, 25n, 37

National Conference of Commissioners on Uniform State Laws, 129

National Conference of Commissioners on Uniform State Laws (NCCUSL), 143

National Conflict Resolution Center, 144

National Institute of Justice, citizen review study of, 35

Navato Police Advisory and Review Board, 237

Nebraska
    Lincoln Citizen Police Advisory Board, 247
    Omaha Public Safety Auditor, 248

networking, in outreach, 149, 190, 197–98

Nevada, Las Vegas Citizen Review Board, 248

New Haven Civilian Review Board, 240

New Jersey, Teaneck Civilian Complaint Review Board, 248

New Mexico, Albuquerque Independent Review Office of Police Oversight Commission, 249

The New World of Police Accountability, 20

New York
    Albany Citizens' Police Review Board, 249
    Civilian Review Board, 145
    New York City Civilian Complaint Review Board, 39, 249
    Ossining Police Complaint Review Board, 249
    public access to information in, 77
    Rochester Civilian Review Board, 250
    Syracuse Civilian Review Board, 250
    Taylor Law in, 89

New York City
    1935 racial disturbance in, 3
    mediation programs in, 6

New York City Civilian Complaint Review Board (CCRB), 3–4, 7, 13, 16, 26, 26n, 36n, 90–91, 136, 249
    revision of, 5

New York City Patrolmen's Benevolent Association (PBA), 90–91

New York Civil Liberties Union (NYCLU), 7

newsletters
    content for, 194
    cost-effectiveness of, 194
    on-going education through, 194
    for outreach, 194
    shortcomings to, 194
    statistical reports in, 194
    target audiences for, 194

North Carolina
    Charlotte Citizens' Review Board, 250
    Winston-Salem Citizen Police Review Board, 250

Oakland Citizen's Police Review Board, 5, 29, 40, 237

Office for Neighborhood Involvement (ONI), Portland, Oregon, 180, 204

Office of Citizen Complaint Review (OCCR), Washington, D.C., 13, 16

Office of Citizens Complaints (OCC), San Francisco, California, 4–5, 13, 16, 27–28, 139

Office of Independent Review (OIR), Los Angeles County Sheriff's Department, 5, 116, 120

Office of Police Complaints, Washington, D.C., 13, 39–40, 137, 139–40, 144–45, 255

official conduct
    "clearly established law" and, 107
    "objective" reasonableness of, 106–7

Ohio
    Cincinnati Citizens' Complaint Authority, 251
    Cleveland Police Review Board, 251
    Dayton Citizens' Appeal Board, 251
    State Employment Relations Board, 87

Omaha Public Safety Auditor, 248

Ombudsman
Flint, Michigan, 246
Los Angeles County, California,
237
Orange County Citizen Review Board,
241
Oregon
Eugene Police Commission, 252
Portland Independent Police
Review Division, 252
Salem Community Police Review
Board, 252
Orlando Citizens Police Review Board,
241
Ossining Police Complaint Review
Board, 249
outreach
agency awareness through, 149
through agency literature, brochures, 191–92
audit, monitor model of, 153
business solicitation through, 149
challenges to, 176
by citizen oversight groups, 147–48
to city council members, 179
coalition building, problem solving,
prevention through, 151
communication tools for, 189
community input, involvement
through, 150, 160–61, 172,
175–76
through community presentations,
198
community relations impact of, 151
to community-at-large, 170, 176
to complainants, appellants, 170–71
through complaint/commendation
forms, 191
through controversy, 211–12
cost-effective, 190
to Crisis Intervention Team, 188
defined, 148–49
through education, 150, 200–201
to elected officials, other agencies,
176–77
to ethnic groups, 171–72
through face-to-face interviews, 219
fairness in, 211

through focus groups, 219
through focused discussion formats,
215–17
through freelance stories, 207
to general public, 171–72
goals and tactics of, 220
goals, performance measures for,
151–52
through hotlines, 217–18
IA, 185–86
to immigrant, refugee groups, 172
inbound v. outbound, 189
through informal discussion,
networking, 197–98
through information flyers, bill
stuffers, 210–11
language barriers in, 172
through local publications, 207
means of contact for, 187
through media, 159–60, 163, 175,
202–12
message consistency in, 182
networking, relationship building
through, 149, 190, 197–98
through newsletters, 194
nonwritten forms of, 197–201
oversight agency mandate in, 152,
154
oversight agency model impact on,
153–56
during oversight agency start-up
phase, 157–58
oversight agency structure impact
on, 152
oversight agency transparency
through, 221
personal contact, networking in,
190
to police chiefs, commanders, 184–
85
to police community, 181–83
on police procedures and policies,
163
in Portland, Oregon, 154
to Portland Police Bureau, 161
through press releases, 203–6
priorities for, 160
to professional groups, 177

public education through, 170–76
through public forums, 213–15
through public inquiries, expert
    panels, 201
through public meetings, case
    hearings, 199–200
public relations through, 150, 155,
    165, 170
through public speaking, 198–99
through purchased media attention,
    209–10
through radio, 208–9
to rank-and-file officers, 186–87
reporters and, 206
reporting/transparency through,
    149
research methodologies in, 218–20
resource limitations for, 153
to special units, 187–88
stakeholder impact of, 152, 157–58,
    165, 169, 220
standardized literature for, 190
standardized presentations for, 198
strategies for, 160, 169
through surveys/questionnaires,
    218–19
tactics for, 169
to targeted groups, 155, 171–75,
    198–99
through telephone surveys, 219
through television, 207–8
time-limited products for, 190
tools for, 189–220
through videos, 209
volunteer recruiting through, 149–
    50
through web pages, 192–94
written communication for, 190–91
to youth groups, 199–200
oversight agencies. *See also* citizen
    oversight groups; citizen review
    boards; police auditor
    advisory committees for, 212–13
    allied professionals and, 180–81
    auditor protocol for, 164
    authority of, 42
    best practices research in, 158–59

case management by, 186
citizen input to, 212–13
citizen review board, 11
city attorneys and, 179–80
community activists, organizations,
    33
credibility of, 21, 24, 66, 68, 135,
    148, 164, 198, 201, 219–20
crises, scandals for, 163, 165–66
customer service by, 162, 170
development success of, 166
disparate treatment by, 173
executive director, staff of, 36
expectations for, 34, 159, 174
experts, consultants and, 38
feedback for, 171
focused discussion formats for, 215–
    17
forms of, 159
funding for, 6–7, 21, 40, 59–60, 62–
    65, 177
high-profile incidents impact on, 32,
    35, 48, 163
hostility towards, 175
IA relations with, 155, 185–86
inbound outreach by, 212–20
independence of, 30
information gathering by, 217
investigation procedures, manuals
    for, 37
law enforcement relations with,
    182–83
life stages of, 156–65
limits of, 166
local challenges, outreach needs for,
    165–66
mandates for, 60, 166, 192
mayor, city council support for, 34–
    45
media outreach by, 159
media relations of, 163
member manipulation of, 177
member terms for, 43
misconduct by, 175
models of, 11–12
ongoing commitments of, 162
operating effectiveness of, 7

outreach mandate of, 152, 154
outreach requirements of, 152
police opposition to, 177
police procedures expertise of, 36
police union relations with, 7–9, 32–
    33, 50–51, 62, 80–82, 85–87,
    132, 183–84
press releases by, 196
problem patterns in, 196–97
public awareness of, 161, 176, 212
public battles for, 164
public forums for, 213–15
public invitation by, 172
public reports by, 38, 195–97
publicity for, 159–60
regular reports by, 195
reputation of, 187
satisfaction surveys for, 171
special reports by, 196–97
stability of, 43
stakeholder involvement in, 157–
    58
technical reports by, 195
training for, 188
transparency in, 147–48, 195, 199,
    221
vacancies on, 40
visibility of, 201
volunteer recruiting by, 212
web pages for, 192–94, 212
workflow in, 160
oversight agencies outreach. *See*
    outreach

PAB. *See* Police Advisory Board
Pennsylvania
    Philadelphia Integrity and Account-
        ability Office, 252
    Pittsburgh Citizen Police Review
        Board, 253
personal capacity suits, official suits v.,
    101
Philadelphia
    Integrity and Accountability Office,
        39, 252
    PAB in, 3–4
    Police Advisory Commission, 83–84

Pittsburgh
    Citizen Police Review Board, 253
    Office of Municipal Investigations,
        7
police academies. *See* citizen police
    academies
Police Advisory and Review Committee,
    Knoxville, Tennessee, 253
Police Advisory Board (PAB), in
    Philadelphia, 3–4
Police Advisory Commission, Clare-
    mont, California, 236
Police Assessment Resource Center
    (PARC), of Portland, Oregon, 38
police auditor. *See also* citizen oversight
    groups; citizen review boards;
    oversight agencies
    advocates of, 18–19
    citizen review boards v., 15–16
    follow-up by, 16
    independent research on, 20
    as oversight agencies, 14
    oversight agencies and, 11
    police monitor v., 14–15
    policy review by, 15
    power of, 14
    review board alternative of, 19
    Seattle's creation of, 5, 7
    selection process for, 31–32
Police Auditor, Independent, Tucson,
    Arizona, 235
Police Board, Chicago, Illinois, 244
police chiefs
    citizen oversight opposition of, 9
    outreach to, 184–85
    in police oversight, 34
Police Citizen Review Subcommittee,
    Portland, Maine, 245
Police Citizens' Review Board, Iowa
    City, Iowa, 244
Police Civilian Review Board, Salt Lake,
    Utah, 254
police commissions
    citizen oversight through, 15
    Eugene, Oregon, 252
    Hawaii County, Hawaii, 242
    Honolulu, Hawaii, 243

Kauai, Hawaii, 243
Maui County, Hawaii, 243
Richmond, California, 238
Police Complaint Review Board,
   Ossining, New York, 249
Police Complaints Office, Washington,
   D.C., 255
police departments
   citizen complaint attention by, 127
   citizen oversight groups relations
      with, 77
   complaint investigation by, 14
   internal process review of, 38
   policy change within, 24
   use of force policies in, 19
police integrity, citizen oversight of, 24
police investigations, public confidence
   in, 164
police management, community
   advocates v., 32
police misconduct
   internal affairs investigations of,
      48–49
   public attitudes towards, 8
police monitor
   for LASD, 39
   police auditor v., 14–15
   selection process for, 31–32
Police Monitor Office, Austin, Texas,
   254
police officers
   allied professionals and, 181
   bias by, 173
   community resentment towards, 166
   community trust impacted by, 146
   conflict groups for, 171
   disparate treatment by, 173
   diversity training for, 173
   impartial review of, 42
   outreach to, 181–83, 186–87
   oversight agency opposition of, 177
   privacy protection for, 53
   public trust in, 1, 24
   union representation for, 88
police oversight
   community confidence in, 44
   high-profile incidents and, 35

mediation use in, 128
   by police chief, 34
Police Oversight Commission, Albuquerque, New Mexico, 26, 249
police performance, surveys of, 45n
police policy
   in community policing programs, 2
   outreach about, 163
police reform
   citizen oversight and, 127
   emergence of, 127
Police Review and Advisory Board,
   Cambridge, Massachusetts, 245
Police Review Board
   Berkeley, California, 236
   Cleveland, Ohio, 86, 251
Police Review Commission (PRC),
   Berkeley, California, 235
police unions, 5–9
   citizen complaint involvement by,
      132
   citizen oversight impact on, 32–33,
      62
   citizen oversight opposition of, 9,
      50–51, 81
   in collective bargaining, 85–87
   interest arbitration rights of, 82
   mediation programs and, 184
   oversight agencies with, 183–84
   police management and, 166
Police-Civilian Internal Affairs Review
   Commission, St. Paul, Minnesota,
   247
police-community relations, improvements to, 24
policy analysts, in citizen oversight
   groups, 67
policy issues, for citizen oversight
   groups, 71
policy review, by police auditors, 15
policymaker liability, under *Monell,* 99–
   100
political process, in citizen oversight, 7
*Pontiac Police Officers Ass'n v. City of
   Pontiac,* 83
Portland, Maine, Police Citizen Review
   Subcommittee, 245

Portland, Oregon
citizen oversight in, 156–59
Citizen Review Committee, 200
city council/IPR relations in, 178
Independent Police Monitor, 137
IPR, 145, 153, 156, 178–79, 252
Office for Neighborhood Involvement (ONI), 180, 204
Police Assessment Resource Center (PARC), 38
Police Bureau Advanced Academy, 162
Police Bureau outreach in, 161
Police Bureau's Crisis Intervention Team, 170
Police Bureau's Internal Affairs, 155
Police Internal Investigation Auditing Committee (PIIAC), 157
PRAB. *See* Cambridge Police Review and Advisory Board
PRC. *See* Police Review Commission
Prince George's County Citizen Complaint Oversight Panel, 245
Privacy Act of 1974, 8
privacy protection, 8, 75
for law enforcement personnel, 53
Professional Accountability Office, Seattle, Washington, 255
professional associations, in civilian oversight, 4
professional standards, for oversight agencies, 5–6
PSAB. *See* Police Safety Advisory Board
public attitudes
towards citizen oversight, 7, 165
outreach impact on, 165
towards police, 165
towards police misconduct, 8
Watergate era impact on, 8
public confidence, in law enforcement, 1, 58
public expectation, for oversight agencies, 34, 159, 179
public opinion polls, on racial profiling, 8n

public records legislation. *See also* FOIA
in Florida, 76
public relations, through outreach, 150, 170
public reports
of citizen oversight groups, 66
by oversight agencies, 38, 195–97
Public Safety Accountability Office, Sacramento, California, 238
Public Safety Advisory Board, Albuquerque, New Mexico, 7
Public Safety Auditor, Omaha, Nebraska, 248
punitive damages, local government immunity from, 103

racial disturbance, New York City, 1935, 3
racial profiling, 218
by police, 49
public opinion polls on, 8n
reasonable cause, public understanding of, 162
research analysts, in citizen oversight groups, 67
Richmond Police Commission, 238
ride-alongs, for citizen oversight group's training, 55–56
Risk Management Bureau (LASD), Corrective Action Manager in, 126
Riverside Community Police Review Commission, 237
Rochester
Civilian Review Board, 250
collective bargaining agreement of, 92–94
New York's Civilian Review Board, 145

Sacramento Office of Police Accountability, 33
Sacramento Office of Public Safety Accountability, 238
Salem Community Police Review Board, 252
Salt Lake Police Civilian Review Board, 254

San Diego Citizens Review Board on Police Practices, 238

San Diego County Citizens' Law Enforcement Review Board, 239

San Francisco
Office of Citizens Complaints, 4–5, 13, 16, 27–28, 239
Police Commission, 26
Proposition H, 28, 43

San Jose Independent Police Auditor (IPA), 14, 15, 39
complaint investigation criteria of, 6

San Jose Independent Police Auditor Office, 239

Santa Cruz Independent Police Auditor, 239

scandals, for oversight agencies, 163, 165–66

Seattle
Office of Professional Accountability (OPA), 17, 26, 40, 255
Police Auditor in, 5, 7

Section 1983 Civil Action, 102
appeals to, 111–12
burden of pleading in, 112
burden of proof in, 113
for deprivation of rights, 97–98
fact-specific requirement for, 108
immunities under, 105–14
judges, jury role in, 109
"state of mind" requirements for, 104
Supreme Court and, 105

Seminole County Sheriff's Office Civilian Review Board, 242

Special Counsel to Board of Supervisors on Kolts Commission, Los Angeles County, California, 237

Special Counsel to Los Angeles Sheriff's Department. See LASD

St. Paul Police-Civilian Affairs Review Commission, 247

St. Petersburg Civilian Police Review Committee, 242

staffing
of citizen oversight groups, 6, 59–61, 63, 66–68

for complaint investigation, 6

Stuart Independent Review Board, 242

supervisory liability
"affirmative link" for, 103
"failure to train," 104
"state of mind" requirements for, 104

Supreme Court
on immunity availability, 109
Section 1983 suits and, 105
on "threshold" immunity, 107–8

survey procedure, of Minneapolis Civilian Review Authority (CRA), 6

sustain rate
for citizen oversight, 18
as performance measure, 19

Syracuse
Civilian Review Board (CRB), 91, 250
collective bargaining agreement of, 92
Police Benevolent Association (PBA), 91

Taylor Law, 89

Teaneck Civilian Complaint Review Board, 248

telephone surveys, 219

television, 207–8

Tennessee
Knoxville Police Advisory and Review Committee, 253
Memphis Civilian Law Enforcement Review Board, 253

Texas
Austin Office of Police Monitor, 254
Dallas Citizens' Police Review Board, 254
Houston Citizens' Review Committee, 254

training
for citizen oversight groups, 37, 47, 51–52, 66, 148, 150, 188
diversity, 173
for mediation, 144
through ride-alongs, 55–56

Section 1983 Civil Action and, 104
transparency impact of, 66
on use of force policies, 37
transparency
in law enforcement, 47, 50, 69, 182
through outreach, 149, 221
of oversight agencies, 147–48, 195,
199, 221
public demand for, 47, 57, 59–60
training impact on, 66
Tucson
Citizen Police Advisory Review
Board, 235
Office of Independent Police
Auditor, 235

Uniform Mediation Act (UMA), 129,
143
applicable statutes of, 143
state status of, 143
unions. *See* police unions
University of Nebraska Omaha
Department of Criminal Justice, 144
U.S. Department of Justice, Cincinnati
Memorandum of Agreement with, 43
use of force policies
litigation and, 120
in police departments, 19
training on, 37
Utah, Salt Lake Police Civilian Review
Board, 254

Violent Crime Control Act, 15

Walker, Dr. Samuel, 144
Washington
King County Office of Citizens
Complaints, 255
Seattle Office of Professional
Accountability, 255
Washington, D.C.
Citizen Complaint Review Board
(CCRB) in, 3, 7, 26, 41
Community Dispute Resolution
Center, 139
mediation programs in, 6
Office of Citizen Complaint Review
(OCCR), 13, 16
Office of Police Complaints, 13, 39–
40, 137, 139–40, 144–45, 255
Watergate era, public attitude impact of, 8
web sites
access to, 193
complaint/commendation forms on,
193
content for, 193–94
cost-effectiveness of, 193
FAQs on, 194
outreach through, 192
shortcomings of, 193
Wickersham Commission, *Lawlessness in
Law Enforcement* report of, 3
Wiengarten rights, 88–89
Winston-Salem Citizen Police Review
Board, 250
Wisconsin, Milwaukee Fire and Police
Commission, 256